Immovable Laws, Irresistible Rights

FEMINIST ETHICS

Immovable Laws, Irresistible Rights

Natural Law, Moral Rights, and Feminist Ethics

Christine Pierce

University Press of Kansas

Published by the University Press of Kansas (Lawrence, Kansas 66049), which was organized by the Kansas Board of Regents and is operated and funded by Emporia State University, Fort Hays State University, Kansas State University, Pittsburg State University, the University of Kansas, and Wichita State University

Library of Congress Cataloging-in-Publication Data

Pierce, Christine.
Immovable laws, irresistible rights: natural law, moral rights, and feminist ethics/ Christine Pierce.
p. cm.—(Feminist ethics)
Includes bibliographical references and index.
ISBN 978-0-7006-1070-9 (cloth)
1. Natural law. 2. Law and ethics. 3. Feminist ethics. I. Title. II. Series.

K428.P54 2000
340'.112—dc21 00-043497

British Library Cataloguing in Publication Data is available.

10 9 8 7 6 5 4 3 2 1

To Beth

Contents

Acknowledgments

This book consists of new essays and some that have been previously published. Those essays that have seen earlier publication have been updated and expanded for this volume. Of the rewritten essays, three were originally coauthored, two with Sara Ann Ketchum. I would like to thank her for her permission to use ideas developed in "Rights and Responsibilities" and "Feminist Separatism" and for the many philosophical discussions we had as colleagues from 1975 to 1982 that influenced my ideas well beyond the scope of these two essays. I would also like to thank Margery L. Collins who coauthored "Holes and Slime: Sexism in Sartre's Psychoanalysis" and Donald VanDeVeer with whom I have coedited two volumes on environmental ethics and another on the ethical and social policy issues surrounding AIDS.

I have read some of these essays in a number of places and have profited from the discussions that followed. My thanks to audiences at the American Philosophical Association, Triangle Ethics Circle (Chapel Hill), University of Chicago, Dartmouth College, Florida State University, University of Florida, San Jose State University, Colorado State University, College of Charleston, Union College (Schenectady, NY), Carleton University (Ottawa), Brooklyn College, City University of New York Graduate School, and several universities in Australia, including Australian National University, University of Melbourne, LaTrobe University, Sydney University, University of New South Wales (Sydney), Queensland University, Newcastle University, Adelaide University, and Western Australia Institute of Technology. I am indebted to the members of the Midwest Society for Women in Philosophy for their presentations, discussions, and comments on my papers. I especially thank Sandra Bartky, Marilyn Frye, Alison Jaggar, and Claudia Card in this regard. Others who have given me valuable comments are Sandra Harding, Rita Manning, and Bat-Ami Bar On.

Thanks also to Claudia Card for her encouragement and comments in her role as editor of this series. Thanks to Nancy Jackson, acquisitions editor at the University Press of Kansas, for making the publication process a smooth one. I gratefully acknowledge the assistance of North Carolina State University and Dean Margaret Zahn in granting me a university research leave for fall 1999. Thanks to my colleague Mary Kathleen Cunningham for alerting me to materials on Mary Daly and to my department head, Harold Levin, for his technological support and good cheer. Thanks to Peter French for sponsoring the Feminist Ethics Revisited conference on October 1–3, 1999, in Tampa, Florida. Thanks to Anne Peterson for our long friendship.

Finally, this book would never have come about were it not for the support I received from my life partner, Beth Timson, and our nonhuman companions, past and present, Portia P. Puss, Georgia Brown, Gypsy, Cady, and Morgan.

Introduction

Much of this book brings into meaningful confrontation two of the great traditions of Western ethical theory, natural law and moral rights, to argue that rights constitute a better basis for ethics than does natural law. At the heart of this confrontation is a crucial conflict between the rights conception of rationality that places the autonomy of the individual at its center and the natural law conception of rationality that prioritizes humans, animals, and things by their places in a natural or "rational" order of purposes—a hierarchy of beings all functioning in the service of some others' ends.

Central also to natural law theory is the doctrine of natural purpose or natural place. As a consequence, many actions are said to be morally wrong because they violate these natural purposes, even if many of these actions are important to the autonomous lives of human beings. For example, to engage in sexual acts with someone of the same sex, to have a child through in vitro fertilization, to end one's life in dignity—all of these choices can be protected by rights, but all are deemed inherently wrong in natural law ethics.

Natural law theory began with the Greeks as a theory that could explain the whole universe. It was thought that everything in the universe or every class of things—rocks, animals, people—had a telos, an end, purpose, or function. To know the purpose of everything was to understand the nature of the universe. For example, Aristotle did physics teleologically. In the *Physics* he develops a doctrine of natural place that provides an explanation of motion: things move in ways they are intended to move. He says: "It is the nature of every kind of sensible body to be somewhere, and there is a place appropriate to each, the same for the part and for the whole, e.g., for the whole earth and for a single clod, and for fire and for a spark. . . . 'coming to a standstill' is generally recognized to be identical or at least concomitant with the locomotion of a thing to its proper place."[1]

Needless to say, no one does physics this way today. All of the sciences as we currently know them have repudiated teleology, with the possible exception of biology, which now and again flirts with the possibility of explaining phenomena vis-à-vis function. However, concepts from natural law persist in ethics in both philosophy and ordinary discourse, although the scope of the theory has severely narrowed from the days of the Greeks. Richard Mohr has said that "the accusation of something being unnatural (where a moral rather than an advertising point is being made) . . . comes up now in ordinary discourse only against homosexuality."[2] Going from explaining the universe to insulting gay people is quite a slide indeed. And although there is some legitimacy in Mohr's claim that homosexuals suffer more from these views today than anyone else, the tentacles of this view still impinge on women's lives and have even been recently recommended as capable of reconstruction and compatibility with a feminist view.

One might wonder why natural law has persisted in ethics when the sciences for the most part repudiated the theory long ago. I want to suggest two reasons, although there may be others. One reason is that the medieval philosopher and theologian Thomas Aquinas, whose work forms the foundation of the ethics espoused by the Roman Catholic Church, followed Aristotle in these views. Relying on the "natural" in its views on suicide, abortion, contraception, and marriage (to name a few issues), the Catholic Church keeps these views alive today.

Another reason may be philosophy's tolerance for old theory. Ethics, although claimed by others as well, has always been a major part of the domain of Western philosophy. But philosophy, unlike physics, does not retire old theory to history textbooks.[3] Imagine a graduate student in physics taking a seminar and suggesting that today's theories of physics are wrong and that what we should do is go back to Aristotle's way of doing physics. Such a person would be thought crazy and her or his assistantship might be gone the next day. On the other hand, a graduate student's suggestion in a philosophy seminar that Aristotle's ethical theory is superior to the more modern theories of rights and utilitarianism would be greeted with, "Oh, why do you think so?" even by a professor who was herself or himself a rights theorist or a utilitarian.

Attempts at bringing back natural law ethics or traditional morality are periodic but common. I examine Alan Donagan's efforts and influence in the 1980s in this regard. Even in ordinary discourse there is much talk of reviving "traditional morality," whereas one never hears anyone talk about reviving traditional physics. Of course, in philosophy, sometimes only parts of old theories are kept. For example, one hears quite a lot today about the virtues and, to a lesser extent, the importance of flourishing. These are old ideas that originated with the Greeks but have been disconnected by many from their roots in natural law. Others, however, have kept the natural law base intact and reached more ethically and politically conservative conclusions as a result.

The book begins with an updated version of an early essay, "Natural Law Language and Women," in which I point out the many ways that the natural law tradition in ethics and theology has functioned to both mystify women's nature and also justify the restriction of women to a predetermined social "place." It extends to the psychology of Jean-Paul Sartre and his views on women's nature as expounded in his discussions of "holes" and "slime" in *Being and Nothingness.*

In more recent manifestations of the theory in "AIDS and *Bowers v. Hardwick,*" I show that natural law arguments contribute not only to bad law but also to bad science. In that same chapter, I argue against Ronald Dworkin's highly qualified version of legal moralism, since natural law reasons can slip through his net to create oppressive legislation on homosexuality as well as block any examination of consequences in the evaluation of proposed legislation. Also in this chapter I discuss Gabriel Rotello's recent ecological explanation of AIDS. I explore the possibility that ecology is a new natural law and contrast ecology's norms with traditional natural law ethics.

There is another significant component in my work on natural law. I argue that Plato's version of natural law theory that supports equal opportunity for women is the best manifestation of that theory, superior by far to the more influential formulations of Aristotle and Aquinas. One of the things I do in the beginning pages of "Eros and Epistemology" is to make clear what an idea of equal opportunity looks like in a natural law view. I do not argue that Plato was a feminist; I only argue that Plato's conception of human nature was not sexist. But his antisexism here is no small thing. Had natural law taken this turn in the history of the West, the absence of gender restrictions on role might have stayed afloat until they could be underpinned by a rights argument. In this chapter I stress not only the antisexist but also the antiheterosexist themes in Plato's work.

Any natural law theory, including Plato's, is fundamentally at odds with the notion of autonomy. I make my case for this claim, and side with the rights tradition, in "Natural Law and Moral Rights." In "Rights and Responsibilities," I defend rights theory (especially in institutional contexts) as an alternative to an ethics of responsibility based on Aristotelian notions of friendship and trust. For the past two decades, an "ethic of care" has been the predominant preoccupation of feminist ethics. With its themes of connection with and concern for others, rights have been rejected as a masculinist valuing of the separateness and autonomy of individuals. More recently, however, with the rise of black feminism, global feminism, and the shaping of feminist ethics by *open* lesbians, rights are enjoying something of a comeback at least as one of the bits worth keeping of a larger moral theory. The reason for this shift is obvious: those without rights can see how important it is to have rights.

In "Postmodernism and Other Skepticisms," I argue that some key Enlightenment ideas, such as universalization in ethical reasoning and equality, not only deserve to survive but do in fact emerge unscathed by postmodernist critiques. Although postmodernists rightly criticize the meaning and functions of universalization in explanations from the disciplines of science, history, and sociology, these same criticisms do not apply to the very different meanings and functions of universalization in ethics. I also question the arguments of postmodern feminists against the concept of equality, claiming that they are led astray by a faulty assumption that equality is identical to "sameness."

Although I defend the idea of a right and key ideas from the rights tradition such as equality and universalization in ethics, I also argue in this chapter that rational ethics of a Kantian sort has its limitations. Moreover, rights theory does not exhaust ethical thought. For example, ideas such as "liberation" and "separatism" do not come from that tradition, nor can they be explained by their political counterpart, liberalism, but both are important ideas in feminist theory.

"Gay Marriage" continues with the themes of equality, rights, justice, and liberation. Indeed, the subject of marriage is a dynamic battleground for rights versus natural law. My arguments in favor of gay marriage are based not only on ethical notions such as equality and rights but also on relevant historical, legal, and psychological considerations.

Contemporary efforts to rely on "nature" for ethical conclusions can also be found in ecology, biology, sociobiology, and religion. In each of these fields I examine the work of some representative author. I single out for special emphasis an attempt to devise a feminist natural law by retrieving Thomism, arguing that this sort of fundamental reclamation does not work. There are *parts* of the Aristotelian tradition that can and have been reclaimed by feminist philosophers for feminist purposes. These ideas are usually general ones such as flourishing or having virtues that can incorporate a feminist meaning if cut loose from natural law. I also argue that natural law cannot be a foundation for rights. Although rights may be only part of a larger moral theory, their status vis-à-vis natural law is one of equal footing and all too often that of a key competitor.

There are clear threads throughout the body of this book, questions that are shifted and turned in attempts to find the best answers: What tradition of rational thought offers the best grounding for an ethical theory? Why does rights theory make a better case for feminist thought? Which pieces of older theories should be kept, which discarded? How do newer liberation theories mesh with the conception of rights? My struggle with these questions is one aspect of the struggle of feminist ethics in these last few decades. It does seem that there is no getting rid of natural law; but it is an immovable object that is meeting—one hopes—an irresistible force in rights theory and feminist ideas.

1

Natural Law Language and Women

"Nature" or "human nature" must be among the most enigmatic concepts ever used. Often, when the "natural" is invoked, we are left in the dark as to whether it is meant as an explanation, a recommendation, a claim for determinism, or simply a desperate appeal, as if the "natural" were some sort of metaphysical glue that could hold our claims or values together.

For centuries people have appealed to the "natural" to back up their moral and social recommendations. The ordinary uses of the term that everyone hears from time to time demonstrate that such efforts are still very much with us. We are told, for example, that suicide, birth control, and homosexuality are wrong because they are unnatural. Now and then, the use takes a positive form: motherhood is natural and hence the duty of women.

My major intent is to examine the language of "proper sphere," role, or function, showing its relationship to the language of natural law and pointing out problems in this kind of reasoning that are overlooked in the discussions of those who use this type of argument against women.

The following four examples characterize in a more extensive way the type of argument to be analyzed here.

- In 1872, Myra Bradwell was refused admission to the Illinois bar by the state supreme court even though she had passed the bar entrance examination. Her suit, based upon the supposed right of every person, man or woman, to engage in any lawful employment for a livelihood, was denied. Justice Bradley, in his concurring opinion, opposed the idea that women might be attorneys on grounds that both God and nature disapprove: "The civil law, as well as nature herself, has always recognized a wide difference in the respective spheres and destinies of man and woman. Man is, or should be, woman's protector and defender. The natural and proper timidity and delicacy which belongs to the female sex evidently unfits it for many of the occupations of civil life. The constitution of the family organization, which is founded in the divine ordinance, as well as in the nature of things, indicates the domestic sphere as that which properly belongs to the domain and functions of womanhood."[1]

- In a statement denouncing abortion, Pope Pius XI assumed that nature assigns duties to women: "However much we may pity the mother whose health and even life is gravely imperiled in the performance of *the duty allotted to her by nature,* nevertheless what could ever be a sufficient reason for excusing in any way the direct murder of the innocent?"[2]
- A paragraph from Etienne Gilson's commentary on Aquinas illustrates the incredible implications of a well-known view that identifies natural sexuality with the reproductive function. On this concept of nature, heterosexual rape is preferable to masturbation: "To violate nature is to set oneself against God who has ordained nature. Now the worst way of violating nature is to carry corruption into its very principle. Fornication, rape, adultery, incest, respect nature's order in the performing of the sexual act. Unnatural vice, however, refuses to respect this order. The worst form of luxury is bestiality, and after it, sodomy, irregularities in the sexual act and onanism."[3] Heterosexual rape, a violent action, is not recommended, but it is not as bad as consensual sodomy or interrupting heterosexual intercourse, because heterosexual rape allows for the possibility of fulfilling the purpose of sexuality, namely, procreation. At the very least, it seems somewhat peculiar to prefer sexual acts that are by definition unloving, violent abuses of persons to acts that need not be and may be quite the contrary. Here we see the natural defined as function or purpose and applied to the sexual organs. It is assumed that procreation is the only purpose of sexual activity; fulfilling its function is what makes a sexual act morally good and deviating from that function is what makes a sexual act morally bad.
- Basing his remarks on Danielle Crittenden's book, *What Our Mothers Didn't Tell Us: Why Happiness Eludes the Modern Woman,* newspaper columnist George Will recently asserted that "feminism's androgeny project fails for an intractable reason: It is unnatural. Today's feminism . . . aspir[es] to rid life of necessity. Feminism's grand dream is to escape the bonds of anatomy and refute the idea that biology is, in any sense, destiny."[4] However, nature seemingly has gotten more liberal since the days of Myra Bradwell. Today, according to Will and Crittenden, women are required to stay home only eight years with young children and postpone their careers rather than forgo them altogether.

Will and Crittenden further cite as a feminist belief that "traditional divisions of labor between husbands and wives, fathers and mothers, make women 'unequal' and sentence them to domestic servitude, beehive hairdos and loss of the vote."[5]

Making light of feminism here has the effect of implying that the consequences of this division of labor are innocuous and that the feminist critique of the practice is overplayed. But there is a real worry here, as we shall see in a later discussion on rights. In the traditional division of labor, women are dependent upon the goodwill of men. If the goodwill runs out, the consequences for women are serious indeed.

As a preface to analyzing these kinds of arguments, it is important to stress how difficult it is for anyone in any social or moral context to say what they mean by "natural" and why it recommends itself as good. Two distinct steps are involved here: defining what is meant by "natural" and arguing that what is natural is good.

It is often assumed that the word "natural" has an automatic "plus" value tag that does not have to be argued for on independent grounds. In other words, it is taken for granted that if someone persuades us that "X is natural," she or he has also persuaded us that "X is good." The Vatican's position on birth control reflects this undue liberty: *Humanae Vitae* assumes that it is sufficient to point out that artificial means of birth control interrupt the natural order of things. The most significant question of all, "Why is 'natural order' a good thing?" is never asked. Apparently, what the "natural order" means in this case is that which will happen if untouched by human invention. This definition, however, yields absurd consequences if we try to use it as a prescription. If "natural order" is a good thing, and we must assume it is because we are told not to interrupt it, why is shaving not a moral issue? Clearly, it is natural for hair to grow on humans' faces, and shaving introduces an artificial means to disrupt the natural order of things.

One thing is evident: We cannot discuss whether the natural is good until we are able to state what we mean by the term. "Natural" can mean "untouched by human invention," but this use is not a coherent basis for normative judgments. A second meaning of "natural" sometimes applied to human beings is that human nature is everything that human beings do. As an explanation, this use is simply vacuous; if meant as a justification, however, it would justify everything. If things are morally right because they are natural, and if everything human beings do is natural, then everything human beings do is morally justified. The third and fourth meanings that I want to consider are particularly interesting, not only because of their relevance to arguments for women's inequality but also because both definitions are currently in use and yet clearly incompatible. Human nature is construed to be either what human beings have in common with the rest of the animal world or what distinguishes human beings from that world.

One of the most amusing efforts to make the third use work against women is the following comment by Mary Hemingway: "Equality, what does it mean? What's the use for it? I've said it before and I'll repeat: Women are second-class citizens and not only biologically. A female's first duty is to bear children and rear them. With the exception of a few freshwater fish, most animals follow this basic rule."[6] Unfortunately, the most obvious consequence of Hemingway's argument is that a few freshwater fish are immoral. What she meant to say, however, was that human duties somehow can be determined by observing animal behavior.

But animal parenting is much more varied than Hemingway realized. Young are raised by same-sex pairs, single parents, and groups of several males or females to name a few.[7] In some cases, homosexual parents have an advantage. "Pairs of male Black Swans, for example, are often able to acquire the largest and best-quality territories for raising young because of their combined strength. . . . And in many species in which single parenting is the rule (because there is no heterosexual pair-bonding), same-sex pairs provide a unique opportunity for young to be raised by two parents (e.g., Squirrel Monkeys, Grizzly Bears, Lesser Scaup Ducks)."[8] Even if many animals reproduce and parent after the teachings of Ernest and Mary Hemingway, it would be hard to get a notion of value from this behavior. The fact that something happens a lot does not argue for or against it.

Interchanging words like "normal" and "natural" illustrates prejudice for the statistically prevalent as opposed to the unusual, the exception. The unusual qua unusual, however, cannot be ruled out as bad; it can be alternatively described as "deviant" or "original," depending on whether or not we like it. Nothing prevents describing the homosexual, for example, as a sexual original rather than a sexual deviant except people's inability to tolerate any unusual behavior in this area; hence, they use statistical concepts with bad connotations (unnatural, abnormal) to discuss it, instead of those with good connotations (original, exceptional).

The fourth meaning of "natural," that which distinguishes human beings from the rest of the animal world, reaches back to Plato. For Plato, to state the nature of any given class of things was to state the features of that class which distinguished it from all other classes of things. Although Plato did not claim that men and women have different natures but rather referred to human beings as the class with the capacity to reason, his use of "natural" lends itself to the defining of classes of things according to function or role that frequently has been used to restrict women. In order to understand how similar our way of talking and explaining things is to the Platonic view, it is first necessary to grasp how the latter has been historically conceived. An increased awareness of the natural law basis of the language of function should help us to be more critical of the language we take for granted and to see what kinds of philosophical commitment we perhaps unwittingly make.

The Greek method of explanation for questions of the sort, "What is the nature of X?" was teleological; explanations were given in terms of function, role, end, or purpose as opposed to mechanistic explanations. The difference between these explanations can easily be illustrated by comparing answers to a simple question such as "What is a lawnmower?" A teleologist will explain that a lawnmower is something used to cut grass; a mechanist will explain about pulleys, plugs, and metal blades. Manufactured items lend themselves to the former type of explanation because we usually have in mind what the function of something is going to be before we start making any of it. Such explanation, however, is not so easily forthcoming for questions like "What is the nature of human beings?" Plato, on the other hand, was interested in this type of question; he wanted to explain the "natural" world. In this realm of nonmanufactured items, functions and roles are discovered, not created.

Although Plato thought he could answer the question concerning the nature of human beings, for the moment what concerns us is not the content of his answer, but the additional philosophical mileage we can expect from success in providing this type of answer. To be able to say what a thing is in terms of its function or purpose is simultaneously to set up standards for its evaluation. Once we can state the function of any "X," we can say what a good "X" is, or, more precisely, we can say that "X" is good to the extent that it fulfills its function. We still have this use of "good" in English; we say, for example, that a good lawnmower is one that cuts grass well, that is, one that fulfills its function.

Plato's effort to apply this teleological framework to human beings consists of his functional analysis of the soul as reason, spirit, and desire. These are analogous to functioning units in the state, namely, philosopher-rulers, soldiers, and artisans. Even as the function of the philosopher-ruler is to govern the state, implicit in the notion of reason as a function is the ability to rule, govern, or control the rest of the soul or personality. When anything does its work well, it is virtuous or excellent. In this case, when reason as well as every other functioning unit is working well and working together, the result is harmony or an order of soul to which Plato gives the name of the overarching virtue, justice. Reason, then, is the ordering principle; a good person is one who has an ordered soul, whose personality is controlled by reason.

Aristotle's agreement with both the teleological method and Plato's application of it to reason is evident when he says, "It is both natural and expedient for the body to be ruled by the mind, and for the emotional part of our natures to be ruled by that part which possesses reason, our intelligence."[9] But, for Aristotle, the soul's capacities vary for different classes of people. Although the parts of the soul are present in women, slaves, and children, "The deliberative faculty in the soul is not present at all in a slave, in a female it is inoperative, in a child underdeveloped," according to T. A. Sinclair's translation.[10] Benjamin Jowett translates this passage a bit differently: "The slave has no deliberative faculty at all, the woman has, but it is without authority, and the child has, but it is immature."[11] Thus, reason in women, according to Aristotle, either does not work or does not count, depending upon one's translation.

Plato may be the only philosopher to have held a doctrine of natural place that assigns social roles on the basis of individual merit rather than assigning places to whole classes of people as illustrated by the commonplace statement "A woman's place is in the home." According to Plato, the nature (distinctive function) of human beings is reason, and a whole spectrum of rational abilities are distributed among human beings. One's nature, then, can be determined only by discovering one's talents, and, as Plato put it, "Many women are better than many men in many things."[12] Aristotle believed the more familiar doctrine that whole classes of people—women, slaves—have their natural places: "As between male and female the former is by nature superior and the ruler, the latter inferior and subject."[13] This type of move usually results in defining women as childbearers and reserving rationally oriented roles for men.

Claiming that men and women have different functions has further implications as well. Women's virtues are different from men's, and what constitutes flourishing for women is also different from that of men because one's virtues and one's flourishing both are dependent upon one's function. Human beings flourish to the extent that we fulfill our function or end. If the ends for men and women are different, what counts as flourishing is different as well. The function or purpose of human beings determines our virtues because the virtues are what lead us to our end or goal. Since men and women have different goals, it stands to reason that they have different virtues, that is, different ways of achieving their different goals.

Plato (and presumably his mentor, Socrates) clearly thought that men and women were capable of having the same virtues. This is so because both men and women have the same natural function of becoming a rational human being. Aristotle said that "the temperance of a man and of a woman or the courage and justice of a man and of a woman, are not, as Socrates maintained, the same; the courage of a man is shown in commanding, of a woman in obeying."[14] Women, according to Aristotle, are naturally ruled rather than rulers so he quotes approvingly the poet Sophocles, who "singles out 'silence' as 'bringing credit to a woman,' but . . . not . . . [to] a man."[15] On the other hand, such Aristotelian virtues as self-restraint, appropriate appreciation of one's own worth, wittiness, how to be gracious toward one's social inferiors without appearing to be condescending, and cultivation of a deep and therefore authoritative voice can be viewed as related to the roles of Greek gentlemen.[16]

Assigning to women the same function as might be appropriate to a female of any species has serious consequences, since in citing the function or role of something, we are setting certain standards that it must measure up to in order to be called good. If we are suspicious of teleology, the quarrel is not with the fact that a use of "good" is generated by defining things in terms of function; the quarrel concerns what sort of "good" we are talking about. Are the standards referred to in maintaining that a good "X" is one that functions well moral standards or simply standards of efficiency? They are at least the latter; the worry is they are perhaps only that. When we say a good lawnmower is one that cuts grass well, we clearly mean "good" in the sense of efficient or effective. If, to take another example, we define poison in terms of its function, good poison is that which does an effective, that is, quick and fatal, job. The good referred to is clearly not moral good, although this conclusion does not imply that a teleological or instrumental use of "good" could not also be a moral use.

There may be cases where the word "good" serves both functions. For example, when Lon Fuller advanced his natural law theory of jurisprudence,[17] he defined good law as laws that are clear, public, and consistent, claiming that such standards are necessary for moral, that is, fair, laws as well as effective ones. Laws that are unclear, secret, and inconsistent are not only ineffective but unjust. Although some jurisprudential scholars have argued against Fuller by maintaining that an instrumental use of good cannot be a moral use, there seems to be no a priori reason why a word cannot function simultaneously in more than one way. Granting this point, the criticism of teleology is not as dramatic as some would have it. Morality based on teleology cannot be scrapped merely because we claim to have discovered that the teleological use of "good" is not a moral use but simply means that things are efficient. However, we must always be on guard to discover from context which use is intended since we cannot assume that fulfilling a function or role is necessarily good in any moral sense.

For example, even if it is accepted that a good woman is one who fulfills her role, it may well be that "good" means nothing more than contributing to efficiency. Although efficiency arguments that condone women's inequality are increasingly rare in American contexts, they still play a powerful role internationally. For example, Amartya Sen, Harvard professor of economics and philosophy, stated in a recent symposium on world development economics that "gender inequality is made acceptable to women themselves (along with the more powerful male members of the society at large) by playing up the demands of efficiency in particular social arrangements. The relatively inferior role of women and the shockingly neglected treatment of young girls are implicitly 'justified' by alleged efficiency considerations. The alternative of chaos and gross inefficiency is frequently presented, explicitly or by implication, in discussions on this subject."[18]

Sen lays the blame for these arguments mainly at the door of utilitarianism, which is not surprising both because of the huge role that utility calculations have played in the field of economics and of the nature of utilitarian theory itself. Sen explains the latter claim: "Utilitarianism is ultimately an efficiency-oriented approach, concentrating on the maximum sum total of utilities, no matter how unequally that sum total may be distributed. If equity is central to justice, utilitarianism starts off somewhere at the periphery of it. It is, of course, possible to use utilitarianism to reject many inequalities, since inequalities are often also thoroughly inefficient. But given a lack of a basic concern with equality in the distribution of advantages, the utilitarian concentration on the promotion of utilities is not particularly oriented toward justice."[19]

But arguments that sex equality is inefficient took the form of natural law arguments in the 1970s in the United States. Just as some American women were beginning to see their lives as unnecessarily constricted, arguments for women's natural function or role appeared in an effort to keep gender roles conventional and mandatory. For example, in a 1970 issue of *Playboy,* Morton Hunt argued against husband and wife sharing equally in all tasks (career and home) on the grounds that "when there is no specialization of function, there is inefficient performance."[20] Although specialization is supposedly one essential aspect of all successful human groups (the other being a system of leadership), it is quite conceivable that a group of two (as opposed to a large corporation) might not prize efficiency as its highest value.

Much depends upon what is meant by "success." Liberty or freedom of role choice may not be very "successful" if success is measured in terms of efficiency. Freedom has never been known for its efficiency; it is always getting in the way of the smooth operations of orderly systems. The conflict between freedom and efficiency can be illustrated by marriage but is hardly confined to it. It may be inefficient for any one person (married, single, or living in a commune) to teach in a university, write articles, buy groceries, go to the gym, and demonstrate for political rights, but if a choice must be made between the freedom to do all these things and efficiency, the choice should at least be portrayed as a legitimate one.

Many corporations and government offices today, although committed to the value of efficiency, would question Hunt's belief that specialization of function is the best means to achieve that goal. Instead, cross-training that provides for interchangeability of role is thought to yield more efficiency than specialization of function. The thinking is this: If one person specializes in making widgets, she or he may be very good at it, but if the widget maker is out sick, the whole plant may be slowed. With cross-training, others will be able to step in and replace the widget maker when the need arises. Indeed, the fact that interchangeability of role has made it easier for corporations to downsize is a mark of its efficiency. At least this new thinking undermines the natural law idea that equality between men and women with respect to whatever tasks confront them will be inefficient.

Downsizing is a paradigm example of a corporate commitment to efficiency. One wonders if efficiency is not considered by some companies to be an ultimate value, given their willingness to permit the disruption, if not the destruction, of the lives of individuals and whole communities that results from throwing people out of work. When filmmaker Michael Moore asks the question, "Why doesn't GM sell crack?" he is suggesting that there are and should be some limits to the values corporations hold dear, that we do not and should not allow corporations to do anything in the name of efficiency and profit. Moore does not object to what he calls "legitimate layoffs," that is, when a company is losing money and cannot pay its workers. However, he argues that downsizing is immoral if done by companies already making record profits just so they can make a little bit more.[21] We can question the importance of efficiency. We can also ask, as we shall see later, efficient for whom?

Hunt further argued that specific roles are attractive: "It feels good, and is productive of well-being, for man and woman to look different, smell different, act somewhat different."[22] He quotes Dr. Benjamin Spock to the effect that the sexes are "more valuable and more pleasing" to one another if they have "specialized traits and . . . roles to play for each other's benefit—gifts of function, so to speak, that they can give to each other." There are heterosexual men and women, lesbians, and gay men who find complementarity of role attractive. Some people even find inferiority attractive. Note once again the remarks of Mary Hemingway: "Equality! I didn't want to be Ernest's equal. I wanted him to be the master, to be the stronger and cleverer than I, to remember constantly how big he was and how small

I was."[23] However, arguing that specific roles are efficient and attractive does not in and of itself determine who is to do what. Telling us in advance what woman's gift of function vis-à-vis men is going to be makes Hunt's argument typical of antifeminist arguments that are couched in the language of role.

The essential content of woman's role is probably best characterized by the concept of "support"—a concept that usually does not get, but certainly deserves, much analysis. Carried to the harshest extreme, slaves played a very important supportive role for their masters; from the masters' point of view, society was the more efficient and hence more desirable for it. Aristotle attested to the efficiency, if not the morality, of his view of natural arrangements when he said that slaves would not be needed if looms would weave by themselves.[24] In its weakest version, playing the supportive role can mean as little as the truism that everyone likes to be fussed over.

What Hunt had in mind is something between the two and closer to the former, since he pointed to the American system as admittedly unfair, but more workable and satisfying than any other alternatives. Hunt, after characterizing the roles of husband and wife as analogous to those of the president and the Speaker of the House respectively, conceded that "although the man is the head, he owes much to his wife's managerial support."[25] To prove the value of support, he appealed to a remark once made by Senator Maurine Neuberger that her greatest single need as a senator was for a good "wife." Neuberger's comment certainly proves that the supportive role aids efficiency; it is undeniably easier to be a senator if one has someone to shake well-wishers' hands, smile with you on campaign posters, repeat your ideas to groups you do not have time for, and answer your dinner invitations. That playing the supportive role aids efficiency cannot be questioned; however, the question remains, efficient for whom? Once it is clear whose projects are to be pursued efficiently or inefficiently, the discussion can be directed toward issues of power—who will say whose purposes, if any, shall be efficiently served.

Being an essentially pragmatic society, we often buy without question the latter half of the teleological framework, that good things are those that function well, although we fail to scrutinize what we mean by "good." We easily overlook that having a function, even a so-called natural one, does not entail that those having it *ought* to use it. As we have seen, to use "X" when "X" is defined as functional is to have a good "X" in some sense of the word. We can explain what poison is by citing its function, but it does not necessarily follow that it ought (in any moral sense) to function. Having children is also a natural function; whether it is good to make use of this function is a separate issue.

Given our current population problems, we might well decide that childbearing is not good in either the moral or efficient use of that word. Whether or not it is a good thing for women to have children, feminist social critic Barbara Ehrenreich says it certainly is no longer necessary: "Maybe there was a time when women had to stay home or at the hearth, and produce baby after baby, and just fill up the earth. God said, Go forth and multiply, and we took that commandment very seriously, this species. That's been done. You could still argue against feminism in the nineteenth century and say, Well, if you want to have these jobs and do this and that, what's going to happen to the species? Now we can say, as women, Wait a minute, we did our work, we overstocked the earth with human beings. We can take a rest now. We can be gay if we want. We can be asexual. The change may be terrifying in some ways, but it's also wonderful."[26]

One might, at this point, legitimately object that the well-being of human beings is more complicated than that of lawnmowers and poisons. If a lawnmower does not function well or is never used to cut grass, the lawnmower is not worse off for it. However, one might say, indeed Freudian conservatives have said, that the human being's biological potential is so integrated that when it is not realized, some kind of "maladjustment" or "unhappiness" results. Of course, some maintain that no such frustration ensues; obviously, to the extent that this view is correct, there is no problem, and, for example, people can decide whether or not to have children on the basis of values already discussed (efficiency, morality) since their "happiness" or "adjustment" is not at stake.

However, if we accept the Freudian conservatives' view, we must apply it consistently. Freudians have also taught us that suppression of sexual and aggressive impulses was necessary for the development of civilization. Even though suppression may result in frustration, we are told that in some cases this is the price that must be paid to purchase other goals. It is certainly not a new observation that one pays in some way for everything that one gets. Certainly, in recent times, humanity has paid for its advanced technological society in increased anxiety, frustration, and, most probably, neuroses. Freudians must allow the same perspective on the question of childbearing as on the questions of sexuality and aggressiveness.

In the latter case, we realize that some sort of suppression, probably resulting in some unhappiness, is required for civilization and/or technology. Some women's deliberate suppression of their biological potential should be regarded as an enhancement of the civilized and rational aspects of experience. If there is some biological or psychological frustration involved in the suppression of biological potential, only the individual woman should decide how she wishes to balance her desire for biological "completion" and her desire to experience the world as an independent human being. To recognize the possibility of such unhappiness is not to condone social arrangements that intensify the either/or character of this choice, but to elucidate once again the importance of liberty and to complicate values (liberty, morality, efficiency) by which we decide which units capable of functioning ought to function.

In the conclusion of his article, Hunt once more called upon natural law, assuring us that we need not fear the eradication of all sex-role differences because "nothing as joyless and contrary to our instinct is likely to become the pattern of the majority."[27] The language of "instinct," a somewhat modern way to refer to those things that we want to call "natural," is usually attached to some variation of philosophical determinism. Instincts are not considered to be matters of value choice, but a small class of desires that are somehow given. Some uses of "natural" lose their force without this built-in determinism; for example, excusing an action on the grounds that one was jealous, and "jealousy is only natural," will work only if the people listening accept the reasoning, "I couldn't help myself." If we do not buy the determinism, we do not buy the excuse.

Hunt's argument, and similar arguments from instinct, assume that that which is not the result of human effort is impervious to human control, since he moves from the claim that these instincts are "natural" (meaning something that happens without our doing anything to bring it about) to the claim that they are unalterable. That empirical assumption is extremely dubious; it would commit us to the position that since gravity "naturally" keeps us on the ground, we could never raise ourselves off the ground. Natural instinct may be just as open to control through education and training as our response to gravity is to the technology of air travel. However, if we assume that the behavior related to instincts is unalterable and inevitable, we can guarantee much more than that their obliteration will not become "the pattern of the majority."

As John Stuart Mill argued over a hundred years ago in *The Subjection of Women,* if the "proper sphere" of women is naturally determined, there will be no need for social and legal coercion to ensure that women stay in that sphere; we need not fear that women will do what they cannot do. There is no point in recommending that people desire what they inevitably will desire, so, insofar as we recommend that people adopt certain roles, we are assuming that those roles are, at least to some extent, items of choice. Thus, Hunt cannot have it both ways: as soon as he uses a claim of naturalness to entail a claim of inevitability, it becomes inappropriate as a support for a recommendation. One does not need to be told to do what one will inevitably do.

In psychoanalytic literature, the notion of instinct is frequently replaced by that of unconscious desire. Freud, in his *New Introductory Lectures on Psycho-Analysis,* defined the unconscious as follows: "We call a psychical process unconscious whose existence we are obliged to assume—for some such reason as that we infer it from its effects—but of which we know nothing."[28] In other words, the unconscious is not a thing, not some kind of container filled with desires that "drive" us to do this or that, but rather an explanatory device, not itself empirically evident but *needed* to explain certain behavior that is. "Needed," that is, in the sense that there are certain "effects" that defy explanation, that simply cannot be accounted for unless we posit an unconscious. For example, if people say they desire one thing but act as if they desire the contrary, and we know they are not lying, we may be tempted to say that they are somehow unaware of what their "real" motivation is.

If Susan says she wants a career more than anything else in the world, but she does nothing all day except stay home and put on makeup, we are puzzled and desire an explanation. If she is not lying or frivolous, we still lack an explanation; anything, including childhood and gene structure, is fair game as far as possible explanations go. But if Leslie has spent eight years preparing for a career and assures a prospective employer that she is serious about it, she does not deserve as an answer, "I would like to believe you, my dear, but all women really desire to be home with their children." Such a remark is unwarranted because there are no "effects" in this case that need to be explained.

I have tried to show some of the muddles that language of the "natural" gets us into. Except in cases where the natural is defined in terms of purpose or function, it carries no automatic value tag and in no case carries an automatic moral implication. After finding out what a person means by "natural," we then have to decide on independent grounds whether what is meant is in any sense good. For example, why is it good to do what animals do, or to avoid invented devices that interrupt what ordinarily happens? Why is what ordinarily happens considered to be a good thing? What is so good about order? Teleological uses of "natural" automatically set up an evaluative context; knowing the function of "X" makes it possible for us to evaluate "X" on grounds of functioning well. But as we have seen, teleological uses have to be morally evaluated; a good bomb is one that destroys, but is a good bomb morally good?

There is no reason to assume that the problem of evaluation would change because some things are created by persons and others are not. Many people, for example, argue that nature is good because God made it. This argument, of course, precipitates the old problem of evil. How can earthquakes and birth defects be good? The answer does not abandon the language of purpose but rather tells us in Platonic fashion that all of "creation" functions for some good end; humans, however, are incapable of knowing this end or purpose. Indeed, part of what it means to have faith is to believe that all natural (that is, created) purposes (in humans or otherwise) are good purposes and work together toward some larger purpose. Since human beings cannot know this larger end, there is no way that they can evaluate it. This belief, however, does not eliminate the problem of evaluation or eliminate the question, "In what sense are things that function well good?" It simply tells us that there is no cognitive answer or, more precisely, that only the faithful, after they have been steadfast in believing the acceptability of God's answer, will receive an answer. The position comes to this: Because we believe in God, we should believe that nature is good in some good sense.

Theological positions, however, in no way exempt us from either defining what we mean by "natural" or from appraising it. Indeed, even if the ultimate evaluation is said to be a matter of faith, the task that Thomas Aquinas referred to as natural or rational theology (the spelling out of the ends of things that are imprinted on the natures of things) is something that human beings must be prepared to perform without divine assistance. This task brings us right back to the beginning of our inquiry, namely, what in the world do people mean when they say that "X is natural"?

2

Eros and Epistemology

What is it in Plato that so angers some contemporary feminists?[1] Of the ancient philosophers, his views on women are the most enlightened, the most egalitarian. In Book V of the *Republic*, for instance, Plato says that women can in fact be philosophers; and this clear assertion has resisted decades of efforts by (mostly male) Plato commentators to argue it away. It is the *Symposium* and the *Phaedrus*, with their emphasis on homoerotic love as the necessary path to philosophic joy, that many feminist critics feel eliminate women from the search for wisdom and rational delight. But if Plato's thinking is consistent, the women he specifically includes as philosophers in the *Republic* cannot then be excluded by the *Symposium* and the *Phaedrus*.

Natalie Harris Bluestone, author of a 1987 book on Plato's *Republic* and gender,[2] categorizes one hundred years of attempts to write women philosophers out of the *Republic*, from 1870 through 1970, as Seven Types of Hostility:[3]

1. Equality as a Non-Issue: Neglect of the Proposals
   The same period of scholarship that discoursed at length on Plato's proposals on the abolition of property and the family often ignored completely the Platonic text on female equality.
2. Women Are Different: The Proposals as Unnatural
   Some of the most famous Plato scholars—Benjamin Jowett, Ernest Barker, A. E. Taylor, and Leo Strauss—substituted their own views on women's nature and role for Plato's, asserting simply that Plato was blind to the facts of human nature or that he forgot the importance of the body. Barker is typical when he says: "The fact of [a woman's] sex . . . colors her whole being; it makes her able indeed to inspire noble enthusiasms, but not to direct a policy or drill a regiment, as Plato would require his woman-ruler or woman-soldier to do."[4]

3. Women Have Better Things to Do: The Proposals as Undesirable
   Richard Nettleship, for example, offers the opinion that Athenian women probably would have viewed Plato's proposal as "dragging them out of a position in which they would rather be left."[5]
4. Plato Didn't Really Mean It: The Proposals as Unintentional, Unwelcome or Comic
   Allan Bloom, for example, suggests that Plato's belief in competent women was a noble lie, a fabrication to cover up the truth that women are placed in the guardian class (or the ruling class) to reproduce guardians.
5. Other Ways of "Explaining Away" the Plan for Gender Equality
   Historical explanations which attribute the idea of equality of role to the historical Socrates and psychoanalytic explanations of Plato's motives tend to detract from the philosophical merit of Plato's claims.
6. Bias in Language: The Consequences of Hidden Assumptions
   Awkward and misleading translations include C. H. Hoole's "woman is the weaker man" and Jowett's phrase, "the female sex in man." Jowett also refers to female guardians as "helpmeets" and to pregnant women as "in the family way" even when there is meant to be no family. Cornford writes that wives must strip for exercise although it is men and not husbands who strip in the gymnasium. The just cause of equal education is not helped by talk of educating the young lad, and the ubiquitous "Philosopher-King" could have been "Philosopher-Ruler" all along.
7. As Long as They Don't Go Too Far: The Warnings of the So-Called Feminists
   These critics cautiously approve of some measure of women's equality while fearing that women will be unreasonable in their ambitions and excessive in their demands.

With the beginning of feminist commentary on Plato in the early 1970s, there was a turning away from the previous hostility to the idea of female philosophers in the *Republic.* Today, with the notable exception of Allan Bloom, one rarely hears a challenge to the gender role equality of the *Republic.*

What does Plato say in Book V of the *Republic*? The argument is this:

Men are better in all pursuits including weaving and baking.
Hence, women have no natural pursuits; there is no woman's place that is hers by nature.
However, "many women are better than many men in many things."[6]
Therefore, each woman must be judged on her own merits.

The argument is one for equal opportunity, a limited but important type of equality.[7] In short, Plato says that generalizations about the abilities of people as a class are not relevant in determining social roles or occupations in particular cases.

The sentiment expressed by Allan Bloom to Plato's first premise above—that the class of men excel that of women in anything practiced by human beings—is especially interesting, because believing it undercuts the notion that women as a class have a natural place. F. M. Cornford translates this first premise a bit differently. Men, he says, are superior to women in any human occupation *except* things like weaving and watching over saucepans and batches of cakes. Although Plato's idea that the doctrine of natural place (or proper sphere) correctly applies to individuals rather than classes of persons is compatible with either translation, Bloom's version has the advantage that Socrates can grant as much as any misogynist could desire and still show the logical implication to be equal opportunity for both sexes. To some feminist commentators, Plato is labeled a sexist for having put forward any version of this premise. Perhaps, instead, the assertion of this premise is an example of the common Platonic practice of having Socrates get his opponent to agree to some outrageous view only to pull the rug out from under him by showing where his views lead. If the argument is accounted for this way, Plato might be absolved of one instance of sexism.

Bloom argues that if ability were the criterion for the role of guardian, there would not be enough women who would qualify. Indeed, it is unlikely that any would be considered because "the best women are always inferior in capacity to the best men."[8] First, according to Bloom's own translation, the class of men is superior to the class of women in all fields, which clearly is not the same as saying that the best women are always inferior to the best men. In fact, a generalization about men's competence is perfectly consistent with saying the best women are more capable than the best men. For example, one could say both that men in general make better physicians and that the best women physicians are better than the best men. Given this possibility, and given Bloom's translation of the relevant passages, some explanation is required for how he arrives at his conclusion that the best men are always superior to the best women.

Second, even if Plato did mean to say that the best women are never as good as the best men, it does not follow that there would not be enough women to be guardians by reason of merit. It might be that 2 men are far and away the best of the species, then 100 women excel to the extent that no man is their equal. After that, the next best are men, but the guardian class is to be made up of 102 people. (This is just the kind of distribution that we are accustomed to seeing in the violin sections of many orchestras.) There is nothing in the Socratic argument that precludes this result, and so there is no way one can know that there will not be enough women guardians on the basis of ability.

According to Bloom, the capacities of men and women are really quite different. Hence, without a fabricated story supporting the ability of women, there would be no reason for treating them the same as men. The fabrication is necessary, Bloom tells us, in order to get women into the guardian class for the purpose of reproduction without denying the Platonic criterion for membership. One would think that assigning women the same social role as men when they do not have the ability to fulfill that role would have devastating social consequences. A myth to support such a possibility would subvert competence and so would run counter to the obvious and plausible purpose of Plato's other myths. The lie or the allegory of metals is to help people face up to an accurate assessment of their abilities, whereas the fabrication about the nature of women would be one that leads everyone to believe that women are capable when they are not. If Plato's statement on the nature of women is a myth, he does not say so, whereas in other cases (the metals, the lottery), he informs us to that effect. Here we would have to assume that there is some reason to lie to the reader.

Plato argues that the same spectrum of jobs should be available to women as to men because it is natural. It is natural because with respect to who holds what job or social role, the differences between women and men are no more relevant than the difference between men who are bald and men who have hair. Although Plato did not argue that either gender has a specific nature, he did insist that human beings as a class do. Plato believed that the nature of human beings is rationality, so the good life for humans is the rational life. To his credit, Plato took it for granted that women were human beings, and thus, in the *Republic,* he is not even tempted to suggest that childbearing is the nature of women, because as human beings their nature is reason. Also, Plato could not remain consistent and claim that the natural end of human beings (or female human beings, had he separated humans into different classes as Aristotle later did) is childbearing or reproduction, because reproduction is not a function peculiar to human beings (or for that matter, female human beings).

Viewing the good life as the rational life means, of course, that the best life is the pursuit of philosophy, but rationality as the standard for good living is not limited to this implication. Plato's meritocracy in the *Republic* is built on the idea that humans are essentially rational creatures. Rational abilities or talents are dispersed among human beings in such a way that some individuals will be good at philosophy, some at carpentry, some at music, some at medicine. Hence, an individual's natural (that is, rational) place is performing the task she or he does best. If only because of the variety of role choice, Plato's view is superior to that of Freud and others who thought there was something unnatural about and wrong with women who did not want to devote their lives to men and children. Of course, Plato would have thought there was something unnatural about and wrong with a woman (or a man) who was good at playing the tuba and did not want to do it.

Perhaps sex roles do not need Plato to liberate them from the concept of nature, for this task is already (and finally) accomplished. Conventional sex roles used to be considered natural; today, at least by many, conventional sex roles are considered merely conventional. Nonetheless, it may be worth noting that had Plato's view prevailed (rather than those of Aristotle, Aquinas, or Freud), the long fight for equal opportunity could have been largely avoided. Still, Plato's framework does not permit free choice with respect to social role; it merely expands the number of roles available to women that count as natural and makes life happier for those who are inclined to do whatever it is they are good at.

Some women are good at philosophy. They, along with the men who are similarly talented, should rule the state. Despite Plato's clarity on this point in the *Republic,* many feminist commentators still feel excluded from the philosophic life by the ties between philosophy and male homoeroticism that pervade the *Symposium* and the *Phaedrus.* Jean Bethke Elshtain's views are a case in point: "[Plato's] debarment of women from the search for wisdom can be explained both by the social milieu within which the search occurred, including its sanctioned homoerotic attachments between older and younger men, as well as the particular nature of the truth at which Plato aimed. That is, a particular homosexual ethos, framed within a society rife with fear of, and repugnance towards, women, especially Mother, fused with what we call the Platonic metaphysic."[9] Elshtain's position is presented by Bluestone as the most vicious and extreme against Plato insofar as she claims that Plato's substantive conclusions were "infected" by the homoerotic as part of the process of acquiring knowledge and that "platonic metaphysics *in its very nature* excludes women."[10]

In truth, platonic metaphysics in its very nature excludes heterosexuals. Throughout the *Symposium* and the *Phaedrus,* the eros that is required for the achievement of knowledge is homosexual. For Plato, reality consists of an eternal, changeless world of Forms of which the physical world is a mere copy. The particulars of our changing, material world (somehow) participate in the forms or essences or perfect exemplars of these particular things. In order to know these perfect exemplars, one must follow a certain process. We cannot, for example, know the Form of the Beautiful without first experiencing beautiful things, and a key step in the ascent of knowledge is homosexual attraction.

As Plato explains in the *Symposium,* the male philosopher begins by gazing upon beautiful boys. He goes on to contemplate beautiful souls and pursuits. Finally, the intense and powerful erotic charge of homosexuality is diverted from physical completion, and the erotic energy is transferred from physical intimacy to an insight into imperishable beauty. As Michael Ruse puts it so nicely, "So, finally, having restrained ourselves in the physical (genital) realm, we come to be rewarded by what is almost literally a philosophical orgasm. As in the physical world, at the moment of climax we get a real sense of oneness with everything."[11] There is no reason that an analogous story cannot be told about women, since platonic metaphysics does not in its nature exclude women. It does, however, require lesbian eroticism as a first step in the ascent of knowledge.

Even a critic as sympathetic to Plato as Bluestone is disturbed by his emphasis on the necessity of homoeroticism; she counters Elshtain's infection thesis by arguing that homosexual eros is "only one device among many." Elshtain, she says, is "mistaken in her belief that homoeroticism is the only, or the chief, or in any sense, an essential element in the doctrine itself." Bluestone maintains further that homosexual attraction has a "metaphorical function" and that although the substitution of heterosexual eros would "detract from the particularity of a special ethos" when the *Symposium* is considered as literature, when it is considered as philosophy just such a substitution can and usually has been made. Generations of Platonists have seen themselves as "followers of a doctrine essentially separable from . . . Athenian homosexual practice." Quoting K. J. Dover approvingly to the effect that Plato *exploited* the homosexual ethos, Bluestone concludes that it is both possible and advisable "to consider Plato's theories independent of his . . . sexual preference."[12]

But the *Symposium* and the *Phaedrus* are not ambiguous on this point: homoeroticism is an essential element in the lover's upward path to the form of beauty. I will argue that Plato's choice of homosexuality over heterosexuality as the model for the ascent toward the knowledge of beauty is crucial, since it reflects his understanding of the nature of that ascent. First, however, I want to call attention to the clear and absolutely straightforward claims that Plato makes about hetero- and homosexuality and their relationship to knowledge and reality. He says that heterosexual eros is, from the point of view of metaphysics, that is, knowing the forms, a dead end. Heterosexual eros is second-rate; it leads to making babies, not to philosophical achievement. In 211C *Symposium,* Plato says, "So when someone rises by these stages, through loving boys correctly . . . This is what it is to go aright."[13]

Susan Moller Okin is correct in her interpretation of Plato that the procreation of the soul that leads to poems, laws, and thoughts is achieved only in homosexual love and that homosexual love is a superior type of love. Even though she finds these views to be hostile to heterosexuality and to women,[14] Okin rejects efforts by Gregory Vlastos to temper Plato's devaluation of heterosexuality by labeling the very use of the image of procreation "a heterosexual paradigm." She says: "If Vlastos is implying . . . that there is any inclusion of heterosexuality in the theory of the higher type of love, his conclusion is unfounded. In spite of Plato's use of an image that, as Vlastos says, has 'a heterosexual paradigm,' it is clearly only the symbolic version of procreation—that of the spirit, which is only achieved in homosexual love—that is thought worthy of philosophical treatment."[15]

Okin is exactly right on this point; Plato is not espousing here—as Bluestone has suggested—some abstract notion of the erotic attraction and fecundity of minds that can be applied to any pair of lovers. Such a view misses completely the importance of the fact that a man's love is for one *like himself.* And though Bluestone, to her credit, admits lesbian attraction as a possible application of the abstract notion she takes to be Plato's, she still wants to include as well the possibility of some idealized heterosexual attraction, agreeing with Erich Segal that Dante's love for Beatrice is a "distinct parallel."[16] Elshtain and Okin are more accurate in arguing the necessity of homoeroticism to Plato's metaphysics, but they both infer wrongly that that eroticism must be male. Okin, in a statement reminiscent of Elshtain, says, "It is quite clear . . . that Plato's vision of love as a pathway to philosophic joy entirely excludes women."[17] Apparently, both Elshtain and Okin are following in the footsteps of Queen Victoria; for them, lesbians do not exist.

Thus, current feminist criticism splits between views denying the importance of homoeroticism in Plato in order to include women in a conventionally acceptable way and views insisting on the necessity of homoeroticism but finding that it bars women from philosophy. Both sides of this unbefitting rift are heterosexist in their assumptions in that they make marginal or invisible the gay experience Plato took to be central. As we will see, feminist critics have reasons for thinking that Plato's criteria for excellence is sexist quite apart from the homoeroticism issue, but before looking at any of these, I want to present what I think is Plato's view on sexuality and knowledge.

Plato disapproved of sexual activity—whether heterosexual or homosexual—solely for the purpose of physical orgasm. But sexual activity is nevertheless important because knowledge of higher types of beauty is not obtainable without the lower level insights into beauty that sex provides. Its primary importance, according to Ellen Shapiro, is to establish the *manner* by which we know the Form. The reason homosexual experience initiates the ascent is because of its unique ability to provide human beings with a method of knowing analogous to the manner in which beauty is known.[18] The Form is known by acquaintance or direct experience—something very much like what Bertrand Russell called knowledge by acquaintance: "We shall say that we have *acquaintance* with anything of which we are directly aware, without the intermediary of any process of inference . . . things immediately known to me just as they are."[19] Homosexual experience best demonstrates the epistemological requirements for the ascent to knowing Beauty; it can provide the type of knowledge needed whereas heterosexual experience cannot.

The idea of beauty in the *Symposium* is not an abstract logical entity; it is absolutely and divinely beautiful, "a love object par excellence . . . a paradigm Form so splendidly and shamelessly self-exemplifying that its own beauty outshines that of everything else."[20] The soul "throbs with ferment" and experiences a "strange sweating and fever" when it encounters (or better, recollects) the Form. Dover is getting at the connection between the direct experience of physical beauty and the direct experience of the Form when he says, "Why eros should play so conspicuous a part in a metaphysical system is not so obvious, but the most succinct explanation is to be found in *Phdr.* 250D, where it is observed that beauty is the only one, of those things . . . 'attracting eros,' which can be directly perceived by the senses so that the sight of something beautiful affords by far the most powerful and immediate access we have to the world of being."[21]

Plato claims that the Form of Beauty is itself beautiful. The self-predicative nature of beauty suggests the suitability of a particular way of knowing, namely, knowledge by acquaintance. Knowledge by description, to use another of Russell's terms, involves knowing that an object has a certain property, though the object itself is not directly known. It is clear from what Plato says that this is not the kind of knowledge one has of beauty. Beauty cannot be separated into constituents and known as a compilation of specific properties: "It is not beautiful in part and ugly in part, nor beautiful at one time and ugly at another, nor beautiful in this relation and ugly in that, nor beautiful here and ugly there."[22] Beauty is a self-referential whole, and to be known it must be experienced as such.

What are the epistemological features of homoeroticism that make it a standard for a method of knowing that in turn enables us to ascend to higher types of love? Simone de Beauvoir, in a passage on lesbian love, discusses relevant epistemological differences between homosexuality and heterosexuality that Plato saw before her:

> It is most important to emphasize the fact that refusal to make herself the object is not always what turns woman to homosexuality; most lesbians, on the contrary, seek to cultivate the treasures of their femininity. To be willing to be changed into a passive object is not to renounce all claim to subjectivity; woman hopes in this way to find self-realization under the aspect of herself as a thing; but then she will be trying to find herself in her otherness, her alterity. When alone she does not succeed in really creating her double; if she caresses her own bosom, she still does not know how her breasts seem to a strange hand, nor how they are felt to react under a strange hand; a man can reveal to her the existence of her flesh for herself, that is to say, as she herself perceives it, but not what it is to others. It is only when her fingers trace the body of a woman whose fingers in turn trace her body that the miracle of the mirror is accomplished. Between man and woman love is an act; each torn from self becomes other: what fills the woman in love with wonder is that the languourous passivity of her flesh should be reflected in the male's impetuosity; the narcissistic woman, however, recognizes her enticements but dimly in the man's erected flesh. Between women love is contemplative; caresses are intended less to gain possession of the other than gradually to recreate the self through her; separateness is abolished, there is no struggle, no victory, no defeat; in exact reciprocity each is at once subject and object, sovereign and slave; duality becomes mutuality.[23]

In homosexual experience, separateness is abolished. The knowledge of the beloved, of how she is aroused, is not inferred because the experience of the lovers is, as de Beauvoir puts it, exactly reciprocal. The subject-object distinction breaks down: the miracle of the mirror. That image of a mirror was used by Plato to depict an important characteristic of homosexual relationships in the *Phaedrus* account of the special happiness that comes to lovers who—after much struggle—resist lust in favor of a life of philosophy together:

> He feels a desire, like the lover's yet not so strong, to behold, to touch, to kiss him, to share his couch: and now ere long the desire, as one might guess, leads to the act. So when they lie side by side, the wanton horse of the lover's soul would have a word with the charioteer, claiming a little guerdon for all his trouble. The like steed in the soul of the beloved has no word to say, but, swelling with desire for he knows not what, embraces and kisses the lover, in grateful acknowledgment of all his kindness. And when they lie by one another, he is minded not to refuse to do his part in gratifying his lover's

> entreaties; yet his yoke-fellow in turn, being moved by reverence and helpfulness, joins with the driver in resisting. And so, if the victory be won by the higher elements of mind guiding them into the ordered rule of the philosophic life, their days on earth will be blessed with happiness and concord.[24]

But it is clear from Plato's account of the dawning of attraction that this swelling and calming of passion is more than physical attraction to some other: "So he loves, yet knows not what he loves: he does not understand, he cannot tell what has come upon him. . . . he *cannot* account for it, not realizing that his lover is as it were a mirror in which he beholds himself."[25] The lover is aware of beauty in the same manner as he is aware of his own existence.

By contrast, heterosexual relationships, at their best, oscillate between subject and object. (At their worst, men are always subjects and women are always objects.) With respect to arousal, a woman knows that her lover desires her, but she does not know this directly. She infers it from his erected flesh, from his behavior. He may tell her so in words, but her experience must always be different and separate from his.

Homoeroticism provides the foundation for acquaintance with Beauty because the immediacy in homosexual encounters is akin to the way in which Beauty is known. Still, as Shapiro notes, it might be objected that the only genuine acquaintance or genuine knowledge is of the Forms, that is, that knowledge of erotic properties is not really knowledge. We might then, she suggests, characterize homoeroticism as a kind of "psychological preparation" for genuine knowledge by acquaintance that will make possible the recollection of Beauty. It is clear that Plato intends that sexuality be the starting point for the ascent, and heterosexuality cannot provide the appropriate preparation because heterosexual "knowledge" of erotic properties must always be inferential.

Even if Plato's talk about homoeroticism is just talk about an image, a metaphor, an analogy, or a model for knowledge, one must get one's images (or whatever) right. Evelyn Fox Keller, who compares various paradigms for knowledge in Western thought, takes this view. For Plato, she says, knowledge is a kind of communion, "a spiritual coupling between mind and form—a union of kindred essences."[26] According to Keller, "Plato's model for spiritual begetting is the love of man for man . . . the union of mind with 'the essential nature of things' is a union of like with like; accordingly, it is taken for granted throughout the *Symposium* and the *Phaedrus* 'that eros which is significant as a step towards the world of being is homosexual.' "[27] When Baconian science in the Renaissance invokes "a new set of images, homoerotic union is superseded by heterosexual conquest." Our understanding of understanding shifts "with the shift from male to female object."

Nature is female for both Plato and Bacon, but in the first instance she is abandoned, in the second, "seduced and conquered." Since Plato clearly recognized (in Book V of the *Republic*) that women could be philosophers, the most we can conclude from this abandonment view is that being a philosopher requires that females (and males) forsake feminine characteristics associated with the earth in favor of abstractions associated with the masculine. But Keller thinks that Plato's conception of knowledge is not merely masculine but male, for she characterizes the Platonic Forms as "a rarefied distillate of male sexuality."[28] It is difficult to know what Keller means by this statement, because none of the elements of Plato's model that she emphasizes—the reciprocity, the importance of like with like, the lack of aggression, the egalitarian factors—in principle exclude women. She could mean that only men are erotically attracted by abstractions, which, of course, is not true.

Still, Elshtain, Okin, and Keller all feel excluded in some way by the homoerotic atmosphere of the dialogues. Only Elshtain and Okin, however, express anger at the exclusion, connect love in the *Symposium* with the belittling of women,[29] and attribute Plato's misogyny (in part) to his homosexuality. But women are neither excluded in theory from becoming philosophers or excluded in principle from participating in the process of knowing. Such points should not be lost on philosophers, that is, those who normally value more highly matters of theory than practice. Why then the accusations by some feminists that Plato's criteria for excellence are sexist?

Plato in fact included women in the pursuit of philosophy, but only some women. He included those with exceptional intellectual gifts who also were devoted to masculine or manly values such as abstract thought and the rational control of passion. Plato's academic world was not so very different from the contemporary one. Few women attended his Academy; one who did wore men's clothing. The historical existence of Diotima, the author of Socrates' speech on love in the *Symposium,* is questionable. As Elizabeth Spelman puts the point so nicely, "Misogyny has always been compatible with having high regard for 'exceptional' (and surely for imaginary) women."[30] Spelman focuses on the fact that Plato favors women who can be philosophers—that is, women who can be like the ideal man—and shows the typical Athenian woman—secretive, gossipy, and emotional—as the model of what to avoid.

Men who act like the typical woman, Plato warns in the *Timaeus,* will be punished by becoming a woman in their next life. Although Plato was not impressed by the typical man either, he did not make continual derogatory remarks about them, the cumulative effect of which is to make it harder for members of the disparaged class—exceptional or typical—to gain equal respect with those who are not similarly discredited. A variety of studies in the past couple of decades show that academic women get less for their achievements even when their achievements are objectively equal to men's.[31] In one such study, for example, psychology department heads judged credentials accompanied by a female name to be one rank lower than identical credentials accompanied by a male name.[32]

Plato's commitment to the so-called masculine virtue of abstract thought also implies much more than might first appear. Luce Irigaray interprets Plato's attachment to reason as a denial of the importance of our birth or, presumably, of giving birth, a denial of our physical origin.[33] Birth, which is a nonrational event and the beginning of a process of becoming, can be conceptually obliterated in a scheme that recognizes only eternal forms as real. Interestingly, recollection allows a philosopher to bypass birth and becoming altogether, for to recollect the forms is to join the realm of being where one existed before birth: "The recollection of 'intelligibles' thus takes one back before the material, matrical conception. It is a matter to be settled 'man to man.' Really man to man? Where, in that case, is the mother? . . . Thoughts on divine truth are available to man only when he has left *behind* everything that still linked him to this sensible world that the earth, the mother, represents."[34]

Irigaray's point that the world of Forms rejects the material world reiterates Keller's that for Plato the *feminine* "Nature" was to be overcome and left behind. In Plato's thinking are perhaps still echoes of the great Earth Mother/Sky Father cultural struggle that had occupied the Mediterranean world for centuries; and feminists who argue that some "earth-connectedness" is central to their philosophy might ultimately find this rejection of the physical more disturbing in Plato than any gender-typing of virtues. Thus, the anger is coming from different sources: some from those who find obnoxious the way in which the idea of the exceptional woman works in society and in the academy; some from those who see mothers rejected; some from those who extol the feminine and "earthy" virtues; and some from those who in their implicit or explicit heterosexism take heterosexuality to be the norm.

Those commentators such as Elshtain, Okin, and Irigaray who fail to see that women are capable of Platonic knowledge because they are capable of homoerotic relations are heterosexist even if they raise interesting points vis-à-vis Plato's idealism or other aspects of his epistemology. Those commentators like Bluestone who say that sexual preference does not matter to how we view reality trivialize the role that gay experience can play as a model for conceptions of knowledge. Keller is right in her view that alternative sexual models modify those conceptions of knowledge and of the relationship of mind to nature. Feminists should take the lead in exploring what new visions become available "if we open up our ways of knowing and of sanctifying knowledge to understandings that are rooted in the phenomenology of being gay or lesbian in the world."[35]

At the very least, the time has come for those who teach and write commentaries on Plato in the twenty-first century to be more truthful. For generations, Plato commentators have written and philosophy professors have taught or implied by their silence that platonic love is heterosexual and spiritual whereas, in fact, it is homosexual and quite physical. It is hoped that those who have worked hard to rid the pre-1970 Plato scholarship of its sexism will be particularly sensitive to the entrenched efforts in Plato scholarship to obliterate gay experience.

3

Natural Law and Moral Rights

Immanuel Kant's moral theory with its central notions of universalization, autonomy, and the Categorical Imperative is among the most important in Western philosophical ethics. Although Kant is perhaps best known for developing a doctrine of moral personhood that forms the basis of a theory of moral rights, there are potentially dangerous inconsistencies in the rights tradition he began. For instance, when philosopher Alan Donagan attempted to reposition Kant's ethical writings from a natural law point of view, he was seizing on a deep inconsistency in Kant's work. In this chapter, I show what Kant's inconsistency—his reluctance to abandon his idea of natural purposes for his much better idea of moral personhood as the basis of a theory of rights—amounts to in both theory and applied ethics. From that, I argue that the Kantian doctrine of moral personhood should lead us to a rejection of the natural law tradition of Aquinas and Aristotle, not the revitalization that Donagan tried to demonstrate.

NATURAL LAW THEORY

The theory of morality that Alan Donagan constructs is a natural law theory that he claims reflects traditional morality and, in particular, Kantian morality.[1] Donagan's theory consists of a fundamental principle—"it is impermissible not to respect every human being, oneself or any other, as a rational creature"—and the precepts that can be derived from it. "The precepts, . . . like the fundamental principle itself, have to do with that part of what the Hebrew-Christian tradition takes to be common morality which does not presuppose any theological doctrine." The precepts, Donagan says, are "mine, in that I think them valid, almost none [are] original. Most of them [are] critically selected from the writings of the moralists whose work has shaped traditional morality."[2] Indeed, most of the precepts are what one would expect from Aquinas or Kant: voluntary sterilization and most suicides are wrong, abortion and infanticide are absolutely prohibited, and so forth.

Central to natural law theory is the doctrine of natural purpose or natural place. Some of the reasoning Kant uses in applying the Categorical Imperative to particular cases clearly displays a commitment to natural purposes. For example, in the case of the person who fails to fulfill his talents, Kant says, "As a rational being, he necessarily wills that all his faculties should be developed, inasmuch as they are given to him for all sorts of possible purposes."[3] Donagan argues for a principle of culture on similar grounds: "Common morality demands of every human being that he adopt some coherent plan of life according to which . . . his mental and physical powers may be developed. Not to adopt such a plan is impermissible, as wanting in respect to himself as a rational creature capable of developing such powers."[4] Kant's argument against suicide is another example of his commitment to natural purposes. The argument assumes a feeling whose special purpose it is to "impel the improvement of life."[5] Otherwise, there would be no contradiction in universalizing the principle of self-love to suicides. The important thing to note about these examples is the fundamental tenet of natural law theory that natural ends or purposes are purposes that are independent of my will.

If we were to dispense with natural law assumptions, the easiest place to do so would be at the level of cases. The cases would be worked out differently if we made no assumption that there are natural ends, functions, capacities, and so on that must be fulfilled. Even at this level the task is not simple, for the notion of rationality employed by natural law theory is one of fulfilling natural ends that are independent of an individual's will. We would have to drop this notion of rationality and mean something else by respecting ourselves as rational agents. One meaning of respecting ourselves as rational agents is contained in the Kantian notion of autonomy—the idea of self-legislation. However, if we accept Kantian autonomy, we must reject the natural law doctrine of natural purposes. Natural purposes are necessarily not an object of my will and are therefore inconsistent with autonomy.

In the *Critique of Judgement*,[6] Kant makes clear that his commitment to natural purposes or natural place extends beyond an occasional invoking of teleology in solving moral problems. The doctrine of natural place, developed in the *Critique* and elsewhere,[7] is the notion that entities or beings—such as plants, animals, women, men—have a natural function or purpose in a hierarchically ordered system of purposes. A rational universe is a universe in which one takes one's place and fulfills one's end in a hierarchy of ends. "The great chain of being," an old metaphysical doctrine expounded by Aristotle, Aquinas, and Kant, is a paradigm example of the doctrine of natural place. The chain of being consists of plants, animals, female human beings, male human beings, and the Unmoved Mover or God. Plants are to be eaten by animals and human beings; animals are to be eaten and otherwise used by human beings since they are "man's instruments," in the words of Kant.[8] Women have their natural place in the home, serving the interests of others, most notably men and children.

In theological versions of the great chain of being, there are two levels beyond male human beings: angels and God. The end of male human beings, and presumably of angels, is to serve God. From the metaphysical point of view, the great chain of being identifies levels of being by their function. Since the function at each level is determined by the needs, interests, or good of beings in the next highest level, each lower kind becomes, morally speaking, a mere means to the ends of the next highest. Animals are to serve human ends, women are to serve the ends of men, and men are to serve the ends of God.

Traditional natural law theory presupposes a hierarchy among persons. In order to show this, we need a distinction between two senses of the phrase "y is x's purpose," where x is a sentient being and y is some state of affairs. (1) Y is x's purpose in that y arises from x's will, that is, y is what x proposes. (2) Y is x's purpose, but y is independent of x's will. In the case of sentient beings who are capable of having purposes in the original sense, how is it possible for x's purpose to be inconsistent with x's purpose? This outcome can only be explained if purpose in the second sense overrules purpose in the first sense. But how is this possible? This result can happen only if purpose in the second sense is the purpose of one with greater moral value or if talk of purposes is disguised talk of moral principles that must then be justified on some other grounds.

Although the latter may be relevant to explaining some natural law claims, it is the former that explains the great chain of being. Aristotle attaches moral superiority to various classes of beings, making it obvious that the purposes of some beings supercede the purposes of others simply because of their greater moral value. If Aristotle had followed Plato's sense of natural function—doing what one is good at—the purpose of human beings might be to serve animals rather than the other way around. After all, we can provide them with shelter and the comforts of life that they cannot provide for us.

For Plato, superiority brings responsibility. The better should rule and serve the inferiors. A talent for ruling creates an obligation to rule, because if I have a talent, everybody will be better off. The right to rule does not mean that I am entitled to the benefit of other people obeying me. Rather, others are entitled to the benefit of my wisdom. For Aristotle, the right to rule implies that others have an obligation to serve me.

When Donagan speaks of traditional morality or natural law morality (which he claims amount to the same thing), he is speaking of Aristotle's views or views that have been influenced by Aristotle. Had Plato's views prevailed, traditional morality would have been very different. As we have seen, for Plato, the nature (distinctive function) of human beings is reason, and a whole spectrum of rational abilities is distributed among human beings. One's nature, then, can be discovered only by discovering one's talents, and, as Plato put it, "Many women are better than many men in many things."[9] On Plato's view, it might be a woman's place to be a musician or a carpenter or a philosopher.

Aristotle and Aquinas, on the other hand, believed the more familiar doctrine that whole classes of beings or entities—women, slaves—have their natural places. Plato's view is the more palatable, because one's nature is at least connected to one's individual characteristics. However, it was not the views of Plato but rather the views of Aristotle and Aquinas that influenced the whole of Western civilization and thus constitute what we think of as traditional morality. On this view, levels of being have a function, and these functions are hierarchically ordered. Not only does each—except perhaps God—have a function, but the function at each level is determined by the needs, interests, or good of beings in the next highest level. The hierarchy among persons can only be explained by attributing moral superiority to some levels of being such that their purposes overrule the purposes of beings with lesser moral value.

MORAL PERSONHOOD

It is generally accepted that persons are the sorts of beings that have rights. Kant provided the original argument that explains what persons are and why they have rights, and he explicates what a person is by distinguishing persons from things. Persons are rational, autonomous beings who are capable of formulating and pursuing different conceptions of the good. That is, persons have ends of their own; things or objects in the world do not.

For example, suppose I walk into a classroom and decide to break up all the chairs in order to use them for firewood. If I do this, it does not matter to the chairs.[10] Now, there may be many reasons why I should not destroy the chairs. The next class may be planning to sit on them. Presumably, somebody owns the chairs and does not want me to destroy them. However, I cannot give as a reason for refraining from breaking the chairs that it matters to the chairs. It can even be said that it is in the interests of chairs not to be broken (or in the interests of lawnmowers not to be left out in the rain), but this assertion is not the same thing as claiming that chairs or lawnmowers have interests of their own if we mean that chairs or lawnmowers care about how they are treated. Persons care about how they are treated; things do not.

According to Kant, things can be used to suit the purposes of persons, but persons are not to be used as if they were mere things, as if they had no ends or purposes of their own. Persons have rights because of their unconditional worth as rational beings, whereas the worth of things is relative to the ends of persons. On this argument, the point of rights is to protect persons from being treated as things. However, a fundamental assumption of traditional natural law theory is that certain classes of persons are rightly treated as things, that is, their function or purpose is to serve the ends of someone else. For example, as we have seen, Kant believed that the function of women is defined in relation to others, not in relation to themselves. They have neither equality of authority nor autonomy, both of which are crucial to the doctrine of moral personhood that supports rights theory.

For Kant, the virtue of a person is radically different from the virtue of a thing. The virtue of a thing consists in being a good means, whereas the virtue of a person consists in being an end. Kant drives a sharp wedge between persons and everything else in the world, but there is no such fundamental difference between persons and things in natural law theory. Plato, for example, means the same thing by virtue whether he is speaking of virtuous knives or virtuous human beings—"doing" that at which they are best. We can talk about the virtue of human beings or knives in terms of means. They are good at something, a good means. For Kant, the goodness of a free being cannot come from being a good means. Therefore, Kant should have rejected the natural law notion of natural function. If the goodness of a free being cannot come from being a good means, it cannot come from fulfilling a natural function, for having a natural function is, morally speaking, being treated as a means to some end outside oneself.

Autonomy is the Kantian notion of self-rule, the ability to formulate and pursue different conceptions of the good. Natural law recognizes only natural ends, not one's own ends. That is, under natural law, persons are not recognized as the source of law. A person's natural end may be to serve the ends of others. Such a conclusion is incompatible with autonomy, for if I am autonomous, I am a source of law, and if I am a source of law, I am not an object to be used by somebody else. Thus, natural law reasoning does not accept Kantian autonomy, nor does it provide a distinction between persons and things, which in Kantian thought helps us to isolate the features of moral persons that rights are designed to protect.

One of the advantages of rights talk is that it portrays persons as autonomous agents who have a legitimate part in moral decisions rather than as mere objects of an obligation or beneficiaries of someone's virtue. As long as we focus on obligations, responsibilities, or virtues, we are talking about the decisions of the person who is in a position to either wrong the other or do good to the other. Rights talk focuses attention on the person to whom the obligation is owed.

Rights can and have been justified on grounds other than personhood, but that does not concern us here. It is also important to note that Kant's notion of personhood can be incorporated into a variety of ethical arguments and theories. That is, it can play a role in ethical argument other than that of establishing moral rights, which is so because the moral insight that persons should not be treated as things or objects is a fundamental one. However, this fundamental insight cannot be incorporated into natural law theory. Traditional natural law theory recommends that persons other than God be treated as a mere means to the ends of others. Moreover, as we shall see, traditional morality reflects this theory in its precepts and applied ethics. It is a devastating criticism of natural law theory that it is incompatible, qua theory, with Kant's fundamental insight about the nature and worth of persons. It is questionable whether such a theory can be called a moral theory at all, let alone, as Donagan calls it, *the* theory of morality.

APPLYING THE THEORIES

One example of how the conflict in theory I have outlined yields incompatible solutions to moral problems can be found in Donagan's treatment of abortion. He concludes that abortion is homicide and that it is absolutely prohibited.[11] However, Donagan also agrees with Judith Thomson that abortion is justified in the case of rape: "Here the unborn child has not been brought into existence by any voluntary action of hers. And so, in my opinion, for her to refuse to have it in her womb would not fail to respect it as a rational creature."[12] A natural law argument could not make an exception for rape, as Etienne Gilson makes clear in his commentary on Aquinas. The natural purpose of sexual intercourse is procreation, and rape does not interfere with the fulfilling of this purpose.[13] The importance Donagan attaches to voluntary action or consent must be derived from a rights argument. Consent cannot be relevant on natural law theory, because one's moral purpose comes from one's nature and that nature is given—that is, my nature cannot be a creation of my will. If my nature could be a creation of my will, then we would not have a contradiction between will and purpose.

Thomson's *primary* concern is to universalize the principle that the bodies of persons ought not to be used as life-support systems without the consent of the person whose body is to be so used. Although Thomson does not explain what is wrong with ignoring consent in these cases, there is a perfectly plausible Kantian explanation. A life-support system is a thing. To use another person as a life-support system without any concern for her will is to treat that person as a thing, as an object useful to the interests and purposes of others.

What matters according to natural law theory is that women fulfill their natural end (reproduction), not whether they fulfill their ends as rational beings or persons. Beginning with Aristotle, the ends of women are limited to the nonrational functions of producing children and caring for the needs of children and men. It is predictable that such a tradition would view women as life-support systems for the use of others (fetuses). As we have seen, natural purposes are always independent of my will. Indeed, according to natural law theory, the purposes that arise from my will have no independent weight. For Kant, the ends of rational beings are self-imposed, which, of course, does not mean that one's purpose cannot be immoral. A rational being must subject its self-imposed ends to the test of universalization.

Thomson is universalizing a right to one's own body, while natural law theory has never been committed to universalization. Examples abound. Defective human beings (biological human beings who do not have rational agency) are thought to be more valuable than animals. The value on rational agency is not universalized. Similarly, if a person with a kidney ailment needs another person's body as a life-support system, consent must first be obtained from the person whose body is to be used. Not until Thomson was it clear that the universalization of the principle behind this case is relevant to the case of abortion.

If the moral importance of consent is acknowledged, abortion is justified in a very large number of cases provided we apply to women the same notion of consent that our moral and legal tradition affords any person. According to this tradition (Locke, Mill, Kant), consent must be informed and uncoerced. There are vast numbers of pregnancies among the very young and the very poor, two groups that are likely to be ignorant and uninformed. If we count along with the uninformed all the cases of coercion in sexual relations of which rape is a blatant example, but not the only example, we have enormous numbers of pregnancies that do not meet the requirements for consent. Thus, to make an exception for rape, as Donagan does, is to defend abortion in a substantial way that is hardly compatible with an absolute prohibition.

It is commonplace for students of ethics to be caught in the kind of theoretical inconsistency found in Kant. For example, with respect to abortion, the students who want to follow a rights argument because of their commitment to a right to life are the same ones who adhere to the natural law tradition of Aristotle and Aquinas. They rely on rights theory in order to claim that fetuses have a right to life while, at the same time, maintaining that women have the natural function of talking care of fetuses. What is not taken into account is that if women are persons and have rights, they cannot be used for the ends of others without their consent.

Donagan faces a similar conflict insofar as he wants to bring back traditional morality, that is, Hebrew-Christian morality or its secular equivalent, natural law morality. What he cannot do, if this is the tradition he wants to revive, is treat autonomy and consent as part of his theory. Kant is inconsistent precisely because he has one foot in traditional moral notions and the other in innovative notions such as autonomy. Donagan, who wants to follow Kant and revive traditional morality, has similar difficulties.

CONCLUSION

Donagan says: "It is unthinkable that a traditional consensus about the substance of morality, maintained for over two millennia . . . should be accidental. Such a consensus may be in error; but if so, its error must lie deep.[14] I have argued that the error does lie deep insofar as traditional morality reduces the significance of persons other than God to their function as a means.

Kant should have rejected the doctrine of natural purpose or natural place for persons as inconsistent with autonomy and equality of persons and the method of universalization. One factor that would have helped him that he did not have at his disposal is the critiques of sexism and speciesism that suggest that there must be a better reason for moral consideration than membership in a given sex or species.

Donagan dismisses the approach in ethical theory that follows Kant's lead in proposing that persons rather than human beings are moral beings, calling it "a do-it-yourself kit for constructing a 'moral community to your own taste.' "[15] Donagan does exactly what he objects to by not taking seriously rationality as the source of moral worth. Like Plato, Donagan claims that rationality is the nature of human beings whether or not there is any evidence that all and only human beings are rational. No one would say of a human zygote (fertilized egg) that it can reason, but it counts as a rational creature, according to Donagan, because it is a member of our species. No one is more deserving of Donagan's criticism—constructing a moral community to your own taste—than Aristotle, who was not only speciesist but insisted that rationality is the nature of men and in women is inoperative or without authority.

According to Kant, rights are a way of showing respect for moral personality, most notably rationality and autonomy. He held what I call the "bag of rights" view. Imagine that all the classical rights (liberty, life, property, and so on) are in a burlap bag or a sack. On Kant's view, if you are a rational, autonomous being, you get the whole bag of rights; if you are not a rational, autonomous being, you get none. Although autonomy may be necessary for possession of a right to liberty, one might ask why a being must be autonomous in order to have a right not to be tortured. But this idea that the various rights have their own relevant criteria or qualifications goes way beyond Kant's thinking or that of any other classical rights theorist.

Donagan further characterizes the choosing of characteristics of personhood as "license" and as "terrifying."[16] However, to say that contemporary philosophers have chosen characteristics of personhood or qualifications for rights that are morally relevant is not to imply anything about license or choosing in an arbitrary way. The choice of these characteristics—to be acceptable—must be based on rational moral argument. However, Donagan's choice of the traditional definition of personhood also stands in need of rational moral argument. In the light of the violent history of the tradition he is appealing to, what is truly terrifying is his assumption that it is only those who disagree with tradition who are being arbitrary.

4

Holes and Slime: Sexism in Sartre's Psychoanalysis

The philosophical acceptance of human nature as a normative concept has dor enormous moral, political, and psychological damage to women. Women have bee denied entrance into the professions because of their nature, yet if they refuse t conform to their nature, they have been declared insane or at best neurotic. Or would expect Jean-Paul Sartre's existential psychoanalysis to be liberatory fc women because Sartre repudiates the existence of human nature and its legitimac as a source of human values. Unfortunately, Sartre's theory of human natu implies a systematic inconsistency in his treatment of women; he insists repea edly that there is no established, immutable human nature, yet in both his philo ophy and his literary works he associates a fixed nature with the female. Th nature, in the psychology, is labeled feminine and in the novels is a factor th determines the roles and behavior of his female characters.

In brief, Sartre claims that human beings are entirely what they make of then selves: "As a for-itself one is not man first in order to be oneself subsequently ar one does not constitute oneself as oneself in terms of a human essence given *a pr ori*. Quite the contrary, it is in its effort to choose itself as a personal self that tl for-itself sustains in existence certain social and abstract characteristics which mal of it a man (or a woman)."[1] Nevertheless, people want to believe that they have fixed nature because such a belief relieves them of the responsibility for definir themselves and provides them with a measure of psychological comfort. A Fo itself tries to discard its freedom and gain security by becoming "serious," that i by treating values or roles as "transcendent givens, independent of human subje tivity."[2] Hence, individuals die for an "honorable peace" without realizing that tl abstraction is of their own making and are loyal to their roles of "soldier," "mothe or "church-member" because such roles are viewed as given rather than chosen

Sartre, however, endorses the Nietzschean insight that if God is dead, we mu ourselves become gods and must be responsible for creating ourselves and our va ues. To rely on God as an external source of values, then, is an instance of bad faith, or self-deception. Although Nietzsche advocates the pursuit of power on grounds that this propensity is "natural," Sartre sees the contradiction inherent in this position and contends that refusing to take the responsibility for our values and our existence by excusing ourselves with an appeal to what is "natural" is as inauthentic as claiming that values come from God. Both are metaphysical props; Sartre diagnoses the effort to derive values from either nature or God as self-deception, an inability to assume our human freedom.

Consequently, we would not expect to find sexism in Sartrean psychology, because Sartre denies the concept of human nature and therefore its legitimacy as a source of human values. Such a view disallows the argument that roles are natural as a basis for assigning particular roles to women. Indeed, anyone who uses such arguments would be guilty of bad faith.

One of the well-known commentaries to expose the sexist implications of Sartre's thought is William Barrett's *Irrational Man,* which attempts to establish that Sartre's psychoanalysis "misunderstands or disparages the psychology of woman,"[4] thus revealing itself as an exclusively masculine theory. Barrett claims that Sartre identifies Being-in-itself as female and Being-for-itself as male by means of the characteristics he assigns to these two aspects of being. Of the In-itself, whose viscosity, excessiveness, and absurdity he duly notes, Barrett contends: "Its softness has the quality of the feminine. Behind all of Sartre's intellectual dialectic we perceive that the In-itself is for him the archetype of nature: excessive, fruitful, blooming nature—the woman, the female." Accordingly, "The For-itself, by contrast, is for Sartre the masculine aspect of human psychology: it is that in virtue of which man chooses himself in his radical liberty, makes projects and thereby gives his life what strictly human meaning it has." Man's humanity, concludes Barrett, resides in the freedom and enterprise of the For-itself, that which allows him to choose and commit himself as he pleases. Consequently, "the woman is a threat, for the woman is nature, and Sartrian man exists in the liberty of his project, which, since it is ultimately unjustified and unjustifiable, in effect sunders him totally from nature."[5] Barrett supplements his case with references to disgust experienced by Antoine Roquentin, in *Nausea,* and Mathieu Delarue, in *The Age of Reason,* at what he terms essentially feminine realities, or revelations of In-itself: the roots of a chestnut tree and the pregnancy of a mistress.[6]

Despite Barrett's basic insight into the sexual identities implicit in Sartre's conceptions, there are several flaws in his argument. Moreover, Barrett himself is far from immune to sexist assumptions and blindness; he fails to discern in this aspect of existential psychoanalysis a most fundamental and conventional sexism and, in fact, contrives to contribute some of his own in the process of faulting the master. First, Barrett's evidence for associating the In-itself with the female, or feminine, rests solely on the flimsy foundation of traditional beliefs expressed in syllogistic form: the In-itself, in its viscous contingency, is soft; women are soft; therefore, the In-itself must possess a female character. Furthermore, the In-itself is the world outside, objects, nature in its fecundity; since women are similarly fertile, they too are nature. He repeats this reasoning with the For-itself: it is aggressive, conscious, and free, as are men, and thus it must be masculine.

Clearly, then, as freedom is threatened by nature, man is threatened by woman, and nausea becomes a male response to female reality. Here, Barrett is practicing a typical and fatuous form of reduction by sexual analogy; he succeeds in relegating women to the nonconscious existence of things and in according human consciousness only to men. He arrives at this conclusion by applying his own deductive logic to trivial, stereotypical notions about women and men and then insists without concrete evidence that Sartre must be exploiting these stereotypes, thereby eliminating women from his psychology. Barrett does not perceive that Sartre's refutation of a fixed human essence should by no means support such an interpretation if his theory is to remain consistent.

The substance of Barrett's quarrel with Sartre's psychology, however, is neither that it is inconsistent in not permitting women human consciousness and freedom nor that it is sexist in rendering the female a mere object, but that it is inadequate in its inability to deal with the natural projects of an obviously natural creature. According to Barrett's analysis, Sartre characterizes accurately the rightful province of the male but cannot account for women and their commitments. Consider, exhorts Barrett,

> a totally ordinary woman, one of that great number whose being is the involvement with family and children, and some of whom are happy at it, or at least as humanly fulfilled by it as the male by his own essentially masculine projects. What sense does it make to say that such a woman's identity is constituted by her project? Her project is family and children, and these do in fact make up a total human commitment; but it is hardly a project that has issued out of the conscious ego. Her whole life, with whatever freedom it reveals, is rather the unfolding of nature through her. As soon as we begin to think about the psychology of women, Sartre's psychology shows itself to be exclusively a masculine affair.[7]

Once again, Barrett assumes that women are beings with a given nature that is fulfilled through a traditional role; he criticizes Sartre for not providing a place in his scheme for such beings. Barrett still fails to make the connection between humanity and the freedom to create one's own identity, a self that cannot be dictated by external or internal necessity, neither by the filling of an established role nor by the "unfolding" of an inevitable nature. Moreover, Barrett overlooks the possibility that marriage and motherhood may be conscious choices for a woman, and that these commitments need not be all-consuming, thereby precluding other projects. He suggests, too, that the term "ordinary" clarifies and justifies a woman's lack of freedom and total, unconscious immersion in natural unfoldings; he carefully refrains from including Simone de Beauvoir in this category, claiming that he is not referring to "that woman, [Sartre's] friend, who wrote a book of feminine protest, *The Second Sex,* which is in reality the protest against being feminine."[8] Presumably, then, she is an unnatural woman and belongs to some variety of abnormal (female) psychology, the positive value of which Barrett renders extremely dubious by remarking that her work and, by implication, her psyche are clearly engaged in protesting against femininity. Although Barrett's sexism is patently obvious in his definition of woman's nature, Sartre's sexism is not necessarily implied, for if there are women who fit Barrett's description of ordinary and adhere to the commitments it entails, Sartrean psychology should be able to explain their behavior quite simply as the practice of bad faith.

Like his theoretical claims, Barrett's literary allusions are peculiarly inappropriate or obscure as support of his argument for the sexual identities of Sartre's two aspects of being. Both Roquentin and Mathieu react with fear and loathing in encounters with a purportedly feminine and threatening In-itself, according to Barrett's rather oversimplified version, but the incidents do not conform to his interpretation. Each character is faced with contingency and forced to recognize that things, despite the overwhelming reality of their presence, are not what they seem or what habit has led him to expect. It is precisely this contingency, the instability of things and their tendency to alter inexplicably, that causes the distress Sartre's characters feel; they are not menaced by some essential, and presumably unwavering, feminine quality that they discover in the world around them. In fact, Roquentin cries out specifically against the unpredictability of things as the source of his nausea, "the inconsistency of inanimate objects!"[9] Furthermore, there is no suggestion in Roquentin's experience with the root of the chestnut tree that its repulsiveness is in any way feminine. He calls the root black, bloated, knotted, obscene, and numerous other epithets, but at no time does he assign to it characteristics that might be regarded as intrinsically female. If anything, his comparing it to boiled leather[10] is quite opposed to Barrett's notion of feminine softness.

By the same token, Mathieu's learning of Marcelle's pregnancy is another confrontation with contingency, with unexpected changes in things, external to himself. In the seven years of their affair, no such unprecedented event has occurred, and Mathieu's confusion arises from his attempt to cope with sudden alteration and the implications of change it might hold for him. It is the potential upset of routine rather than the factual evidence of female fertility that disturbs Mathieu, and he is by no means physically repelled by Marcelle or her condition. On the contrary, he is secretly fascinated by the fetus and guilt-ridden at the thought of destroying it by abortion. Certainly, his freedom may be jeopardized by this contingency, but he does not demonstrate the physical disgust Barrett would have us see. Whatever distress Mathieu experiences is turned more toward himself than against Marcelle; he exclaims, "It is I who have done *this* to her!"[11] For that matter, Sartre persistently presents Mathieu's jealously guarded freedom equivocally, as the self-deception of utter lack of commitment rather than as a genuine project; thus, the threat of the feminine loses much of its force if Mathieu is not actually involved in masculine freedom.

Hence, despite an accurate assertion on Barrett's part that Sartre's In-itself is imbued with intrinsically feminine qualities, a contradiction of his contentions about human nature, Barrett's evidence is largely ambiguous or irrelevant, and his conclusion fails to encompass the charges of either inconsistency or sexism that Sartre incurs by employing this sexual identification. Sartre's existential psychoanalysis and his fiction both offer instances in which the In-itself is associated with distinctly feminine, or female, qualities,[12] thereby implying that a typical female nature does exist and function. Moreover, this female essence is invested with an utterly negative value, making Sartre guilty of blatant sexism.

This specific feminine nature, with its negative value and behavior, is particularly evident in Sartre's discussion of holes and slime in *Being and Nothingness*. In his analysis of slime, Sartre insists that it is a horrifying image, soft, clinging, leechlike, and, regardless of its docility, threatening. Normally, the phenomenon of possession is characterized by the For-itself asserting its primacy, yet the slimy reverses these terms. "The For-itself is suddenly compromised. I open my hands, I want to let go of the slimy and it sticks to me, it draws me, it sucks at me. . . . It is a soft, yielding action, a moist and feminine sucking. . . . I cannot slide on this slime, all its suction cups hold me back. . . . it is a trap. . . . Slime is the revenge of the In-itself. A sickly-sweet feminine revenge which may be symbolized on another level by the quality 'sugary.' "[13] This "sugar-like sweetness," furthermore, poses an ultimate threat: "A sugary sliminess is the ideal of the slimy; it symbolizes the sugary death of the For-itself (like that of the wasp which sinks into the jam and drowns in it)."[14]

Sartre's analysis of slime leaves him in an ambiguous position at best, for what emerges here is a traditional concept of the feminine, a sweet, clinging, dependent threat to male freedom. Like his predecessors Nietzsche and Schopenhauer, Sartre identifies his concept of femininity with female and rails against these qualities in women as if they were natural characteristics, evidence of a given nature. In the discussion of holes, however, it becomes clear that it is not culturally acquired or chosen qualities but actual female anatomy that constitutes the threatening In-itself. Here, the translation "feminine sexual organ" undoubtedly denotes female.

One of the strongest sources of nausea is the human body through its perpetual revelation of contingency. Nonetheless, in his remarks on sexual organs, only the female, corresponding obviously to the hole, is labeled obscene: "The obscenity of the feminine sex is that of everything which gapes open."[15] This gaping obscenity prompts Sartre to conclude: "In herself woman appeals to a strange flesh which is to transform her into a fullness of being by penetration and dissolution. Conversely, woman senses her condition as an appeal precisely because she is 'in the form of a hole.' This is the true origin of Adler's complex. Beyond any doubt her sex is a mouth and a voracious mouth which devours the penis. . . . The amorous act is the castration of the man; but this is above all because sex is a hole."[16]

Clearly, Sartre suggests here that Adler's complex in women, their inferiority feeling, is caused by inferior and obscene anatomy; something is missing. The "masculine protest," for Sartre, is not against the feminine role, as Adler argued, but against being female. The conventional piece of wisdom expressed by this quotation is derived from the view that all holes are obscene, and that filling holes is a fundamental human tendency. Sartre is careful to distinguish his view from Freudianism. He does not explain holes in terms of sexuality but rather explains sexuality in terms of the ontological meaning of holes: "The hole, before all sexual specification, is an obscene expectation, an appeal to the flesh."[17] Apparently, all holes are appeals to the flesh, that is, the objective nature of a hole is a nothingness that we fill with flesh. Hence, children crawl into holes, put fingers in their mouths, and so on. If we take seriously the view that all holes are obscene, then we should by extension view these activities as obscene. Consequently, we should also recognize that such items as Swiss cheese and bowling balls are obscene. Filling holes, Sartre claims, is a fundamental human tendency, but the opposite tendency, to poke holes, is also of considerable importance. From this type of vacuous psychological statement, it is difficult to ascertain anything at all.

Even if there is a fundamental Parmenidean urge to fill holes, we need not deduce that the female sexual organ will be filled by a penis. Notwithstanding, Sartre does draw this conclusion and, significantly, characterizes the plugger as For-itself and the plugee as In-itself: "To plug up a hole means originally to make a sacrifice of my body in order that the plentitude of being may exist; that is, to subject the passion of the For-itself so as to shape, to perfect, and to preserve the totality of the In-itself."[18] Since a hole is admitted by Sartre to be a nothingness, one might hope that he would associate it with freedom. Instead, we see that holes and slime are obscene qualities of the In-itself that are identified, in anatomy and behavior, with the female.

Sartre's literary work provides similar and telling instances of his conception of the female as a sickening, obscene essence of the In-itself that threatens the For-itself, usually embodied in a male character. In *No Exit,* for example, Garcin rejects the advances of Estelle, an extremely "feminine" woman who demonstrates throughout the play the kind of nonconscious cloying dependence that Sartre has associated with the In-itself. Garcin repels Estelle's open-armed invitation, retorting, "I won't let myself get bogged in your eyes. You're soft and slimy. Ugh! Like an octopus. Like a quagmire."[19] The threat of the female as In-itself is evident here in the characterization of Estelle as soft, slimy, and sucking, as is the loss of identity by the For-itself in the bog of the In-itself. This notion of losing or forgetting oneself is reinforced later, when Inez chastises Garcin, "Oh, you coward, you weakling, running to women to console you!"[20]

Likewise, although Roquentin is nauseated by everything physical, and thus contingent, his disgust at the physical, especially sexual, reality of a woman carries strong overtones of a confrontation with the overwhelmingly obscene, unlike his simpler nausea at things like a glass of beer, his own face, or even the celebrated chestnut tree root. His dramatization of his response to a casual sexual episode is certainly one of the most repellent in the novel; he describes the woman's genitals as black, hairy, beastly, horrible, and crawling with insects, and ultimately associates them with vomit, scarcely a winsome image: "I played distractedly with her sex. . . . Ants were running everywhere, centipedes and ringworm. There were even more horrible animals: their bodies were made from a slice of toast, the kind you put under roast pigeons; they walked sideways with legs like a crab. The larger leaves were black with beasts. Behind the cactus and the Barbary fig trees, the Velleda of the public park pointed a finger at her sex. 'This park smells of vomit,' I shouted."[21] Without question, woman is endowed with a nature that is menacing and obscene; she becomes here the personification of the In-itself, contingency notwithstanding. Significantly, this scene is followed immediately by a dream or fantasy sequence in which Roquentin and some friends thrash a colleague for referring to a hole (in the head) that they all possess but do not mention.[22] This is heavy punishment; obviously holes are taboo, even in conversation.

Although Maurice Cranston has pointed out that none of the ways to freedom pursued by Sartre's characters is ultimately workable or successful,[23] it is noteworthy that the only persons permitted engagement in such projects are the fictional men; in fact, *Troubled Sleep,* the last volume of the trilogy, becomes an exclusively masculine novel, dealing only with male prisoners of war. Even when a critic detects essence in Sartrean personages, he fails to note its constant presence in women. Typically, Barrett's complaint about *No Exit,* accusing Sartre of creating fixed natures in his characters, is mistaken and irrelevant in its application: "Beyond a certain point they hold no surprises for us, they are without contingency—and this from an author who denies the existence of 'character' as a fixed thing."[24] The people in *No Exit* have been guilty of bad faith, which explains their erroneous insistence on some essence in themselves, but beyond this guilt they cannot be contingent because they are *dead* and of course can no longer change anything about themselves. If Barrett is representative, the critics consider the dead unentitled to fixed natures, but such natures in women pass unremarked.

Sartre's trilogy *The Roads to Freedom* offers several succinct examples of essences attributed to female characters. The women in these novels behave according to established natures or roles of which they are virtually unconscious and therefore unable to manipulate or escape. Moreover, Sartre does not judge them as practitioners of bad faith but seems to accept their actions as dictated by some internal or external necessity that applies, apparently, only to women. All Sartre's women are conventional, natural, instinctive, submissive; they seldom reflect or analyze, they are emotionally swayed, and they exhibit the pettiness and malice of narrow-minded creatures. In short, Sartre relies heavily on stereotypes, refusing to allow his women the individual consciousness his male characters demonstrate. His women seem complacently, rightfully, and inevitably imprisoned in their essences, a condition never acceptable for male characters who correctly struggle against their role and whose reduction of self is portrayed as bad faith.

Ivich, Lola, Marcelle, and Odette, the four major female characters of Sartre's trilogy, all seem to have rational intelligence and consciousness; their insights into

Mathieu are accurate and are meant to stand as valid comments from trustworthy sources. Yet all of these women are systematically reduced in the course of the novels to the expression or pursuit of a ruling passion that seems to spring from some inner nature or external need. Lola is ruled by her sexuality, exhibited primarily in her passion for Boris; Marcelle is dominated by the need for motherhood, for a child; Ivich is a slave to caprice and escapism; and Odette fills a sexual and social role without which she ceases to exist. In each case the woman is a stereotype who exercises some inevitable nature or role; she is never a free agent who creates these things consciously for herself. A brief examination of these characters in the trilogy will serve to clarify each woman's essence and the behavior it inexorably provokes.

Ivich, a young student and friend of Mathieu's, presents a curious study, for in her Sartre suggests that even if a woman attempts to create a self through free choice she is doomed to defeat. Ivich is petulant, capricious, and, if not unintelligent, unable to concentrate her attention on anything for long; it is just these intrinsic qualities that drive her to the choices she makes, and sometimes in effect make her decisions for her, so that even she cannot avoid seeing that her freedom is illusory. In *The Age of Reason,* Ivich fails her university examinations; her intellectual or discipline limitations eliminate freedom there. When, in *The Reprieve,* she tries to exercise sexual freedom, she cannot prevent the man's using her as an object, especially since pure whim had dictated her choice of partners, a man nearly a stranger to her. Sartre emphasizes the helplessness of Ivich's position narratively by alternating with her defloration the presentation of the Munich Pact to the Czechs, thus comparing woman's sexual experience to the selling or parceling out of property, and damaged goods at that.

Married, miscarried, and bored by the time of *Troubled Sleep,* Ivich still combats her inescapable lot as a woman by rejecting her natural role and assuming male toughness and aggressiveness, but she is still powerless to alter her situation through her own action except by fleeing with her brother Boris, exchanging one dependent role for another. For her "unnatural" masculine behavior, Ivich is judged and condemned through Boris: "Ivich had become a pretty tough customer; she now gave back as good as she got; but nostalgically he recalled the old days when, shaken by anger, she used merely to toss her head so that her hair fell over her face and growl. It had caused a good deal less trouble."[25] Ivich's own nature has caused her unhappiness, but unlike a man she is not free to change that nature or create an alternative self; her attempt to do so, her "unfeminine" behavior, is criticized as artificial, implying a violation of nature, and troublesome, suggesting that women cannot escape or refuse roles as men can. Seemingly, Ivich should, and in fact must, remain the petulant, powerless, feminine essence that Sartre describes and Boris celebrates and that, by its very fixity, precludes freedom and change. Possession of a female nature imprisons Ivich and dictates her role.

Odette, Mathieu's brother's wife, who appears only as the perfectly groomed, smiling hostess in the first volume, is introduced more fully as a person in *The*

Reprieve. She is the only one of Sartre's women who achieves any consciousness of herself and her condition, but the final result of this self-awareness is the knowledge that she is inevitably locked into the role she recognizes herself as playing; she does not enjoy the freedom she comes to appreciate for the simple reason that she is a woman. Odette begins as a stereotype, a woman filling a given role, "sensible and discreet, with a lot of rules of conduct, one being never to think anything out to its logical end," for "she knew she would soon be told all that she must think and say and do." Later, she is referred to as having "the grace and tranquillity of a domestic animal; she sat down, went away, came back, and sat down again, certain that she would pass unnoticed." Thus, she commands both an essence and a role, neither of which seems open to choice or criticism. As she gradually becomes conscious of her position, she achieves only a feeling of futility. Life, she thinks, "is interminable,"[26] and she questions the use of living at all.

In *Troubled Sleep,* Odette realizes that she is responding to demands and expectations engendered by her role as Jacques' wife and society matron, but she cannot transcend it and become independent because, Sartre implies, of the limited knowledge and reasoning powers of a woman: "What is the truth? Until now it has always been what Jacques said; if I stop believing in him, in whom can I believe?" Finally, Odette admits in despair, "I don't know enough about it."[27] The consequence, then, of Odette's dawning consciousness is the discovery that she is imprisoned in her sex role; as a female, her mind is circumscribed by her sex, and although she has the acuity to understand her situation, she has neither sufficient initiative nor intelligence to act on this insight. Odette is trapped because she is a woman.

Lola is effectively juxtaposed with Odette, for what rules her life exactly contrasts to the deciding factors in Odette's. Instead of being fixed by her mind and role, Lola is restricted by her emotions and ultimately her biology; if anything, her progression is downward from consciousness to physiological necessity. Throughout the trilogy, Lola is obsessed with her love for Boris, a man twenty years her junior; the natural fact of aging, traditionally tragic for women, sparks in her a desperate desire for love at any price. As Boris himself explains, "Older people grow embittered and behave as though their lives were at stake."[28] In Lola, Sartre is trading on typical generalizations about women: for a woman in transit through middle age, unmarried and childless, every relationship is crucial because she has nothing to look forward to save old age and death. Lola becomes, then, the stereotypical frightened older woman clinging to life through a youthful lover. She cries passionately to Boris, "If I think of my life, I want to throw myself into the river, I have to think of you all day. . . . you're all I have left. . . . don't ever hurt me—I'm all alone."[29]

In *Troubled Sleep,* Lola learns that she has a tumor of the womb and must undergo surgery, and once again biology dictates her response. Lola is stripped of all emotions; her love for Boris disappears completely, and she can be concerned only with her ailment and its consequences. For a male character, the processes of aging and disease would constitute confrontations with contingency, causing nausea at first and then a gradual sense of freedom, but for Lola such experience only leads to acceptance and definition of herself through the inevitable. A woman is no more than her aging and atrophied body; nature in her dominates all her responses and determines her very ability to respond. Lola escapes the exigencies of her middle-aged status and role only to lose herself in direct preoccupation with her anatomy, in which her essence consists.

Marcelle, Mathieu's pregnant mistress, is the most strictly typical of Sartre's female essences, even though she has, at the outset, great promise as a consciousness. She is opinionated and somewhat testy, certainly able to think, but as soon as she begins to accustom herself to pregnancy she moves unswervingly into motherhood in a state of dreamy acquiesence: "She was no longer thinking of anything. . . . She looked at her belly, and the placid abundance of those rich pastures revived her girlish impressions at the sight of women suckling their babies in the Luxembourg. . . . She shrugged her shoulders; yes, that foolish, burgeoning body was indeed created for maternity."[30] Marcelle's acceptance of Daniel's offer of marriage, then, is not an act of cowardice or fear of abortion or society, but merely a propulsion toward fulfillment of inner necessity, Barrett's "unfolding of nature through her." Significantly, Sartre does not suggest that having or not having a child encompasses any issue of Marcelle's freedom; only Mathieu's liberty is in question here.

In *The Reprieve,* Marcelle's participation has dropped to one brief appearance in which she smiles at children, drinks milk, and sleeps, exercising only the instincts of an unconscious animal; this behavior corresponds more closely to Being-in-itself than to any human freedom. Sartre even calls her "the pregnant belly."[31] She is limited to her mere physical presence. *Troubled Sleep* refers to Marcelle only once as "pupping at Dax"; she is reduced here to a biological function, the sexual role of reproduction.[32] All this takes place not through any conscious choice on Marcelle's part, but rather as a result of the assertion of nature in her body. There is a female essence and role, then, that a woman cannot choose or escape but naturally, unconsciously agrees to fulfill as the opportunity arises.

A sexual interpretation of the For-itself and In-itself changes Sartre's view of intimate relationships from a theory about the way human beings relate to each other to a theory about the way men and women relate to each other. Intimate relationships, according to Sartre, must be characterized in terms of the alienation of a subject from an object, so that a partner as subject tries to possess or entrap the liberty of the other, thus making the other an object. Love is impossible, for love would be the meeting of subject with subject, but there can never be a mutual recognition of freedom. In other words, one of the partners is always an object. Although none but these limited options that Sartre dramatically describes as sadistic or masochistic are available to them, without sex-specific categories of being, the partners could at least take turns. If men are subjects and women are objects, even these limited options are unavailable.

Iris Murdoch in her book on Sartre finds it arbitrary and inexplicable that the "we" that is often experienced is not among Sartre's basic ontological categories.[33] But if one reads Sartre on the subject of holes and slime, it is not at all surprising that the basic categories are those of subject and object, dominance and submission, actor and acted upon, sadist and masochist. Traditional relationships between the sexes became for Sartre the model of human relationships in general because the basic categories of being are nothing more than a universalization of conventional masculinity and femininity.

Thus, in both his psychology and his fiction, Sartre associates essence and roles with women, which both violates his theory and makes of him a traditional sexist. Women possess a fixed nature, determined by their unfortunate sexual anatomy, which limits them to roles approximating the nonconscious, unliberated Being-in-itself. Female attempts at freedom and self-creation are, as we discover in the novels, doomed to ignominious failure; women are forever enmeshed in their physical necessities and established functions. It is gravely disappointing that a major contemporary effort to refute the existence of human nature and its legitimacy as a source of human values fails to encompass women, one of the groups of human beings to suffer most from essentialist views.

5

AIDS and *Bowers v. Hardwick*

During the beginning of the AIDS crisis, natural law arguments turned up again not only in relation to antisodomy arguments but even as parts of important claims about AIDS prevention made by the medical and scientific community. Such arguments were invoked by the State of Georgia in the 1986 Supreme Court case *Bowers v. Hardwick,*[1] in which the Court held that the Constitution does not confer a fundamental right upon homosexuals to engage in sodomy. As we shall see, the Court accepted a version of legal moralism, ignoring both the relevance of a right to privacy and two friend-of-the-court briefs urging them to consider the public health implications of prohibiting homosexual sodomy. I want to argue against legal moralism both in its standard form and in a more sophisticated version that permits natural law arguments a place in legal reasoning. Natural law arguments aggravated the AIDS crisis by contributing not only to bad law but also to bad science. More recently, natural law arguments have surfaced in the national debate on (same-sex) marriage, threatening once again to create bad law as state legislatures scramble to deal with judicial rulings.

Natural law arguments that attempted to fix blame for AIDS on gay sex are variants of arguments from design. For example, former Representative William Dannemeyer (R-Calif.), a leading proponent of AIDS legislation, stated on the House floor that "God's plan for man was Adam and Eve, not Adam and Steve."[2] Ken Kesey, author of *One Flew Over the Cuckoo's Nest,* remarked: "It seems to me it's one's job to put sperm in a place that's designed for it. You don't put crankcase oil in your power steering system. And when God says, 'Do not put crankcase oil in your power steering system,' he's not saying 'if you do, you'll go to hell,' he's saying, 'if you do, you'll blow the seals out of your power steering.' "[3] If blowing the seals out of one's power steering system is analogous to getting AIDS or any sexually transmitted disease, then the best designed sex between or among human beings is lesbian sex. As physician Barbara Herbert put it, "Only nuns have less incidence of sexually transmitted diseases (STDs) than lesbians. . . . where you see an STD there's been a penis in the picture."[4]

NATURAL LAW AND BAD SCIENCE

I now want to examine some serious attempts on the part of the contemporary medical and scientific community to use natural law arguments in their effort to show that AIDS would not spread in any significant way into the heterosexual population. The first is a so-called efficiency thesis, popular in the 1980s. An efficiency thesis is important and understandably was incorporated into safe sex guidelines, for such guidelines needed to be explicit as to who was at risk. Some scientists maintained that HIV is more *efficiently* transmitted through anal sex than vaginal sex with the implication that heterosexuals who practiced only vaginal intercourse were at very low risk. However, the fact of heterosexual transmission was not in question. The *New England Journal of Medicine* reported an example of sexual transmission of HIV from a man to a woman to a man in 1986.[5] A thirty-seven-year-old married man engaged in homosexual activity while on business trips in New York. He and his thirty-three-year-old wife had vaginal intercourse accompanied by heavy mouth kissing about twice a month. After her husband died from pneumocystis carinii pneumonia (PCP), she had a sexual relationship with a twenty-six-year-old male neighbor. She too died from PCP. The neighbor, who developed AIDS-related complex (ARC), reported no drug use and no sexual contact except the above-mentioned relationship that included only vaginal intercourse and deep kissing.

Comparatively few cases of vaginal transmission (particularly woman to man) existed at the time, and the efficiency thesis attempted to explain that fact. It was thought that the lining of the anus is easily torn, thus facilitating the entry of infected semen into the bloodstream. "The rugged vagina," in the words of John Langone, unlike "the vulnerable rectum," is "*designed* to withstand the trauma of intercourse."[6] Even if it were true that rectums and vaginas are respectively tender and tough, it had not been demonstrated that a traumatic event was necessary for the transmission of HIV. For example, artificial insemination[7] is not a traumatic procedure and yet women can get AIDS from undergoing this process if the sperm is contaminated.

Although scientific research already pointed to the possibility of direct infection of cells without trauma or tears, conventional assumptions about proper sexuality continued to influence both the design of experiments and the interpretation of results. For instance, in late 1986, a team of federal scientists headed by Dr. Malcolm Martin found that HIV can directly infect cells from the colon and rectum in the test tube, suggesting that AIDS could spread in anal intercourse without any breakage in tissue. Dr. Martin's team tested thirteen other types of cells representing a wide range of human tissues such as breast, lung, pancreas, and ovary, none of which proved to be susceptible to the AIDS virus. Though he neglected even to test vaginal cells for any susceptibility to HIV, the new finding, according to the *New York Times* interpretation, "may help to explain the high incidence of AIDS among male homosexuals practicing anal intercourse."[8]

Scientist or science reporter, heterosexuals had a vested interest in believing that AIDS would be largely confined to the gay male population—that AIDS really was the "gay plague." Moreover, the efficiency thesis relied, as does the next argument under consideration, on beliefs about the proper place for depositing sperm that historically have been used to support the view that heterosexuality is good and homosexuality is bad.

Steve Witkin and a team of researchers from Cornell University conducted experiments intended to show that the mere introduction of semen into the bloodstream during anal intercourse—not the trauma—adversely affected the immune systems of males. Witkin theorized that in order for the species to continue, "females have evolved immunological mechanisms to deal with exposure to sperm."[9] A woman, he thought, was not at risk for AIDS even if her partner ejaculated inside her rectum. Men, however, had not evolved such mechanisms, hence, the implication that from an evolutionary point of view gay anal sex was biologically unnatural. Witkin's thesis explains why the rabbits described in the following experiments were male. The researchers engaged in what David Black, author of *The Plague Years,* called "bunny bondage." In an effort to test the thesis that depositing semen from one male into the rectum of another might cause the receiver to produce antibodies to foreign semen and in turn suppress the immune system, researchers "took rabbits and gave them rabbit semen rectally once a week. . . . Healthy males were restrained and 1 ml of fresh semen . . . was deposited . . . to a depth of 5 cm . . . with a No. 7 French rubber catheter."[10]

Like so many religious explanations for disease, says Richard Goldstein, a reviewer of David Black's book, Witkin's theory "not only wrongly fixes blame but falsely reassures."[11] Views like Witkin's including the efficiency thesis suggested that "prevention may ultimately be a matter of harmonizing with the natural order."[12]

IS ECOLOGY ANOTHER NATURAL LAW?

Both the efficiency thesis of the 1980s and a conception of the natural order such as Witkin's are wrong, according to views developed by Gabriel Rotello in his 1998 book *Sexual Ecology: AIDS and the Destiny of Gay Men.* Regarding the efficiency thesis Rotello says: "The difference in risk between anal and vaginal sex is nowhere near sufficient to account for the several-thousand-fold difference in HIV prevalence between gay men and comparable heterosexuals in the developed world. True, the rectum is somewhat more susceptible to infection than the vagina or the mouth, but not by very much."[13] The reason, then, for the catastrophic levels of infection in gay males, Rotello continues, had "less to do with anal sex *per se,* and more to do with specific ways that gay men practiced it."[14] The primary practice to which Rotello refers is anal sex in the context of a very high level of promiscuity.

A fuller explanation, however, of why AIDS spread so quickly in the gay male community and did not spread in a similar fashion into the middle-class heterosexual population involves what Rotello calls an ecological explanation. "Ecology" is the study of the interaction of living things with their nonliving environment. Sexual ecology, then, is how groups practicing particular sexual behaviors interact with one another and their environment. Rotello puts it this way: "Nothing in our varied biosphere just happens, especially not disease. The microbial world, the chemical world, the realm of toxins and pollutants, parasites and microbes, are intimately connected to our behavior, our physical condition, our diet, all of which are intimately connected to the economic world, the cultural world, the social and religious and technological world around us. All ebb and flow in a seamless web of cause and effect. It remains for us to seek, so far as we are able, to understand these processes. Or, if we cannot or will not, to suffer the consequences."[15]

Ecological awareness is the understanding of the connections between and among biology, chemical substances, culture, economics, and so on. Thus, in explaining the spread of AIDS in the gay male community as a matter of sexual ecology, Rotello is saying that specific sexual practices and their interconnections are causally implicated. In turn, these sexual practices are related to certain cultural ideas, certain chemical substances, economic considerations, and so forth. Rotello claims that "the primary factor that led to increased HIV transmission was anal sex combined with multiple partners, particularly in concentrated core groups."[16] Gay men, he argues, constitute a core group or risk group, that is, a "collection of people who . . . suffer from and transmit STD's at much higher rates than the rest of the population."[17] There are cores within cores. For example, the core of prostitutes and their customers may include a core of military men and long-distance truck drivers.[18] In similar fashion, those gay men who regularly visit commercial sex establishments such as bathhouses form a kind of subcore. They do so because of their engagement in an extraordinary level of sexual behavior with concurrent partners as opposed to serial partners and because of experiencing many other risk factors such as "recreational drug abuse, repeated waves of STD's and constant intake of antibiotics, sexual tourism and travel."[19]

Using this example, ecology looks like a new natural law. After all, Rotello talks about the importance of finding "a new equilibrium with nature."[20] Also, there is a sense in ecological ethics that "nature" can tell us what we ought to do and that behaviors that interrupt the natural "processes" will cause their actors to "suffer the consequences." However, there are significant differences between the project of ecology and the project of the traditional natural law ethics of Aristotle and Aquinas. The *conclusions* drawn from ecology are different from those of traditional natural law, and the *bases* of the conclusions are also different.

Rotello's conclusion is not that male homosexuality is unnatural but rather that high levels of promiscuity are not sustainable. What is needed, he argues, is self-restraint and moderation on the part of gay men and some cultural support—such as legalizing gay marriage—for these values. Sustainability is a key concept, some would say a buzzword, in ecological ethics. It is a slippery but important term. One general characterization is that a sustainable ecosystem is one whose essential practices can be carried on indefinitely while maintaining its population of living species at a certain level of well-being. By this definition, a population of gay males that is suffering a high rate of AIDS-related deaths is obviously not pursuing sound behaviors; the behaviors themselves are not good or bad, but they are ecologically unsustainable as the population is decreasing.

This notion of sustainability is linked to the desire for future generations and to the preservation of their welfare. Such a link presents a problem of motivation that runs through many issues in environmental ethics such as reducing pollution and population, avoiding increased global warming, preserving biodiversity and old growth forests, and so on. We are asked to care enough about generations living in the distant future to alter our behavior now. Advocates of sustainability predict that catastrophic costs lie down the road if we do not adopt sustainable practices now. However, most or all of the alterations recommended to save the future would impose significant costs on some group or other today.

For instance, Rotello argues that the world's population explosion (6 billion and counting) is the "ecological issue most analogous to AIDS prevention."[21] "Both deal with the unwanted side effects of human sexual desire and behavior (getting pregnant, getting AIDS), effects that have both a personal and ecological impact. The solutions to both require that people modify their personal and sexual behavior in ways that many individuals find undesirable in order to alleviate ecological problems that these individuals don't feel personally responsible for. The proposed solutions to both often conflict with deeply held cultural values as well as with many individuals' immediate and powerful psychological and biological desires."[22]

One thing I want to call attention to here is the contrast in how the two "natures"—ecology's nature and natural law's nature—suggest dealing with the population issue. On November 18, 1992, the Union of Concerned Scientists issued a warning to humanity on behalf of over sixteen hundred scientists, including a majority of the living Nobel laureates in the sciences, that "human beings and the natural world are on a collision course."[23] These scientists recommended not only effective and voluntary family planning but also sexual equality, since women who are educated and have life options tend to have fewer children. Moreover, these same scientists say there must be a "guarantee [that] women [have] control over their own reproductive decisions."[24]

On the other hand, natural law as interpreted by the Catholic Church led the Vatican and its supporters to oppose United Nations proposals on abortion and sex education at the 1994 International Conference on Population and Development in Cairo, Egypt, which were designed to curb the world's population. In 1999 the Vatican continued to stall efforts to implement the program agreed upon by 179 countries five years earlier.[25] Special objection was made by the Vatican in 1994 to a principle that referred to "ensuring women's ability to control their own fertility."[26] Indeed, in 1996, in the Roman Catholic Diocese of Lincoln, Nebraska, a bishop excommunicated anyone who was a member of Planned Parenthood.[27]

With respect to the differing bases of these conclusions from ecology and natural law, ecology is at least to some extent connected to facts. An attempt is made to discover connections in the world that are established by science; and, significantly, respect for the interconnectedness of things is encouraged in order to avoid harmful consequences. For instance, according to Rotello,

> ecologists consider it perfectly moral to build a small bonfire on an empty prairie since that does not damage the environment, while it is plainly immoral to burn millions of tons of urban refuse in unfiltered incinerators, since that would lead to ecological disaster. The point is that the activity itself, in this case combustion, is not by itself moral or immoral. What is immoral is polluting an ecosystem in a harmful and unsustainable way, especially in a way that is almost certain to destroy human life. In the same way, individual sexual behaviors that traditional moralists might consider "always wrong" can still be considered perfectly moral so long as they don't produce widespread harm. But those behaviors must be considered immoral when they do. Harm is the key.[28]

As the "scientist's warning" put it, "A great change in our stewardship of the earth and the life on it is required, if vast human misery is to be avoided and our global home on this planet is not to be irretrievably mutilated."[29]

In the next section, however, I argue that traditional natural law ethics is not a consequentialist theory, does not consider behaviors in some ecological context, and therefore does not decide issues on the basis of whether or not harmful consequences can ensue from them. Natural law theorists are interested in seeing that people do what they consider to be the natural thing regardless of the consequences. The Catholic Church, for instance, in opposing the availability of contraceptives, abortion, and sex education is able to overlook a few weighty, cosmic consequences by ignoring the harmful effects of the burgeoning human population such as unwanted children and poverty and the danger of running out of food and water on the planet.[30] Likewise, in condemning homosexuality, natural law theorists are not looking at the consequences to a whole community, as Rotello does, but are focusing on a particular behavior in isolation and applying theoretical moral rules.

BOWERS V. HARDWICK: NATURAL LAW AND BAD LAW

In the 1986 *Bowers* case, the Court was presented by the petitioner with natural law arguments that were admissible because the Court embraced legal moralism, rejecting, to the surprise of many, the rights approach it had been developing in sex-related cases over the past twenty years. A brief review of the facts surrounding the *Bowers* case follows.

Michael Hardwick was arrested for sodomy in his own bedroom.[31] Police arrived at his door to see him about an unrelated charge—a ticket for public drunkenness that Hardwick claims he had long since paid. Hardwick, a gay bartender, received the ticket as he was leaving his place of work. According to him, he left at 6:00 A.M. because he had been working on a sound system. Although he did not pay the fine on the appointed date, he did settle the matter in person at a later time. Thus, Hardwick was not expecting to be visited by the police. A house guest answered the door and let the officer in. Not knowing that Hardwick had company, the guest said that Hardwick was in his room. The officer went to Hardwick's bedroom, caught him in the act of consensual fellatio, and arrested him. Although the charges were later dropped, Hardwick sued Michael J. Bowers, the attorney general of Georgia, in hopes of achieving Supreme Court review of a law that had, he thought, "inadequate rationale."

The Georgia statute in effect at the time read as follows: "A person commits the offense of sodomy when he performs or submits to any sexual act involving the sex organs of one person and the mouth or anus of another." It is important to note at the outset that the issue before the Court in *Bowers v. Hardwick* was whether to affirm a lower court ruling that Georgia, in order to keep its sodomy statute, would have to demonstrate that it promoted a compelling state interest. Michael Hardwick's winning the case would not have made the law unconstitutional; it simply would have required Georgia to show that the statute served some legitimate state objective and was the most narrowly drawn means of achieving that end.

As it turned out, the ruling in *Bowers* allowed, and still allows, states to have sodomy laws (or laws prohibiting "crimes against nature" as they are sometimes called) without providing any justification for them. Significantly, the Georgia statute that triggered the *Bowers* ruling was struck down by the state supreme court in *State v. Anthony Powell* in November 1998.[32] Ironically, as a Supreme Court case *Bowers* is still the law of the land. However, a 1996 case, *Romer v. Evans,*[33] shows that even the Supreme Court has moved away from the homophobic and simplistic rhetoric of *Bowers.*

In *Romer,* the U.S. Supreme Court struck down Colorado's amendment to its state constitution that nullified existing civil rights protections for gays and lesbians and forbade any new antidiscrimination laws based on sexual orientation.[34] Amendment 2, as it was called, was said by the Court to lack a rationale related to legitimate state interests. Moreover, the Court made clear that animus toward the class affected would not do as a rationale.[35] The Court concluded that "Amendment 2 classifies homosexuals not to further a proper legislative end but to make them unequal to everyone else. This Colorado cannot do."[36]

Legal scholar David A. J. Richards maintains that "a reasonable interpretation of *Romer v. Evans* suggests implicitly that [*Bowers v. Hardwick*] has been [overruled],"[37] even though the Court in *Romer* did not overrule *Bowers* and in fact said absolutely nothing about *Bowers*. Richards's "reasonable interpretation" consists of noting that in *Romer* simply citing majoritarian morality is not sufficient for denying gays and lesbians their constitutional rights.[38] It is true that *Romer* has upped the ante by requiring a rational basis for laws that pertain to gays and lesbians. In doing so, the Court has undermined legal moralism in its most simplistic form. However, there are more sophisticated forms of legal moralism that do require reasons for laws but still allow bad reasons, which may spell trouble ahead despite the advance of *Romer.* In any event, *Bowers* is an interesting case study in the influence of natural law ethics on contemporary law.

Bowers is an example of legal moralism par excellence. Legal moralism, as characterized by Joel Feinberg, is the view that "it can be morally legitimate to prohibit conduct on the ground that it is inherently immoral, even though it causes neither harm nor offense to the actor or to others."[39] A view often associated with Patrick Devlin, legal moralism is also put forward in a more sophisticated form by Ronald Dworkin in an article critical of Devlin. I want to argue against Dworkin's proposal that the legal enforcement of morality might be acceptable as long as certain minimal rational requirements are met. Dworkin distinguishes between moral views that ought not to be legally enforced because they are based on prejudice, emotional reaction, false claims or arguments from authority (what Dworkin calls parroting), and genuine moral convictions that might be legally enforced. As Dworkin puts it, "Not every reason I might give will do."[40] Among the reasons that will do, however, as a legitimate basis for prohibiting X, is "X is unnatural." As we shall see, the reasoning in *Bowers* arguably meets neither the minimal standards outlined by Dworkin nor even the lower requirements advocated by Devlin.

Patrick Devlin takes the view that, ultimately, morality is a matter of feeling, in particular, feelings of disgust, indignation, and intolerance on the part of ordinary people. Moreover, he claims that moral views should be legally enforced if these feelings are sufficiently intense (reach "concert pitch," as philosopher of law H. L. A. Hart put it), and these feelings need not be based on any rational considerations. In essence, the majority of the Court in *Bowers* said that there is no fundamental right to homosexual sodomy because people have strongly disapproved of it and have done so for a very long time.

For example, the majority said, "Sodomy was a criminal offense at common law and was forbidden by the laws of the original thirteen States. . . . In fact, until 1961, all 50 States outlawed sodomy, and today, 24 States and the District of Columbia continue to provide criminal penalties for sodomy performed in private and between consenting adults."[41] Chief Justice Warren Burger said, "Decisions of individuals relating to homosexual conduct have been subject to state intervention throughout the history of Western civilization."[42]

The Court, in *Bowers,* did not take a critical view of history. It did not consider the possibility that popular prejudices can undermine individual rights in societies that are deeply rooted in sexism, heterosexism, and racism. However, the Court has not always thought of history as buttressing moral claims. Thirty years ago, section 20-59 of the Virginia law stated that "if any white person intermarry with a colored person, or any colored person intermarry with a white person, he shall be guilty of a felony and shall be punished by confinement in the penitentiary for not less than one nor more than five years."[43] In *Loving v. Virginia,*[44] a unanimous Court found Virginia's ban on interracial marriages a product of "invidious racism."

In that case, the Court was unpersuaded either by tradition or by the trial court's argument from design that "Almighty God created the races white, black, yellow, malay, and red, and he placed them on separate continents. And but for their interference with his arrangement there would be no cause for such marriages. The fact that he separated the races shows that he did not intend for the races to mix."[45] The Court was also unpersuaded by the fact that antimiscegenation statutes had been common in Virginia since colonial times and that Virginia was one of sixteen states that prohibited interracial marriage. Nonetheless, when Michael Hardwick claimed that "the presumed belief of a majority of the electorate in Georgia that homosexual sodomy is immoral and unacceptable" is an "inadequate rationale to support the law," the Court said simply, "We do not agree."[46]

There is an important feature of Devlin's legal moralism that is relevant to the outcome of *Bowers*. Devlin notes that "the limits of tolerance shift." Although, on his view, we are justified in passing laws on no other basis than deeply held feelings of disapproval, when the limits of tolerance shift, we should change the laws. Polls conducted in 1986 by *Time* and *Newsweek* magazines showed an absence of majority approval for the outlawing of any of a variety of specific sexual practices, including oral and anal sex, between consenting adults.[47] Thus, one might argue that the Supreme Court did not even realistically apply legal moralism of the sort articulated by Devlin.

It is also important to note, for example, that the trend of states to repeal laws against sodomy or interracial marriage has been interpreted as cutting both ways. Virginia, as we have seen, was one of the sixteen states to prohibit interracial marriage in 1967; fifteen years earlier thirty states prohibited interracial marriage. These data were taken by the Court as showing that the limits of tolerance shift. A similar trend vis-à-vis sodomy laws was used by the Court to show that many people still oppose sodomy.[48]

Natural law arguments figured into the *Bowers* case since the petitioner, Michael J. Bowers, appealed to the beliefs of Western philosophers who thought that homosexuality was unnatural. As Bowers argued, "No universal principle of morality teaches that homosexual sodomy is acceptable conduct. To the contrary, traditional Judeo-Christian values proscribe such conduct. Indeed, there is no validation for sodomy found in the teaching of the ancient Greek philosophers Plato or Aristotle. More recent thinkers, such as Immanuel Kant, have found homosexual sodomy no less unnatural."[49]

In the *Laws* (the work of Plato's cited by Bowers), Plato, himself a homosexual, characterizes homosexual sex as unnatural, whereas in earlier dialogues he portrayed the intensity and delights of homosexuality, even suggesting that homoerotic experience is an important prerequisite for knowing the essence of Beauty.[50] In the *Laws,* Plato's last work, he maintained that heterosexuality with its procreative end was inherently orderly; he approved of the use of the law to enforce what he saw as natural, that is, orderly sexuality. Some commentators have charged Plato with inconsistency, while others have said that he got increasingly conservative in his old age. However, there is another possible interpretation here. Plato, in the *Laws,* was legislating for a public that, by and large, did not consist of philosophers. Not above considerable elitism and (some say) a bit of totalitarianism, Plato thought—as did petitioner Bowers—that marriage, family, and procreation were institutions designed to promote social control.

Bowers says that "homosexual sodomy is the anathema of the basic units of our society: marriage and the family. To decriminalize or artificially withdraw the public's expression of its disdain for this conduct does not uplift sodomy, but rather demotes these sacred institutions to merely other alternative lifestyles. One author has described that result as the promotion of indifference toward these foundations of social order, where historically there has been endorsement."[51] Unlike the attorney general of Georgia, Plato made an honorable pederastic exception for philosophers—an exception not needed (in the *Laws*) for members of the general public who lived their lives in the realm of opinion, not the realm of knowledge.[52]

Although Bowers cites Kant as a philosopher who disapproved of sodomy, other legal scholars such as David A. J. Richards have found support in Kant for the opposite point of view. Richards cites Kant as an author of the idea of human rights, as one "who best articulated its radical implications for the significance of respect for moral personality."[53] Extending the Kantian notion of autonomy to sexuality, Richards says, "Sexuality . . . is not a spiritually empty experience that the state may compulsorily legitimize only in the form of rigid, marital procreational sex, but one of the fundamental experiences through which, as an end in itself, people define the meaning of their lives."[54] Rights, typically, protect certain basic interests or desires of persons even if doing so makes the majority unhappy. Being able to love, according to Richards, is central to human lives. Moreover, "freedom to love means that a mature individual must have autonomy to decide how and whether to love another."[55]

Despite Kant's talk about rights as guarantees of proper respect for moral personality or rational autonomy, he did not see the implications of his theory for sexual autonomy. Of course, whenever one is developing a new theory, one may fail to see the whole range of its possible applications. Kant, for example, never asked whether nonhuman animals were capable of rational autonomy. He also thought women were quite lacking in rational ability and therefore did not see that they had any need for the rights of "man." Moreover, he referred to masturbation, same-sex intercourse (male and female), and intercourse with animals as *crimina carnis contra naturam* that "degrade human nature to a level below that of animal nature and make man unworthy of his humanity. He no longer deserves to be a person."[56]

Thus, in citing Kant, both Bowers and Richards are right: Kant was a very conventional man with many beliefs stemming from traditional natural law. He was also one of the originators of a theory of rights with radical implications for moral and social thought.

On a view like Devlin's, there is no theoretical limit to the legal enforcement of morality. Principles such as J. S. Mill's principle of liberty or a right to privacy are designed to function as just such limits. Justice Harry Blackmun, in his dissent, laments the "overall refusal" of the Court to "consider the broad principles that have informed our treatment of privacy in specific cases."[57] The word "privacy" does not appear in the Constitution. Nonetheless, a series of Supreme Court decisions has established a right of privacy, which is said to exist in the penumbra of certain amendments and, more philosophically, in the concept of liberty itself. (The word "liberty" is in the Constitution.)

A number of cases have established the constitutional status of a right of privacy.[58] *Griswold v. Connecticut*[59] held that a right of privacy protects the use of contraceptives by married persons. In this case, much was made of the fact that if contraceptives were illegal, police could enter the bedroom and search for them. *Eisenstadt v. Baird*[60] held that unmarried persons, under the equal protection clause, also have the right to use contraceptives. *Roe v. Wade*[61] held that the right of privacy encompasses a woman's decision to have an abortion. *Stanley v. Georgia*,[62] upheld the right to private possession of obscene material. Although a First Amendment case, the Court stressed the importance of the privacy of one's own home. In the words of Justice Thurgood Marshall, "[Stanley] is asserting the right to read or observe what he pleases—the right to satisfy his intellectual and emotional needs in the privacy of his own home."[63]

One way to explain a connection between the concepts of privacy and liberty is to borrow some thoughts from J. S. Mill, who advances roughly the following principle of liberty: People (competent adults, not children) should be allowed to voice their opinion and direct their lives as they see fit as long as no one else is wrongfully harmed. It follows from this principle that what one does to oneself, as long as no harm comes to another, is one's own business. A private action then is one that concerns oneself and does not wrongly harm others. Mill adds that if more than one party is involved, all parties must give their consent. Thus, what consenting adults do, as long as others are not wrongly harmed, is private, that is, their own business and not the business of the law. On such a view, it would be natural to suppose that a right of privacy would include sexual intimacies between consenting adults in their bedroom. The recognition of a right to sexual autonomy—something very much like Mill's view—was believed by many, including David Richards and dissenting Justice Blackmun, to be the Court's view in its development of privacy law. Thus, many were surprised that the Court did not extend the right of privacy to the facts in *Bowers*.

With respect to prior cases on privacy, the Court said: "None of the rights announced in these cases bears any resemblance to the claimed constitutional right of homosexuals to engage in acts of sodomy. . . . No connection between family, marriage, or procreation on the one hand and homosexual activity on the other has been demonstrated."[64] The majority produced no principle for this distinction. Nan D. Hunter, former American Civil Liberties Union attorney, calls the Court's statement one of "unmasked contempt . . . as if gay people don't create families, belong in families, raise children, or have the staying power for those 9.4-year-long average marriages that are the bedrock of civilized society."[65] It is not insignificant that the majority here aligned itself with Bowers who in turn sided with Plato in thinking that a legitimate function of law is to bolster the conventional institutions of heterosexual marriage, family, and procreation.

The complaint here is not simply that the Court did not extend privacy to consensual sexual conduct between adults in their bedroom, but that the Court did not even recognize the right of privacy as the fundamental right at issue. Blackmun, in the opening sentence of his dissent, says, "This case is no more about 'a fundamental right to engage in homosexual sodomy,' as the Court purports to declare, than *Stanley v. Georgia* was about a fundamental right to watch obscene movies."[66] To push the point, in Kansas in 1986 and in Alabama in 1998, the legislature passed a law banning sex toys in general and vibrators in particular.[67] If a challenge to these laws should ever reach the Supreme Court, no one would expect the Court to find in the Constitution a fundamental right to own a vibrator. However, since the Kansas legislation was part of a pornography package, we might anticipate that the right of freedom of expression would count as a fundamental right at issue. The right to privacy might count as fundamental in either case.

Recognition of a fundamental right by the courts triggers heightened judicial scrutiny. Very good reasons (a "compelling interest" in the language of law) must be given by a state if a law restricting some fundamental right is to survive this heightened scrutiny. In a case where no fundamental right is recognized, almost any reason, however weak, will do. As we have seen in *Bowers,* moral beliefs were used as reasons without meeting any rational requirements such as those suggested by Ronald Dworkin. For example, Dworkin would not count as genuine moral convictions those claims based only on arguments from authority such as appeals to the beliefs of Plato, Aristotle, and the Judeo-Christian tradition.

Assuming an ordinary person (Dworkin's "man on the bus") does produce a reason that is not disqualified on Dworkin's grounds, that reason, he says, "will presuppose some general moral principle or theory, even though [the man on the bus] may not be able to state that principle or theory."[68] Presumably, it is unreasonable to make everyone who rides the bus take a course in moral philosophy; hence, Dworkin's standards of rationality are minimal, requiring only that one be able to produce a reason for one's view and use it consistently. "X has harmful consequences," "X violates my rights," "X is unnatural," even "The Bible forbids X," all count as genuine reasons and, if used consistently, constitute a genuine moral conviction. Joel Feinberg objects to Dworkin's version of legal moralism when he says, "Even if there is a *genuine* moral consensus in a community that certain sorts of 'harmless' activities are wrong, I see no reason why that consensus should be enforced by the criminal law . . . even a genuine 'discriminatory' popular morality might, for all of that, be *mistaken*."[69]

Bad reasons slip easily through Dworkin's net. To condemn homosexuality because it is unnatural is to give a reason that can be expressed in a principled form and is attached to a theory developed by Greek and medieval philosophers. Yet it is a bad reason on many grounds. The biological data do not support it.[70] There is no reason why the purpose of sexuality should be procreation rather than intimacy or pleasure even as there is no reason why the purpose of the mouth should be for eating rather than kissing. "Nature" does not rank purposes for us when something has more than one, so we cannot get very far with minimal rational standards. In not requiring the ordinary person to recognize moral reasons in their principled form or to know anything about the moral theories to which the reasons are attached, Dworkin does not and cannot require a citizen to have a good reason for his moral point of view. Without a knowledge of ethical theory or metatheory, there is no basis for judging between competing kinds of reasons.

It is easy to think that in adopting legal moralism one simply adds a principle of legal moralism to the harm principle, the offense principle, and so on, in an effort to sanction increasingly invasive restrictions on personal liberty. In some instances, however, endorsing legal moralism is costly to society, that is, personal liberty is not the only cost. For instance, a friend-of-the-court brief accompanying *Bowers* filed jointly by the American Psychological Association and the American Public Health Association argued, correctly I believe, that "from a public health standpoint, the [Georgia] statute is simply counterproductive. . . . the statute does not deter conduct that spreads AIDS, but it may deter conduct essential to combating it."[71] Briefly, the two organizations argued that sodomy statutes adversely affected scientific investigation directed toward containing AIDS and finding a cure and interfered with health education efforts designed to encourage safer sexual practices. Specifically, the associations supported their claims in the following way:

> A statutory scheme that creates a realistic fear of punishment if certain behavior is disclosed runs the risk of obscuring important data, as individuals simply refuse to volunteer for studies or provide needed information, and of creating false data, as individuals try to conform what they reveal to what they believe is legal. . . . With respect to at least two important issues—the existence of potentially high risk to recent immigrants from Haiti and the transmissibility of the AIDS virus from women to men—there is reason to believe that falsifications of information, caused by fear of punishment, have distorted the epidemiological picture. Finding these and other crucial pieces of the AIDS puzzle should not have to depend on the ability of epidemiologists to guess whether patients are not telling the truth because they fear being punished. . . . community effort and support [for major educational efforts] are made more difficult in an environment in which a concomitant of participating in educa-

> tional efforts is self-incrimination. Attending an educational presentation on "safe sex," for example, could be seen as an admission of engaging in sexual practices prohibited by the statute. Criminalization is likely to compromise the efficacy of informal educational networks by making people more cautious about what they reveal about themselves to acquaintances. It also presents state public health officials with the awkward choice of appearing to suppress information about safe sex techniques or appearing to condone felonious conduct.[72]

The associations also pointed out that the Georgia statute did not further any mental health objectives and caused substantial psychological harm by fostering homophobia among heterosexuals and internalized homophobia among gay people. Roy Cohn, a queer-baiter in the McCarthy era who died of AIDS in the mid-1980s, is a classic case of the destructive behavior that results from internalized homophobia. It is worthy of note that Cohn's medical records showed him as "reluctant" to be celibate[73] and his public statements showed him as reluctant to tell the truth.

Rather than relinquish the idea that homosexual sex is wicked, some would even deny condoms to those who need them, preferring to see people die of AIDS. For instance, the Corrections Department in New York State made condoms available to married prisoners enrolled in a family-visitation program, whereas condoms were not offered to prisoners who were not in the program even though officials realized that some prisoners engaged in homosexual sex and could use the condoms to protect themselves against AIDS.[74] Of course, if natural sex is procreative sex, then the use of condoms by heterosexuals is equally unnatural. This point was not lost on Archbishop Renato R. Martino who recently said that "the Church's stand . . . includes the prohibition of the use of condoms in AIDS prevention programs."[75] However, somewhere between Aquinas and *Bowers* a new use of "natural" emerged for convenience-oriented consumers. In defense of a company decision not to portray gay users of condoms in television commercials, Susan Smirnoff, spokesperson for Trojan, said that condoms "are effective against infection when used properly. A condom's proper use is for vaginal intercourse."[76]

The point I want to make here is that natural law arguments and consequentialist arguments are incompatible. As we saw in Chapter 1, Aquinas said that rape is not as bad as consensual sodomy or interrupting heterosexual intercourse, because heterosexual rape allows for the possibility of fulfilling the purpose of sexuality, namely, procreation. Nor would natural law theorists be interested in some new data developed by University of Chicago economist Steven Levitt and Stanford law professor John Donahue that suggest that the reduction in crime rates in certain states in the United States is linked to liberalized abortion laws in those same states following *Roe*. Unwanted children bring about unwanted consequences in a society.[77] However, consequences, no matter how destructive of individuals or society, do not matter a whit in the face of what is claimed to be the natural order.

Regardless of one's assessment of the foregoing arguments regarding the social costs of prohibiting homosexual sodomy, the fact remains that to advocate such a prohibition because it is believed to be wicked or unnatural is to dispense with any discussion of harmful consequences that may result from that prohibition. Had the Court ruled in Hardwick's favor, Georgia could have made its case for its sodomy statute on the basis of public health reasons or whatever. But Georgia did not have to give any good reasons for its law, nor did the Court concern itself with arguments to the effect that the public health was ill-served by the prohibition of sodomy. The Court, as has been pointed out, dismissed these arguments in favor of traditional views that were poorly supported or wholly unsupported: Bowers said that Kant said that homosexuality is unnatural.[78]

NATURAL LAW AND MARRIAGE

Natural law reasoning was once used against gay men with AIDS with the effect of impeding scientific research. We did not hear AIDS examples of natural law reasoning in the 1990s, nor will we in the new century, because AIDS is now primarily a heterosexual disease and nobody says that heterosexuals are doing anything unnatural. AIDS has moved in one direction and natural law arguments in another—as arguments against gay marriage, to give one example. What remains constant here is that natural law arguments are forever being used against gay people, even as the topic of the decade changes. In the 1980s it was AIDS; in the 1990s it was marriage.

Early legal arguments against interracial marriage, that they were "unnatural" and "by definition not a marriage," are repeated today against lesbians and gay men.[79] Gays cannot marry, according to John Finnis, because "sexual acts . . . are not marital unless they have . . . procreative significance."[80] Even the sexual intercourse of sterile heterosexual married couples is claimed by Finnis and his followers to have "procreative significance" because "nature has designed the human body to allow heterosexual couples to unite biologically in a way it has denied homosexuals."[81] Thus, as David Richards characterizes the views of Finnis and other Catholic conservatives, "The exclusively procreational model of sexuality [is] the measure of the right to marriage."[82]

Finnis argues that homosexual couples, because they do not constitute a "biological unit," cannot experience the common good of marriage. Paul J. Weithman argues against Finnis that homosexual relationships are capable of complementarity and realizing a common good.[83] Nonetheless, Weithman sees Finnis's argument against homosexuality and gay marriage as an "advance in natural law thinking" because it is based on respect for "basic goods" rather than the wrong of frustrating natural functions. The basis of Finnis's argument, Weithman claims, is more plausible than that of earlier natural law thinkers, and "his arguments do not depend upon the naturalistic fallacy."[84] According to Weithman, Finnis's "claim is that human beings must never choose to act against the good realized by the 'biological (hence personal) units' constituted by voluntary, uncontracepted, heterosexual union."[85] If it is more plausible to say that sexuality has only one good[86] rather than that sexuality has only one legitimate function, each position supports the procreational model.

Philosophers generally acknowledge G. E. Moore's naturalistic fallacy, that is, the idea that normative conclusions are not logically entailed in descriptions of fact. But teleological uses of "natural" do not commit the naturalistic fallacy. Although many uses of the term "natural" are mere descriptions of fact, teleological uses are not. The language of function or purpose is normative from the outset, containing standards of evaluation within it. Those standards, as we saw in Chapter 1, are not necessarily *moral* standards and in any event require ethical critique of the standards themselves. Finnis also escapes the naturalistic fallacy by claiming to know the "basic goods" in life and who is capable of having them.

The procreation model of sexuality has been dismissed in legal arguments about constitutional rights, says Richards, by granting heterosexuals the right to contraception in *Griswold* and the right to abortion in *Roe*.[87] Thus, an equal protection of the laws argument ought to free lesbians and gay men from this type of argument at least. Richards may be right here in his logic, but there is more than logic at issue. After all, Richards thought that the Court in *Bowers* would apply the right to privacy to the facts of the case and define privacy as sexual autonomy; the Court did neither. In *Baker v. State*,[88] a 1999 Vermont same-sex marriage case, the subject of procreation played a prominent role. Indeed, this case was on appeal to the state supreme court precisely because a trial court found that the state was justified in using marriage to promote procreation. The state argued that, because same-sex couples cannot conceive a child on their own, excluding them from marriage promotes a "perception of the link between procreation and child rearing," and that allowing lesbians and gay men to marry would "advance the notion that mothers and fathers . . . are mere surplusage to the functions of procreation and child rearing."[89]

In the final analysis, the Vermont Supreme Court rejected these procreation arguments against gay marriage, noting instead that "to the extent that the State's purpose in licensing civil marriage was, and is, to legitimize children and provide for their security . . . many same-sex couples are no different from opposite-sex couples with respect to these objectives."[90] Further, after pointing out that it is mostly infertile heterosexual couples who conceive a child using assisted reproductive techniques (often involving genetic material from only one of the married partners), the court took the following line of argument: "The State does not suggest that the use of these technologies undermines a married couple's sense of parental responsibility, or fosters the perception that they are 'mere surplusage' to the conception and parenting of the child so conceived. Nor does it even remotely suggest that access to such techniques ought to be restricted as a matter of policy to 'send a message that procreation and child rearing are intertwined.' Accordingly, there is no reasonable basis to conclude that a same-sex couple's use of the same technologies would undermine the bonds of parenthood, or society's perception of parenthood."[91] The court also pointed out the obvious, that is, that many opposite-sex couples never intend to have children or are incapable of having children. Thus, the law as it stands "extends the benefits and protections of marriage to many persons with no logical connection to the stated governmental goal [of procreation]."[92]

The fact that the "procreational model" of marriage did not succeed in Vermont does not mean that it will necessarily disappear from the legal scene. Some less progressive state may try again. The Vermont case cannot go on to the U.S. Supreme Court,[93] and even if it could, its reasoning could be rejected. It would have been hard to succeed with bad reasons of this type in Vermont or in states like it because in such states these kinds of reasons typically are thrown out. For example, the Vermont legislature had already removed legal barriers in order to allow a partner of a biological parent to adopt, if in the child's best interest, without reference to sex. It takes a little explaining to allow gay parents but not gay marriage.

It may be, as Richards believes, that the Supreme Court will have to overrule *Bowers* before a gay marriage case can be successful, even as school desegregation came before the right to interracial marriage.[94] Apparently, being free to have sex is perceived as less radical than being able to marry. As strange as the priority of values here may seem to some, there is an important conceptual connection between the two issues. In both instances, lesbians and gay men are seeking to gain access to the private sphere, in the former case as individuals and in the latter as people who have important relationships.[95]

It is true, however, that because of *Romer* the constitutional rights of lesbians and gay men must now be taken seriously. And it is also true, as lawyers at the Lambda Legal Defense and Education Fund say, that because of *Romer* "same-sex couples cannot be singled out for discrimination for no reason at all, for the sake of 'tradition,' or for the sake of catering to the prejudices and fears of the majority."[96] Nonetheless, it remains true that natural law arguments are still used in courtrooms and still pose an obstacle to equality and justice.

6

Rights and Responsibilities

The rights approach to ethics has been more criticized than defended by feminist philosophers in recent years. The notion of rights has come under fire as reflective of Western masculinity in its emphasis on the individual rather than the community. According to Susan Bordo, "Our students still experience this moment of critical and empowering insight when, for example, they learn from Gilligan and others that the language of 'rights' is not the ethical discourse of God or Nature, but the ideological superstructure of a particular construction of masculinity."[1] The implication is that the notion of rights can be dismissed because its foundation is not solidly based but rests upon comparatively weak pillars. But whether God, Nature, or masculinity is considered a foundation of a philosophical viewpoint, they are all equally weak. To say that a principle should be followed, for instance, because "God says so" is not to give a reason at all but to cite an authority, and unless the authority has reasons, we have done little more than assert that someone in power is the source of our view. Nature, as we have seen, has little to say on the topic of the relative values of points of view. It may indeed be that the whole concept of rights reflects typically masculine values such as individuality and self-assertion; but it may also be that certain ideas such as autonomy and liberty have value independent of the fact that men historically have prized them.

FEMINISM AND RIGHTS

Much of the feminist criticism of rights stems from the publication of Carol Gilligan's 1982 book *In a Different Voice*,[2] referred to earlier by Bordo. In the value systems described by Gilligan, an ethic that relies on rights is portrayed as setting up adversarial if not hostile relationships in contrast to caring and loving relationships and efforts to build connections and consensus.

Carol Gilligan once told the following story to an academic audience at a 1985 conference on women and moral theory in order to illustrate the differences between what has come to be called the justice (and rights) perspective (associated with men) and the care perspective (associated with women). The story is about a mole and a porcupine.[3] The mole and the porcupine make their home together in a hole that formerly belonged to the mole alone, but over time their relationship is not working out. The hole is too small, and the mole gets pricked by quills when the porcupine brings friends home for dinner. Problems multiply. What to do?

In her work as a psychologist and moral development theorist, Gilligan gathered empirical data on ethical problem solving by asking men and women how they would answer this prickly question. Generally, women came up with the most accommodating of solutions in an effort to save the relationship. One said the mole and the porcupine could look for a different place to live. Another said that together they could dig a bigger hole. One woman even suggested throwing a blanket over the porcupines' quills when friends came to visit. Many men, on the other hand, saw the issue involved as one of property rights. The solution was simple: the mole should evict the porcupine. Those men who saw the issue this way were later asked what they would do if the porcupine refused to leave. A significant number of them, Gilligan reported, said "shoot the porcupine." At this point the audience erupted with laughter. It seemed clear that masculine rights talk was adversarial, hostile, and even violent.

Although there may be some merit to this critique of rights, there is also a sense in which it is clearly not appropriate to criticize rights for not promoting caring and concern for others. After all, the concept of rights was created to protect certain basic interests of individuals, not to promote loving relationships and/or caring connections with others, so it should not be surprising if rights do not serve these ends.

Certainly ethics must question how people relate to each other in a community, but a crucial issue here is whether or not we think that certain basic interests of individuals—such as the desire to live an autonomous life—ought to also be protected. If we agree, we try to think of ways to rein in rights rather than dismiss them altogether. Property rights, for example, are an individual right that is regulated in widely differing ways. Although in Europe an owner's use of his property must also consider his neighbor's views and sunlight, zoning ordinances in the United States rarely if ever take such considerations into account. Similarly, the United States makes no attempt to regulate salaries, while other countries do not allow CEOs to make vast fortunes. Perhaps placing a value on the autonomous life is not the problem here. Perhaps, instead, the masculinist tendency to push rights in a selfish, hostile way can be explained by the character that lies beneath the rights.[4]

Although feminist criticism of rights dates back to Carol Gilligan's work, the notion that asserting rights within some personal relationship will destroy that relationship has a long history. For example, in marriage law, it has long been argued that the recognition of rights undermines domestic harmony. Specifically, "The argument of dangers to domestic harmony [has been] used by the courts in refusing to adjudicate civil, and in some [instances] criminal, cases between spouses."[5] As one judge in 1858 put it, "The flames which litigation would kindle on the domestic hearth would consume in an instant the conjugal bond."[6] Thus, any legal redress for personal wrongs was denied to women in order to preserve the stability of marriages.[7] Many other "special" relationships have been seen as so based on trust and intimacy that asserting the rights of one of the individuals is perceived as inherently adversarial and destructive: teacher/student or religious leader/suppliant. In the late 1970s, John Ladd used this criticism of rights to argue against them as the basis for physician/patient relationships.

Ladd proposed, as an alternative to rights theory, an ethics of responsibility based on interpersonal relationships. These relationships, described as friendships, are personal in nature, founded on trust, and obtain between doctor and patient, parent and child, and so on. A major disadvantage of relationships based on rights, Ladd said, is that they threaten the friendly interaction between doctor and patient: "Requests for help from family and friends are not and perhaps ought not to be based on who has a right against whom. For if a request is based on a right, it will more than likely destroy the relationship altogether, because it implies an absence of trust. That is why the appeal to rights is sometimes inappropriate, improper, and immoral."[8]

What is consistently overlooked in these arguments is the fact of inequality of power between the parties and the ultimate effect of this inequality on the nature of their relationship. If, for example, a physician operates without a patient's consent, it would be absurd to blame the patient for ruining the harmony of the relationship by asserting his right not to be treated this way.[9] Even when a patient appeals to individual rights prior to any negative action on the part of the physician—for example, a patient might start a physician/patient relationship with an assertion of his rights in order to make his position clear—it is not obvious that the assertion does imply an absence of trust or that, if it does, that the absence of trust is unreasonable (or, to put it another way, that it is the responsibility of the patient to trust the physician).

The need for patients' rights and a clarification of those rights before surgery is illustrated by the growing practice in thousands of U.S. hospitals of reusing medical instruments designed to be used only once.[10] Referred to recently in *U.S. News and World Report* as "medicine's dirty little secret," the practice involves "quietly recycling millions of disposable sawblades, biopsy forceps, and catheters for use in procedures from cardiac angioplasties to orthopedic surgery, putting unwitting patients at risk for injury, infection, and worse." Documented examples of the "risk from what appears to be recycled disposable instruments that were contaminated or defective" include "cases of premature babies stitched with unsterile sutures; a crumbled tube lodging in the pulmonary artery of an elderly women; a fractured catheter becoming stuck in a patient's facial artery; a biopsy patient possibly being contaminated with hepatitis B; and two catheters breaking during the brain scan of a 50-year-old woman, requiring surgery."[11]

Of great importance here other than the possible risks is the fact that "patients are almost never told about reuse in the first place." Jose Nazari, a Chicago area electrophysiologist, compared his hospital's "patient consent policy on recycling" to the military's policy of "Don't ask, don't tell." As the title of an insert to the magazine article put it, "If you don't ask, they won't tell." Some professionals recommend that patients get a written statement from their doctor or add a sentence to the traditional consent form to the effect that single-use devices are not to be reused.[12]

Reminding people of the moral dimension of their conduct may offend them if it seems to suggest that one is not taking their acting morally on faith. However, there seems no reason for believing that basing such a reminder in the language of rights would be any more disruptive to the relationship than basing it on talk about responsibilities or utilities or character. It is the calling of attention to moral mistakes (or their possibility) that may cause disruption, not the theoretical language that is used to characterize the mistake. Moreover, if it is inappropriate for the patient to make moral claims on the physician, then the patient has no legitimate part in the moral aspect of the decision making. Unless the patient asserts his "rights"—or alternatively, his beliefs about the physician's responsibilities—the physician may unknowingly be making decisions about the patient's life on the basis of moral principles contrary to those the patient holds.

Some feminists are now viewing rights with a new acceptance—not necessarily as the whole of one's moral theory but at least as a possible important component in it. Ideas closely related to rights, such as the value of autonomy and certain concepts of the self, are being reevaluated and reworked by feminists today.[13] The fact that social relations enter into many of these analyses of autonomy and the self shows the impact of Gilligan's work on feminist thought. Directly in line with this social dimension approach is the view that rights can be rehabilitated as relational. Samantha Brennan, for example, argues that although classical rights are flawed because they rest on individualistic assumptions, rights as relational can become a feminist project. She claims that, at both the conceptual level and at the level of practice, rights clearly are relational; at the concrete level, rights can be made relational if feminists create rights with relational content.[14]

Conceptually it is true that rights are relational since one individual is making a claim against another individual or individuals. But this truth, as I see it, just moves the original feminist objection to rights to a different plane. Now, instead of claiming that rights presuppose a self that exists like an atom with no relation to others, the objection must be phrased in terms of the *way* individuals who claim rights relate to one another, namely, badly.

Constructing rights with relational content can be a useful idea, but only if some rights that protect the basic interests of individuals are kept. Eva Kittay has suggested a "right to care" as an example of a right with relational content. For example, in a recent case, a woman who was a single parent was fired from her job because she could not put in the many extra hours her employer asked her to work if she expected to care for her child at all. No court would recognize a public interest on the part of the child in a case like this, but Kittay's point is that they should.[15]

However it may evolve with feminist reworkings of rights theory, I argue that rights must include some protection of individual interests such as the desire to make important decisions concerning one's own life. As such, rights will continue to be a better alternative than an ethic of responsibility based on interpersonal relationships. Let us examine just one relationship model more closely—the physician/patient one as proposed by John Ladd. I will argue that the notion of autonomy rights for individuals and the corresponding institutional model of medicine are indeed appropriate to the physician/patient relationship. In fact, given the growing interjection of health maintenance organizations (HMOs) into the physician/patient relationship, the assertion of individual rights becomes even more crucial.

EQUALITY AND FRIENDSHIP

Ladd presents his views in a most appealing way—helping the needy, being friends with the doctor, and so on—but his ethics of responsibility is plausible only because he ignores the facts of power that rights theory was designed to take into account.

The interpersonal relationship from which moral duties stem is characterized by Ladd as "not . . . of a casual or transient sort, but the kind of relationship that Aristotle called 'friendship,' which includes family, companions, colleagues, and perhaps even doctors and patients!"[16] The friendship Aristotle extended to his colleagues and his family, however, includes two entirely different kinds. Thus, it is not clear what sort of friendship Ladd thinks doctors and patients can have.

Aristotle's "perfect friendship"[17] applied to upper-class Greek males whose natural superiority made it possible for them to be alike in virtue. A second kind of friendship applied to unequal parties, for example, "that of father to son and in general of elder to younger, that of man to wife and in general that of ruler to subject."[18] Aristotle explains the implications here: "By nature a father tends to rule over his sons, ancestors over descendants, a king over his subjects. These friendships imply superiority of one party over the other. . . . The friendship of man and wife, again, is the same that is found in an aristocracy; for it is in accordance with virtue—the better gets more of what is good, and each gets what befits him."[19] In short, the inferiors have less virtue and thus their receiving less of what is good is justified. Ladd can recommend either this model of friendship for doctors and patients or the colleague model.

Applying the colleague model to doctors and patients is problematic, for, as Ladd admits, the patient's position vis-à-vis the doctor is one of dependence and inequality. Ladd characterizes the inequality as basically one of knowledge.[20] However, the inequality between doctors and patients amounts to much more than an inequality of knowledge. Medicine in the United States is an institution with enormous power and wealth. Whereas doctors have power in virtue of their affiliation with this institution, most patients are ordinary individuals with no such connection or comparable power. This vast inequality between doctors and patients makes Aristotle's "colleague model" an inappropriate one for their relationship.

If the colleague model is inappropriate, we are left with the model of friendship that presupposes inequality. Under this model, those without power must rely on the goodwill of the powerful. Aristotle was very much in favor of the power structure he delineated so clearly: kings rule over subjects, men rule over women, slaveholders rule over slaves, and so on. He did not think that inferiors had any rights; instead, superiors and inferiors had their different virtues and responsibilities. There are, of course, particular powerful individuals who are concerned and caring and responsible, but this fact in no way detracts from the point that good intentions are no substitute for equality of power.

INSTITUTIONS AND INSTITUTIONAL RELATIONS

Ladd insisted that, in applying rights theory to medical contexts, one is taking rights out of the context of politics, laws, and institutions to apply them to personal relationships.[21] Perhaps today, with corporate control of health care in the existence of HMOs, no one could fail to see that medicine is institutional and political. However, even two decades ago, the physician/patient relationship was political, not only in the extended sense in which any power relationship is political but also in the straightforward conventional sense of being organized, constituted, and created by laws, institutions, and government actions.

That medicine is political in this conventional sense might be illustrated by a comparison between medicine and auto repair. I am dependent on both my physician and my auto mechanic for their knowledge—that is, they have knowledge of processes and technologies that I need to be able to control. However, my relationship with my auto mechanic is significantly less political than my relationship with my physician in the following respects: if I were to acquire the knowledge necessary for the performance of anything from routine tasks to complicated repairs on my car, I could perform them with no legal hindrance. I would not need a licensed mechanic's written permission to buy parts or to rent or buy complicated machinery, and I would not be guilty of illegally practicing auto mechanics without a license. Whereas, even if I gained the appropriate medical knowledge, not only would the law prevent me from purchasing necessary supplies (drugs) without written authorization from a licensed physician, but it also would prevent me from directly hiring the services of other health professionals (medical technicians, nurses, pharmacists) who might have precisely the expertise that I need.

The profession of medicine is an institution defined by laws, practices, and rules. An institution is not a thing over and above the people in it; rather it is a way of structuring human relationships. The profession of medicine is, among other things, a structured relationship between physicians and those people who stand in need of health care. Therefore, the physician/patient relationship is an institutional relationship. My relationship to my physician qua physician is not (as Ladd suggests) a relationship between two persons that is fundamentally based on differences in our individual noninstitutional characteristics, my lack of medical knowledge and his or her possession of medical knowledge. If that were the case, there would not be a qualitative difference between the physician/patient relationship and, for example, the pharmacist/patient relationship, or, for that matter, between a physician/patient relationship and my relationship to someone who is an expert on human biology and organic chemistry but who holds no license or membership in a profession.

Medical ethics should be concerned with the responsibilities arising out of the physician/patient relationship, but it is precisely because of the institutional nature of this relationship (rather than because of its noninstitutional nature) that physicians have special responsibilities. Because of the position they occupy within the institution of medicine, physicians have responsibilities, and patients have a right to insist that those responsibilities be carried out because of their position within the institution. Thus, a physician who perceives the physician/patient relationship as a personal rather than an institutional one will be less able to recognize his responsibilities qua physician and more likely to act irresponsibly than one who thinks in terms of the institutional relationship.

Ladd suggests that legalism (and, presumably, rights theory that is an instance of legalism) "gives a means for coping with individuals who *perceive* their relationship to us in impersonal terms, e.g., doctors whose relationship to us is legalistically defined by their professional role."[22] It is not the *perception* of the relationship as either institutional or personal that makes it so. Whether or not A's relationship to B is institutional is an objective fact about them, having to do with rules and structures that go beyond their particular case; since it is not a fact about their beliefs, it cannot be altered by a simple alteration of their beliefs. Moreover, experience suggests that it may be the physician who disregards the institutional nature of the relationship and conceives of it in personal terms (particularly, in paternalistic terms) against whom the patient will be most likely to need the protection of rights.

The responsibilities of the physician qua physician do indeed go beyond obligations correlative to basic rights; that is, they go beyond that which any adult human being can claim against any other adult human being. This actuality does not commit us, however, to the claim that they are not correlative to rights at all. After all, there are special rights we can claim, as citizens, of government, of police officers, of judges; as students, of teachers; as employees, of employers; and, presumably, as patients, of physicians.

EQUALITY AND RIGHTS

While Ladd admits the inequality of the doctor/patient relationship, he contends that it still argues against the use of rights theory: "The rights relationship . . . is based on the assumption of a certain kind of antecedent equality between the two parties, as is supposed to exist between those entering a contractual agreement. . . . in critically important ways the patient is likely to be in an initial state of dependence and inequality vis-à-vis the doctor; to speak of rights—for example, contractual rights—in such cases is an absurdity."[23]

But rights theory was designed to handle cases of inequality of power; a fundamental model of the assertion of a right has traditionally been that of a citizen vis-à-vis government or a government official, who is presumed to have power over the citizen. This assertion of rights is theoretically supported by the assumption of an antecedent *moral* equality (rather than an antecedent equality of power). This view makes puzzling Ladd's assertion "that the ethics of responsibility implies another sort of equality that is not as obviously a part of an ethics of rights, namely, the equal worth and dignity of individuals."[24] The only theory Ladd appeals to as an instance of the kind of theory he is advocating, that is, Aristotle's ethics, assumes an antecedent moral inequality and an antecedent inequality of legitimate moral authority.

For Aristotle, some individuals are antecedently morally superior—because they are aristocrats, male, or otherwise "virtuous"—to those who are morally inferior—because they are slaves, female, or otherwise lacking in virtue. Rights theory, in particular, the social contract version developed by Locke, is concerned to deny this purported natural right to rule and substitute for it an equal moral authority over one's own life. Where there is an inequality of power on the part of contractees is precisely where an institutionalization of the rights of the weaker party (backed up by state or other institutional power) is most appropriate. Whatever weaknesses rights theory may have, the initial assertion that empirical inequalities (of strength, intelligence, knowledge, and so on) do not confer moral authority (the right to rule) on the superiors may serve as a needed antidote to the Aristotelian tendency to confuse superiority of power with superiority of virtue, which in turn is presumed to confer legitimate political power.

In talking about patient's rights, we portray the patient as an autonomous agent who has a legitimate part in the decisions about his or her medical care rather than as a mere object of an obligation. As we have seen in Chapter 3, as long as we focus on obligations or responsibilities, we are talking about the decision of the person who is in a position to either wrong the other or do good for the other. Rights talk focuses attention on the person to whom the obligation is owed. In stating the special moral concerns of the profession in terms of the obligations and/or responsibilities of the professional while suggesting that it would be improper for the patient to claim these as rights is, at least by implication, to place the locus of moral decision making in the hands of the professional and to suggest a model quite different from the model of autonomous agents.

If A is related to B in such a way that B's (reasonable) assertion of a right against A is interpreted as a violation of the relationship, then A and B are not relating as autonomous and morally equal agents. Indeed, A's taking offense at B's assertion of a right (qua assertion of a right) is at least prima facie evidence that A either expects or desires to be granted unquestioned moral authority. If A regards B as an autonomous and equal moral agent, A will regard B's assertion of a right as an occasion to assure B that they are in agreement as to what B's rights are or, if they are not in agreement, either to change his behavior toward B or to pursue rational discussion of the disagreement about B's rights and needs. If A (as a physician) believes that B needs an operation that B is not consenting to, then A has a responsibility to provide whatever knowledge he can to support this contention, but he should also recognize that B is the final arbiter of his own needs. Any suggestion that B's continued assertion of his right to withhold consent is necessarily inappropriate is to assume that the physician's medical authority confers moral authority—the right to make decisions about other people's rights.

Ladd avoids specifying who the final arbiter should be by stating his principles as if the patient's needs were unproblematic: "To do what a right-holder demands may be inconsistent with one's responsibility to him; for giving someone what he has a right to may in fact not be good for him at all."[25] It is difficult to imagine a situation meeting this description that does not represent a disagreement between the physician and the patient about what the patient's needs are—for example, a patient who is opposed to certain medical procedures and thinks his religious principles are more important than his health; or a patient who resists radical surgery (for example, a mastectomy) in order to maintain a sense of bodily integrity and wholeness or even for reasons of vanity.

Ladd claims that the underlying principle of his ethics is nicely expressed in the old socialist slogan: from each according to his abilities, to each according to his needs. That is, the physician helps the needy, the patient trusts the one with the ability to help. The socialist slogan, however, is a principle of distribution designed to change social and political institutions. It tells us nothing about what ethics might be appropriate until the power structure is changed. Ladd's use of this slogan as an individual moral maxim again highlights his attempt to convert institutional problems to individual and personal ones.

CONCLUSION

As we have seen, physicians and patients cannot simply step outside their institutional relationship by perceiving or declaring it to be a personal one. Even though the intrusion into the relationship of a third party, the HMO as the financial watchdog, has altered the dynamics of the power, still the physician cannot relinquish at will the power that is his qua physician. In fact, many of the relationships for which an ethic of care is claimed as superior to an ethic of rights are implicitly relationships of power inequality such as patient and physician, as one partner in the relationship is backed up by some overarching institution. When the institution is generally perceived as benevolent—marriage, religion, education, medicine—then the partner with less power—the wife, the supplicant, the student, the patient—is encouraged by both internal and external pressures to depend for just treatment on the goodwill engendered by the relationship. An assertion of individual rights by the less powerful partner is perceived, as Ladd suggests, as an attack upon the morality or trustworthiness of the more powerful partner. It can also, as early feminists learned in their critiques of the husband/wife power dynamic, be perceived as a blow at the underlying institution itself.

But an adequate analysis of the political, social, and technological bases of an institution must be a part of any analysis of the relationship between participants in it. Denial of the power of one party over another, when that power differential really does exist, is hardly the likeliest road to morality. It is true that an ethics based on rights can be perceived as divisive, as with Gilligan's home-sharing mole and porcupine. Although the divisiveness may be real, its source, I have argued, does not lie in the language of rights or even the assertion of a right. Moreover, an ethics based on rights avoids both the explicit inegalitarianism of Aristotle and the kind of irresponsible paternalism that could result from encouraging those with institutional power—such as physicians—to ignore that context and view their relations with others—the patients—as mere friendships.

7

Postmodernism and Other Skepticisms

Feminist theory, according to some of its practitioners, is a subset of postmodern philosophy.[1] With respect to the possibility of knowledge, Jane Flax, for instance, sets up the choices for feminists as an either/or proposition: postmodernism or the Enlightenment. Feminists, she says, cannot have it both ways: either what is called "truth" is tainted by history and social practice, as deconstructionist philosophers have shown, or some absolute truth of the whole universe is possible: "We cannot simultaneously claim (1) that the mind, self, and knowledge are socially constituted and that what we can know depends upon our social practices and contexts *and* (2) that feminist theory can uncover the Truth of the Whole once and for all. Such an absolute truth (e.g., the explanation for all gender arrangements at all times is X . . .) would require the existence of an 'Archimedes point' outside of the whole and beyond our embeddedness in it from which we could see (and represent) the whole."[2] Flax's argument follows a recognizable inference schema:

- Postmodern philosophy or Enlightenment philosophy.
- Enlightenment notions are untenable.
- Therefore, "feminist theory . . . belongs in the terrain of postmodern philosophy."[3]

She goes on to elaborate this claim: "Feminist notions of the self, knowledge, and truth are too contradictory to those of the Enlightenment to be contained within its categories. The way(s) of feminist future(s) cannot lie in reviving or appropriating Enlightenment concepts of the person or knowledge. . . . [D]espite an understandable attraction to the (apparently) logical, orderly world of the Enlightenment, feminist theory more properly belongs in the terrain of postmodern philosophy."[4]

Without a doubt, Enlightenment philosophers such as Kant were overconfident regarding the powers of reason and promised much more than they could deliver. However, even though both feminists and postmodernists are critical of so-called Enlightenment projects and the universalistic theories associated with those projects, feminist skepticism in recent decades has been a moderate one compared with the radical skepticism of postmodern philosophy. Moreover, the insight of postmodernism most attractive to recent feminist theory—that advances in knowledge are tentative, limited, constrained by culture, race, class, gender, sexual orientation, and other biases, and applicable only to a fraction of folks—can be salvaged without buying the radical skepticism and relativism of postmodernism.[5]

Flax's own use of the term "contradiction" in her rejection of Enlightenment conceptions indicates that she thinks the notion of contradiction can be employed in some legitimate way despite the dismissal of the principle of noncontradiction by contemporary French feminists Luce Irigaray and Hélène Cixous as paradigmatically male—penile, to be exact. And since Flax's criticisms of various postmodern thinkers suggest that only some of the conclusions of postmodernism should be saved, it seems equally plausible that some of the ideas of the Enlightenment might be worthwhile as well. If both philosophies can be critiqued for salvageable portions, perhaps feminism ought not to be classified as a subset of either postmodernism or the Enlightenment.

Flax sees feminism and postmodernism as common allies in their criticism of reason—that glory of the Enlightenment—as being ahistoric, transcendental, disembodied, impersonal, and abstract.[6] And, in fact, feminists have rightly been concerned with situatedness and the importance of relationships and context in areas such as theories of self. Nevertheless, feminist conceptions of notions in ethical or political theories—justice, for example—can be strengthened by, if not grounded in, certain abstractions. While postmodernists engaged in the unraveling of rational structures cannot take reason as a ground for anything, feminists can appeal to reason unless they choose to abandon it altogether. Which techniques stay and which go can be decided on the basis of relevance. For example, an ahistorical, disembodied concept of the self would be poor psychology; but just such an abstract self in a concept like the "veil of ignorance" might work well to explain justice. The fact that all concrete particular situatedness disappears may be exactly what is needed in order for people to understand what it is like to live in somebody else's shoes.[7]

My preoccupation is with rethinking ethics from a feminist perspective in the midst of the current struggle over which epistemology is more feminist. Reason, I argue, can play a role, albeit a small one compared with Enlightenment hopes, in establishing feminist ethical principles. In particular, I will focus on two concerns: how what has come to be the accepted or politically correct feminist view of affirming differences affects interpretations of a principle of equality, and how the postmodern critique of universal (or universalizing) claims overlooks the difference in the process of universalization between ethical theories and explanatory theories.

Explanatory theories such as those found in psychology, history, and metaphysics are under attack by feminists and postmodernists because the generalizations—sometimes referred to as universal or essentialist statements—they generate inevitably turn out to be false. Explanatory theories are designed to give an account of isolated phenomena, and some theories attempt to account for an extraordinary range of them. Authors Nancy Fraser and Linda Nicholson give as examples the metanarratives of Marx and Enlightenment humanism and the quasi-metanarratives of Nancy Chodorow and Carol Gilligan. However, efforts to explain the oppression of women by reference to a single cause will unavoidably extrapolate from the experiences of some while leaving out the stories of others. For example, such a theory might single out a domestic life that is typical of white, middle-class, heterosexual women but fail to capture the experiences of lesbians, black women, and working-class women. General claims about gender, in the words of Susan Bordo, create "a false unity out of heterogeneous elements relegating the submerged elements to marginality."[8]

From this enlightened perspective, Gilligan is criticized for ignoring differences in race and class in much the same way that Gilligan criticized Lawrence Kohlberg for ignoring gender differences. Just as Gilligan doubted that Kohlberg's single standard for human moral maturity was really anything of the sort, given that the data for his conclusion included only the moral reasoning of males, so too have some feminists suggested more recently that the type of moral reasoning Gilligan associates with women is better identified with subordinate or minority status.[9] This moderate skepticism regarding universalizing claims is typical of feminist theorizing of the decades preceding postmodernism.

Postmodern skepticism is radical skepticism. Gendered explanations of the kind Gilligan offers are rejected not because she, like Kohlberg, is guilty of false generalization but because of new skepticism about the use of gender as an analytical category.[10] It is not that Gilligan and Kohlberg have the wrong categories; under postmodernism, categories are abolished altogether. Every generalization leaves out something of importance, and our efforts to capture the item left out are endless and lead to a radical particularity. The view is well known: the world as text, subject to endless commentary and particular interpretations, the continual displacement of one text by another. It is reminiscent of the philosopher Cratylus, who, when convinced of radical skepticism, "did not think it right to say anything but only moved his finger."[11] The feminist celebration of difference that began by discarding false generalizations moves in postmodernism to a radical particularity, what Bordo calls, "the view from everywhere." The feminist worry that some stories are marginalized or not told shifts in postmodernism to the view that there are only particular stories, that no rational standards arbitrate between discourses.

The notion of life as literary criticism—ceaseless textual play—has unsurprisingly prompted some feminists to claim that no (practical) politics can come from postmodernism. When one refuses to order thoughts into concepts, categories, and theories, one eliminates politics. If we have no political theory, we have no practical politics. If we have no feminist theory, we have no women's movement. Some feminists have even been tempted to claim there are no "women," following Michel Foucault's idea that "the homosexual" is an invented classification. Teresa de Lauretis, for example, says the subject of feminism is "not only distinct from Woman with the capital letter, the *representation* of an essence inherent in all women . . . but also distinct from women, the real, historical beings and social subjects who are . . . actually engendered in social relations. The subject of feminism . . . is a theoretical construct . . . not women."[12] Even if academics can understand perfectly well what is meant, one cannot go into the street and talk about a women's movement if there are no women. One might as well join Cratylus in the bending of a finger. But before we become overly pessimistic regarding the possibility of ethics or political theory, it must be noticed that the postmodern disparagement of universalistic claims applies only to discussions that try to capture truths about the world.

ACTING ON PRINCIPLE

Universalization in ethics is not the same thing as universalization in nonnormative, explanatory principles and theories, such as those found in psychology, history, or metaphysics. Universalization in ethics is a purely formal approach to procedures requiring consistency, insisting that people not make an exception for themselves. As a formal process, it makes statements that do not contain content in the usual narrative sense; that is, universalization in ethics delineates some abstract content such as the notion of equality with some criteria of relevant similarities rather than describing a condition of the external world. Thus the postmodern critique of universalization and generalization in explanatory theories cannot be applied to universalization or generalization in ethics. Universalization in ethics does not fail to tell the stories of some because it tells no stories at all.

Gilligan appeals to ethical universalization in her normative claim that women should be less self-sacrificing and men should be less egoistic.[13] From an empirical standpoint vis-à-vis moral worth, many women are likely to count themselves for less than others, whereas many men tend to count themselves for more than others. To be less inclined to self-sacrifice is to view one's own moral worth on a par with that of other folks. To argue that a woman ought to have such a view is to assume a universalization, that is, a consistency of the standards of moral worth, as the right way to proceed. Without such a view we have only particular stories: the stories of those women who undervalue themselves and the stories of those men who do not. Gilligan's appeal to the principle of universalization arbitrates between these discourses.

Acting on principle, according to Kohlberg, is the highest stage of moral maturity. It makes sense—from a psychological point of view—that acting on principle would be a late stage in moral development because certain rational capacities must be acquired in order to recognize and apply principles that are not needed, for example, at the authority stage ("X" is wrong because Mom says so) or even at utilitarian stages ("X" is wrong because doing "X" raises the level of unwanted suffering in the world). Kant, of course, was not a psychologist and therefore did not use the jargon of "maturity," but he did believe that ethics is a matter of acting on principle. Now, part of what is meant by acting on principle is that one must be prepared to ignore the social consequences of one's actions, indeed, if necessary, to ignore the sufferings of others. Acting on principle can be a dangerous thing because people already disposed to do possible social damage might in addition act on the wrong principles.

Kant's standards, it must be noted, are even higher than acting on principle; we first must formulate the principles according to formal considerations of reason, such as universalization and not violating the principle of noncontradiction—in other words, the content of principles is determined by abstract, formal rules of reason. Here is where the confidence in reason so typical of the Enlightenment can be seen very clearly in Kant's ethics. Because we are rational beings testing our principles against rational standards, we will come up with the right principles. There is no need to worry about our having the right principles because the rational principles are the right ones, and as rational beings we know what principles have survived the tests of reason.

REJECTING PRINCIPLES: THE DEMISE OF EQUALITY AND NONCONTRADICTION

In recent feminist scholarship, acceptable projects attend to the recognition of differences among women—in particular, those differences due to race and class. Bordo describes as a feminist dogma the idea that "the only 'correct' perspective on race, class, and gender is the affirmation of difference" revealing itself in "criticisms which attack gender generalizations as *in principle* . . . totalizing."[14] Presumably, to generalize about gender is to intentionally marginalize others. Two lamentable consequences of the celebration of difference for principled ethics is Flax's interpretation of equality as similarity that results in the problematizing and demotion of the principle of equality and the rejection of the principle of noncontradiction by Irigaray and Cixous because of its association with masculine sameness.

Justice, says Flax, is a potentially more useful concept than equality because justice allows for a consideration of differences whereas equality does not: "Equality as currently understood and practiced is constituted in part . . . by a denial . . . of differences. . . . I cannot imagine equality apart from some measure of sameness."[15] By assuming equality as similarity, Flax creates the following paradox: "If equality requires and reflects sameness, the nature of this sameness itself must be questioned. For it did not escape attention that the concepts different/same were also constituted dualistically and were gendered. The feminine is the 'different' to the masculine 'same.' Hence to attain equality it would appear necessary for women to cease being feminine, at least in the public sphere. . . . Yet if women must cease being feminine to be citizens, to speak of *women's* political emancipation would be an oxymoron since we must eliminate our 'difference' before entering the public world."[16]

The assumption here is that egalitarian arguments are based on similarities between the sexes and that arguments based on sex differences constitute a rejection of egalitarian arguments. It is hard and often unproductive to talk about equality without saying whether one means moral equality, economic equality, equal opportunity, equal representation, and so on. The point of arguments for representation is not to show that differences win out over equality. Rather, the issue here is that whether or not differences are relevant depends on what kind of equality one is talking about. If one is talking about *equal opportunity,* differences should be ignored; however, if one is talking about *equal representation,* differences are important.

For example, I believe there is good reason to suppose that some groups, such as blacks, gays, and women, need representation. One case can be found in Richard Wasserstrom's account of an all-white jury and a black defendant. Police testified that the black defendant, without provocation, threw an empty Coke bottle at their passing car. The defendant said he had been selling copies of the Black Panther newspaper when the police slowed down and said, "Nigger, if we see you on the street with those newspapers again we'll kill you." He replied, "You @#$!'s can't scare me." The police insisted they had seen the defendant clearly and that he had thrown the bottle with a pitching motion of the right arm. An eyewitness testified that no bottle was thrown, and it was demonstrated that the defendant was left-handed. Nonetheless, it took the jury over seven hours to return a verdict of acquittal.

The difficulty the jurors had in reaching the correct decision, says Wasserstrom, requires an explanation. Wasserstrom conjectures that the jurors had a hard time convincing themselves that the police would fabricate a story against the defendant. After all, there is nothing in their white, middle-class experience that would cause them to take seriously the possibility that the police would deliberately and flagrantly lie. However, many black people have had experiences that make them doubt the credibility of the police. On Wasserstrom's analysis, whites bring with them to the jury box a general point of view that affects the way they see the facts. Thus, a case can be made for representational juries on the ground that these different points of view should find their way into the jury's deliberations.[17] Since there exists a standard liberal analysis of equality that can accommodate differences, the fleeing to postmodernism in order to escape the paradoxes within Western liberal democracies seems unwarranted in this instance. If we do not interpret equality as similarity, the paradox disappears.

As creator and practitioner respectively of a woman's discourse—*écriture de la femme*—Irigaray and Cixous abandon coherence, consistency, and noncontradiction as reflective of male anatomy. To have a penis is to be the sort of person who would think up such ideas as the principle of identity and the principle of noncontradiction: "Phallic language is based on a semantic economy of 'has' and 'has not' and endless repetition of the same. . . . The 'one' of the male subject becomes the two of the vaginal lips, constantly in touch with each other in an interaction in which the two are not separated by negation but interact and merge. . . . Instead of the relation of identity, vaginal symbolism suggests contiguity. The law of non-contradiction does not rule because the point is not a repetition of the same. Asked for clarification, a woman cannot answer; she has already moved on, or turned her back on her own thought, in a kind of a vaginal 'fold' within herself."[18]

Even as a woman's sexuality is plural, goes the argument, her speech would encompass multiplicity, rejecting rules of grammar, rigid concepts, and boundaries in favor of a language and a philosophy that flow. It is true that the very form of an academic discourse makes ideas such as those of Irigaray and Cixous difficult to describe and comprehend, and so they must turn to metaphor to explain. And metaphor is notoriously easy to laugh at; my love is not *really* like a red, red rose at all. But even within the bounds of metaphor, anatomy is a poor choice to explain the gendering of language; men have two testicles, after all, and the duplication of organs is basic *human* anatomy. If one is going to accept the possibility of rational discourse, as presumably is axiomatic for scholarship to continue, then one must cite some reason for rejecting the principle of noncontradiction other than genitalia.

REASON'S SMALL ROLE

Reason can establish that dominant-subordinate relationships of a carefully specified type are contradictory and a violation of the principle of universalization. A principle opposing the idea that some persons should be dominated because they have less moral worth is a fundamental if limited feminist principle of the sort that is implied by formal rationality. Interestingly enough, Sarah Hoagland, who is very skeptical of principled ethics—although not from a postmodernist perspective—nevertheless articulates the connection between a principle with content regarding dominance and subordination and Kant's formal principle of universalization in a way that surpasses Kant's own efforts to bring form and content together. She says:

> Reason . . . can determine moral laws. . . . Now, these laws . . . can't be just any laws. They must be laws that are a matter of pure reason. . . . And to be rational, these laws must be universal (or "categorical"). So Kant offers a formula, what he calls the "categorical imperative": "Act only on that maxim through which you can at the same time will that it should become a universal law."
>
> The idea of this formula is that every rational being be treated as an end in itself and not merely as a means. For example, by this formula I could not will

> slavery, for according to the formula I would have to will slavery universally: Always enslave everyone. But if I willed it universally, then I would be included among those to be enslaved; and as a slave I would not be a being who could will laws. In other words, I would be willing myself to be a being who could not will anything—a contradiction. Thus, it is not possible for me to will such a law morally. It is logic—pure reason, not inclination—which prohibits the willing of such a principle.
>
> More generally, we could not will a universal law that treats everyone merely as a means. Since we are one of that group, it would mean willing a law that treats us as a mere means; and if we were merely a means, we would no longer be the sort of being who could will laws. On the other hand, if we willed such a law for everyone but ourselves, the law would be no longer universal or categorical, hence moral, since it would be excepted in our own case, and thus based on inclination or desire, not reason. It is logically impossible to universally will such laws.[19]

What reason can do is very limited. Moreover, skepticism about principled ethics is justified. Furthermore, what we know about the limitations and pitfalls of principled ethics (sketched in the next section) we certainly did not learn from the Enlightenment.

THE PROBLEMS WITH PRINCIPLES

People Act on Bad Principles

Although acting on bad principles is a problem that does not arise in a Kantian universe, it does in fact happen frequently. Condemning as "sins of omission" the policy of Catholic agencies to refuse even to mention condoms let alone teach safer sex to Hispanic teenagers in New York City at enormous risk for AIDS, a *Village Voice* article quoted a Brooklyn priest as saying, "My fear . . . is that we may be sacrificing lives for the sake of a principle."[20] In saying that lives are worth more than principles or at least more than the principle at work here, he hints at the possibility that many have died and more will die for the sake of the wrong principle. The principle (unstated in the article) is that possible people (remember, possible people are not anybody) are worth more than actual people.[21] It is connected to the belief that the sole acceptable purpose or good of sexuality is procreation.

Ronald Dworkin, as we have seen, is committed to a principled approach to ethics and law. He defends the legal enforcement of morality but only if the conception of morality enforced meets certain rational standards. With these standards in place, laws based on ignorance, hate, fear, and prejudice will be ruled out. However, even though Dworkin's rational standards block laws based on the worst of reasons, laws based on bad reasons are possible in his system because the requirements of reason are so minimal.

Consequences Are Ignored

As was evident in the discussion of ecological issues and natural law, it can be taken as a criticism of a principled approach to ethics that social consequences are ignored. However, as implied above, ignoring consequences can be a good thing or at least unproblematic as long as one is acting on the right principle. Rights, for example, are principles that are designed to specify when even great amounts of social happiness can be ignored or declared illegitimate. For instance, if we take considerations of rights seriously, the many people who might be made happy by denying fundamental rights to gays, women, and blacks would have to forgo that happiness.

Principles Can Be Sabotaged

Principles, says Sarah Hoagland, at most "serve as guides for those who already can act with integrity. Thus, for example, we have fairly intricate strategies for fair fighting or conflict resolution, and yet we can use them to sabotage mediation."[22] Illustrations of Hoagland's point involving academic males using principles to justify their large share of goodies will spring to the minds of feminists in academe. Here is one example: a former law dean in a discussion of university day care argued that a lottery is not equitable. (It was assumed that the university could not provide day care for all.) So in the name of equality, the university did nothing. Instead of trying to do as much as they could, they justified the status quo without any recognition that the status quo benefited them.

Hoagland goes on to note that "principles are not something we can appeal to when all else fails."[23] This is an important point because many who defend reason have a strong tendency to talk as if pure reason can save us from bigotry and other irrationalities in the world.

Particularly apt as an example, given Hoagland's observation, is the handling of gay marriage cases by various courts and legislatures. The Hawaii Supreme Court, unable to find a legitimate or compelling reason against gay marriage, delayed their decision for three years until the legislature and voters amended the state constitution against gay marriages. As Joseph Melillo of one of the gay couples who sued the state said, "We have such wimps in our judicial system."[24]

Courts are not supposed to work this way. They are supposed to provide a principled check on the legislature rather than waiting for the legislature to bail them out of a decision they do not want to make. It is not surprising that courts can get away with this sort of behavior, however, given the misunderstanding of their legitimate function of critiquing conclusions arrived at by democratic means. Speaking of a gay marriage case in the Vermont Supreme Court, Matthew Daniels, writing in the *Wall Street Journal,* recently said, "If the state Supreme Court does decide to radically remake the moral, legal and social landscape of the state by judicial fiat, it will have done so by declaring our most important democratic institutions and traditions null and void."[25] Daniels is ignoring the basic function of courts, which is to hold legislative decisions up to constitutional scrutiny to see if they measure up to that standard.

Principles Are Not Applied Correctly

Principles themselves do not tell us how to apply them. Consequently, even the most apparently straightforward translation of normative principle to actual case can go awry. On an annual basis a colleague who administers a "survey of beliefs" to students discovers that large numbers who will agree with the principle that "consenting adults should have free choice in their sexual activity" will simultaneously agree that "homosexuality is not permissible."

A similar example can be found in the way Michael J. Bowers, attorney general of Georgia, and legal scholar David A. J. Richards used Kantian principles to opposite ends. Bowers, in his petitioner's brief for *Bowers v. Hardwick,* cited Kant as a philosopher who disapproved of sodomy, whereas Richards saw Kant's talk about rights as guarantees of proper respect for moral personality or rational autonomy as implying a right to sexual autonomy that is incompatible with a prohibition of homosexuality.

Examples in Kant scholarship abound. It is commonplace to admit the failure of at least some of Kant's own examples of how his system is supposed to work. For example, although he defended a principle that prohibits suicide, there is no logical contradiction if some or all decide to take their own lives.

Making Sure You Come Out Right

John Rawls describes and favors a process used in finding answers to ethical and legal questions called "reflective equilibrium" that consists of going back and forth between our rational principles and our intuitions. Intuitions, that stock of beliefs not subjected to rational scrutiny, play some role in the framing of principles. We can find a nice illustration of this function in Joel Feinberg's caution regarding the formulation and application of the offense principle. He says: "Bigoted prejudices of a very widespread kind (e.g., against interracial couples strolling hand in hand down the main street of a town in the deep South) can lead onlookers to be disgusted and shocked, even 'morally' repelled, by perfectly innocent activities. . . . For [this reason], the offense principle must be formulated in a very precise way, and supplemented by appropriate standards or mediating maxims, so as not to open the door to wholesale and intuitively unwarranted legal interference."[26]

The use of this process of reflective equilibrium assumes that reason is not transcendental, and the reliance on intuition makes the process open to sabotage. Luckily, Feinberg's intuitions tell him that "walking hand in hand down the main street of a town is just as much a right of homosexual as of interracial couples,"[27] although his occasional reference to homosexuality as abnormal shows his intuitions on this topic to be a bit shakier. It never occurs to him that some interracial couples are also gay couples.

Feinberg talks about drafting and redrafting the principle that results in protecting the behavior of the interracial couple from legal interference. Clearly, he is seeking a justification for his liberal intuitions; if one principle fails to do the job, he can find another:

> In my previous writings on this subject, I fell into a trap . . . by forgetting the useful scales analogy, and resorting too quickly to an absolutist mediating maxim which I called, rather grandly, the "standard of universality." If I wanted a reason against *ever* criminalizing interracial hand-holding and the like, all I had to do was cite the reasonableness of the conduct it would forbid. . . . Instead, I recommended a stringent standard to be met before the "extent of offense" could be put on the scales at all, namely that "in order for the offense . . . to be sufficient to warrant coercion, it should be the reaction that could reasonably be expected from almost any person chosen at random, taking the nation as a whole." . . . The chance of these conditions being satisfied, I assumed, should not cost the liberal any sleep.
>
> My own dogmatic slumber, however, was quickly interrupted by another kind of liberal nightmare, caused by application of the universality standard to examples like . . . public cross-burnings. . . . To prevent this unhappy consequence . . . I proposed an *ad hoc* amendment to the standard of universality itself, so that the special class of offensiveness that consists of abusive, mocking, insulting behavior of a sort bound to upset, alarm, anger, or irritate those it insults, the offense principle could be applied, even though the behavior would *not* offend the entire population. . . . Like most hasty *ad hoc* patch-up jobs, this one put the theory in even worse trouble.[28]

Ultimately, philosophy is no freer than any other discipline from the pulls of larger intellectual currents. The struggles of postmodernism and feminism with the heavy weight of rational structures are continuations of the Romantic movement of the early nineteenth century. Poet John Milton had told the men of the seventeenth-century Enlightenment that reason was their special gift, a gift specifically *not* granted to women. Adam and Eve in Eden are not equal,

> Not equal, as their sex not equal seem'd;
> For contemplation hee and valor form'd,
> For softness shee and sweet attractive Grace,
> Hee for God only, shee for God in him.[29]

The works of thinkers such as Newton and Kant convinced men that reason was their most godlike tool, the facility that would explain the order of the universe if not today, then certainly tomorrow. When Goethe and Rousseau and Blake began to reject the claims of reason, they seemed compelled to reject also its rampant masculinity. Imagination and inspiration became either feminine or androgynous, and reason became the deity of the mechanistic, obviously patriarchal establishment. Reason, as we have found, makes a bad deity, but it does make a good tool. Physicists who consider Einsteinian relativity and quantum mechanics to be our current best models of the universe still use Newtonian formulas to plot rocket trajectories. Feminist attorneys who understand the origins of civil rights in property protection invented in the capitalistic Renaissance can still use those rights in court to empower minorities.

Where postmodernism will go in its deconstruction of the philosophies of the Enlightenment has yet to be seen. It is easy to understand how the postmodern repudiation of the one true universal story dovetails with much of feminist thought. After all, most of the one true universal stories in Western history, psychology, and so on have been about white, heterosexual men. Patriarchal resistance to multidimensional accounts is at least as big a problem as relativism (some feminists would say greater) in terms of damage to women.[30] Moreover, multidimensional accounts do not entail relativism.

To deny that there is a single right view of history, for example, is not to agree that any view of history is as good as any other. But if there are only discourses and no rational way to arbitrate between or among them, then relativism seems to be an obvious consequence. Feminism as a force in the world must keep a balance: understanding the skepticism toward reason as a masculinist, historically weighted method of organizing knowledge while recognizing that not all of the laboriously created works of the past are useless for our own liberation. Certainly you can destroy the master's house with the master's tools.[31]

8

Can Animals Be Liberated?

In *Animal Liberation,*[1] Peter Singer argues that supporters of liberation for blacks and women should support animal liberation as well and that the basic principle of equality used against racism and sexism should be extended to animals to eliminate speciesism. Singer is right in claiming that animals have not received the moral consideration they deserve, but it is not clear that the term "animal liberation" is anything more than a flashy way to call attention to the problems of animals. Singer says: "The title of this book has a serious point behind it. A liberation movement is a demand for an end to prejudice and discrimination based on an arbitrary characteristic like race or sex."[2] This definition, however, would more accurately characterize a civil rights movement than a liberation movement. Singer talks as if liberation is no different from gaining equality; as if classical liberalism, which has no concept of liberation, would be up to the task of giving an account of animal liberation.

My objective is to develop the concept of liberation in order to make obvious the differences between liberation and rights. I will argue that liberation is not reducible to either the right to liberty (with which it is often confused) or equality. Singer rightly rejects the argument that humans deserve moral consideration (or rights) because they are human, but the revelation of speciesism does not support a liberation of animals that would be parallel to the liberation of women and blacks provoked by sexism and racism.

SPECIESISM AND RIGHTS

The literature on animal liberation and rights indicates a weakness in traditional rights theories. For example, classical rights theories typically do not explain what it is about human beings that gives them rights, and raising the issue of animal rights points out the inadequacy of the claim that human beings have rights because they are human. Such a claim is truly speciesist in that it restricts rights to a given group without justifying the restriction in terms of morally relevant characteristics that only members of that group have.

If we no longer rely on speciesist argument, then rights must be based on some morally relevant characteristic(s) that may turn out to be shared by animals and humans alike. One such method is to identify the morally relevant qualifications for the possession of specific rights (liberty, property, the right to life, the right not to be tortured, and so on) in order to determine what rights, if any, a being has. With respect to some rights, a plausible case can be made that certain qualifications are morally relevant. To do this, however, one needs to know the specific function of each right. For example, the right not to be tortured protects the basic interest that certain beings have in not suffering. The right to liberty protects the interest in directing one's life as one sees fit without unjustified interference from others. If a being is capable of suffering but not capable of autonomy or self-rule, it can have a right not to be tortured but not a right to liberty. On this model, the right to life must protect some specific interest or desire. One plausible candidate, suggested by Michael Tooley, is a desire to continue into the future, that is, a desire to continue to live.[3]

The desire for continued existence presupposes the capacity to have a concept of oneself as a continuing self, as an entity existing over time. Of course, each right, according to this view, presupposes some morally relevant capacity. The right not to be tortured presupposes a capacity for suffering. The right to liberty presupposes a capacity for autonomy. Once we figure out the morally relevant capacity for any given right, only those beings that have the relevant capacity have the right. Thus, only sentient beings have a right not to be tortured, only autonomous beings have a right to liberty, and only self-conscious beings have a right to life. Most adult human beings can meet the self-awareness or self-consciousness requirement, as apparently can some animals.[4] However, as Tooley points out, some adult human beings do not have the requisite capacity, nor do human fetuses or newborn infants.[5] It is worth noting that the self-consciousness requirement is a fairly sophisticated one. According to a view like Tooley's, mere consciousness or sentience may be sufficient for having a right not to be tortured, but not for having a right to life.

According to the above approach to rights, many animals fare rather well. Some animals most certainly have a right not to be tortured and quite possibly a right to life. However, it appears that animals do not qualify for a right to liberty because they are probably not autonomous. The whole liberal tradition in political philosophy (Locke, Mill, and Kant) conceives of the right to liberty as the right to live my life according to my own understanding of the moral law. If we are applying the same right to animals that liberal philosophers give to people, then we can restrict another's actions only with that being's informed consent. But I cannot persuade my cat that a rabies shot is in her best interests, yet if we grant her the right to liberty as traditionally understood, any restriction of her action without her consent would be a violation of her right to liberty. The classical right to liberty presupposes abilities to follow moral rules and give informed consent, morally relevant capacities that animals do not have.

Animals are not autonomous, yet they have legitimate freedom interests that need attention. In recognition of this fact, David DeGrazia sees liberty as a lack of external constraints and the right to liberty as protecting sentient animals against unnecessary confinement.[6] He defines "confinement" as "the imposition of external constraints on movement that significantly interfere with one's ability to live a good life."[7] Surely DeGrazia knows that the interests cited here having to do with confinement do not represent the core interests concerning autonomy that the classical right to liberty is designed to protect. Perhaps he would side with pragmatists such as Anthony Weston on this issue. Weston says that ethical theories like theories of rights or utilitarianism are not exhaustive; they leave out important values. And when an ethical theory is incomplete, Weston continues, "The conclusion is surely not: so much the worse for animals. Why not, so much the worse for rights?"[8]

One option here is to claim that animals have a right to liberty but to construe this right in different ways—as the "right not to be unnecessarily confined" for animals and as the "right to pursue one's own conception of the good life without unjustified interference from others" for people. Another option is to reserve the term "right to liberty" for the classical right, admitting that rights theory has its limitations and that many ethical problems that need attention, such as the freedom interests of animals, must be dealt with outside of rights theory.

However, we must not gloss over the fact that many humans do not qualify for a right to liberty if we use the standards as set by Kant. As we have seen, Kant requires not only that moral rules be followed but also that they be formulated and tested by the principles of universalization and noncontradiction. Many people have no idea what such an intellectual procedure entails and would be unable to carry it out, yet we grant them the right to liberty. So it seems that we are willing to abandon at least some version of classical standards for autonomy in order to include some humans in the class of those who have a right to liberty. Thus, one can ask why, if we are willing to loosen up the concept of autonomy for humans, we could not do the same for animals.

One other dispute relevant to whether or not animals can have any rights at all is a disagreement over the relationship of rights and duties. Rights can be correlated with duties. For example, correlated with *my* duty not to kill you is *your* right not to have me kill you. Some people argue that beings cannot have rights unless they are capable of performing duties or obligations or responsibilities. Scientist Frans B. M. de Waal recommends "making care, not rights, the centerpiece of our attitude" toward animals in part because "rights are part of a social contract that makes no sense without responsibilities."[9]

It is doubtful that animals can act from a sense of duty. Promise-keeping is a paradigm case of a duty or obligation. Suppose I say to my cat as I leave in the morning, "I want you to meet me here at 5:00 P.M." Can I seriously expect her to make and keep such a promise? Animals kill and eat one another (and occasionally us). As unfortunate as these actions may be, it does not seem to make sense to say that animals have duties not to do them.

In arguments about the correlativity of rights and duties, it is often pointed out that, while infants and retarded persons may be incapable of duties, they may still have rights. If the only requirement for rights is to be capable of having certain interests, then beings that have those interests have rights whether or not they can meet additional requirements for being able to perform duties. Rights and duties are two different things. Acting out of a sense of duty presupposes certain rational capacities, whereas possession of the right not to be tortured, for example, presupposes only a capacity to suffer.

Some of de Waal's examples of rights rely on a context of frivolous litigation that has the effect of making the idea of animal rights dubious. For example, he says, "After a narrow escape, the Thomson gazelle calls her attorney, complaining that her freedom to graze wherever she wants has once again been violated. Should she sue the cheetah, or does the lawyer perhaps feel that predators have rights too?"[10] This type of example obscures any serious discussion of basic moral rights such as the right not to be tortured or the right to life.

EQUALITY

Singer's case against the torture and eating of animals is not based on any conception of animal rights. The equality he wants to institute is an equal consideration of interests, and his argument is that the interest animals have in not suffering far outweighs many trivial interests of humans, such as testing hundreds of new cosmetics every year. The central claim of Singer's book that animals have an interest in not suffering[11] is a fairly uncontroversial one. However, the capacities relevant to equality of consideration are not the same as those presupposed by liberation, so that finding a sense in which animals and humans are equal does not imply either the need for or the possibility of animal liberation.

According to Singer, every being is entitled to equality of consideration of interests if that being is capable of having interests. The only requirement for having interests is the capacity for suffering and enjoyment, and some animals clearly satisfy this condition. Therefore, they are entitled to equal consideration.

Equality of consideration of interests is the principle to which Singer refers in his chapter "All Animals Are Equal or Why Supporters of Liberation for Blacks and Women Should Support Animal Liberation Too." Because the principle is one of equal consideration and not equal rights, it is too weak to be acceptable to feminists and black liberationists. Even if the principle of equal consideration is itself a right, it guarantees only a hearing that may result in unequal rights.

Women, like animals, are due equal consideration of interests, but Singer explicitly states that this requirement does not entail equal rights with men. Important differences between humans and other animals give rise to differences in the rights of each. Analogously, "the differences that exist between men and women are equally undeniable, and the supporters of Women's Liberation are aware that these differences may give rise to different rights."[12] Singer gives one example: "Many feminists hold that women have a right to abortion on request. It does not follow that since these same feminists are campaigning for equality between men and women, they must support the right of men to have abortions too. . . . The basic principle of equality does not require equal or identical treatment."[13]

Singer does not distinguish here between equal treatment and identical treatment. Even the most conservative feminists argue for equal treatment and equal rights. Feminists claim that women and men have the same basic rights that, when applied to different circumstances, may entail different, although not *unequal,* treatment. There is no reason why abortion should pose a problem for equal rights or equal treatment. For example, abortion can be seen as an instance of the right to one's body. Women and men, then, have an equal right to their bodies, but the application of this right to them may not result in identical treatment.

I am not alone in thinking that Singer's view of equality is inadequate. Gary Francione argues that both Singer's principle of equality and his ethical theory of utilitarianism are weak, the latter to the point of being incapable of eliminating animal exploitation.[14] He argues further that only a rights theory—a theory that eliminates the property status of animals—can afford animals any serious protection.

It makes sense that the principle of equal consideration, whether or not it is weak in itself, is made weak by connecting it to the principle of utility. In Singer's utilitarianism, once all relevant interests have been identified, the interests that prevail are those that make the greatest contribution to the general happiness. As Francione and others have pointed out, animal interests are always being traded away in favor of human interests because those of humans are said to be more significant.[15] But Francione argues that animal interests are continuously sold out in the utility calculus because the interests of property owners are pitted against the interests of those who are property.[16]

In contrast, David DeGrazia views the principle of equal consideration as a strong principle that would "rule out . . . the routine overriding of animal interests in the name of human benefit."[17] According to him, the principle of equal consideration is presupposed in a number of ethical theories, but its importance and interpretation have been overshadowed in philosophical discussions of animal ethics by the rights versus utility debate. The principle would mean giving animal interests the kind of weight we give to similar human interests and "would constitute a revolution in attitudes" if extended to animals. DeGrazia maintains that "there is little question that such practices and institutions as factory farming, hunting for sport, trapping, and common methods of cosmetic testing involve less-than-equal consideration for animals."[18] In addition, he reaches a number of moral conclusions about the human treatment of animals supported by the principle of equal consideration. A representative list includes such strictures as the following:

- Don't cause significant suffering for the sake of your or others' enjoyment.
- Apply equally any standards allowing the causing of suffering.
- Don't kill sentient animals unnecessarily.
- Don't confine sentient animals unnecessarily (where "confinement" is understood as the imposition of external constraints on movement that significantly interferes with one's ability to live a good life).
- There is a presumption against disabling sentient animals (that is, damaging their ability to function in ways that significantly interfere with their ability to live a good life) and, if they are non-dangerous, the presumption is virtually absolute.[19]

What is interesting here about the basis for these conclusions is that equal consideration is claimed to be stronger support for most of them than is needed. For most, it would be enough support, DeGrazia says, if people gave *serious* consideration to the interests of animals.[20]

Despite DeGrazia's arguments for the strength of the principle of equal consideration, he admits that "equal consideration . . . does not entail . . . a moral requirement to treat humans and animals equally."[21] Suppose DeGrazia made (as he does not) this same statement about men and women. It would read: Equal consideration does not entail a moral requirement to treat men and women equally. Such a principle of equality would be and should be rejected by feminists as too weak. Still, if the principle of equal consideration would do all the things for animals that DeGrazia claims it would, it is a strong principle for them.

It seems that whether the principle of equal consideration of interests is considered to be a weak or a strong one depends a lot on who you are. Equal consideration is a weak principle from the point of view of women; it is a strong principle from the point of view of animals. From an animal's standpoint, having one's interests considered or count for something as they can and should in utilitarian theory is a huge advance over having those interests dismissed out of hand or count for nothing as happens in traditional natural law theory. Still, having such consideration is not as strong as having rights, because rights guarantee that certain of one's interests have to be protected and not simply taken into account.

The claim that animals have an interest in not suffering, although morally relevant to equal consideration, has nothing to do with liberation. The relevant capacities for liberation are the ability to construct one's own sense of oneself and one's own purposes, not simply a capacity to feel pain and experience suffering.

LIBERATION

Liberation for women is the dismantling of the social practice of defining the behavior of a woman in terms of the responses of men rather than in terms of her own intentions or the responses of other women. Since male-centered values pervade our tradition, law, custom, language, division of labor, and so on, any successful liberation will require not only a psychological ability on the part of women to see their own responses as legitimate but also changes in the social structure that support their efforts.

The following is an example of the kind of oppression just described. A woman who is whistled at may be assumed to enjoy it even though she shows signs of anger. The fact that women sometimes take such negative experiences as proof of something wrong with them shows they have adopted the attitude that men's responses are what count. Similarly, the way a woman dresses is interpreted in terms of the sexual reactions of men rather than in terms of her own needs and interests. While styles of dress that are designed for comfort or practical value may be interpreted as antisexual or antimale if men do not find them attractive, they are likely to be interpreted as sexual invitations if men do find them attractive. Mihailo Marković once said that feminists who reject the pursuit of beauty do so "only in order to punish men."[22] Few people assume that the man who refuses to curl his hair and wears baggy pants is doing so to punish women. Such an inference is only possible when the actions of one sex are defined in terms of the sexual responses of others. Liberation begins when a woman sees her own responses and the responses of other women as legitimate, and no longer associates legitimacy with the intentions, responses, and purposes of men.

Both animals and women are viewed in our culture as items of consumption. One bit of contemporary evidence that attests to women being so viewed is travel brochures that tell where to find good food, good wine, and women.[23] Being viewed as an item of consumption is not entailed by being eaten. There are circumstances under which one can be eaten and still retain respect from others and self-respect. For example, there is the textbook favorite of the marooned travelers with no food and no hope of immediate rescue who decide that one of their number must be eaten. In this case, each person might still be treated with equal respect as an autonomous individual and as having a legitimate interest in survival—the decision might be made by a lottery giving each an equal chance. Whereas if beings are viewed as objects of consumption (whether culinary or sexual), they are not viewed as having any interests of their own, and their purpose in life is viewed as that of the consumer rather than their own. Thus, those who are viewed as objects of consumption are ipso facto not being treated with respect.

Undoubtedly, people are guilty of defining pigs in terms of human purposes. The consumption of pigs is even claimed to be in their interest and here again is a similarity with women's oppression. However, arguments for these claims with regard to animals are typically means-end arguments; most pigs would never have lived if we did not raise them for food. Arguments used against women in this respect are often based on a notion of female nature that questions the very existence of women's ability to define their own interests. Such arguments and theories prompt self-doubt in women. Even if subjected to this type of reasoning, it is unlikely that animals suffer adverse effects from listening to the arguments humans make about them. Moreover, an attempt is made to convince women to take on the purposes of their oppressors as their own. It is not clear whether animals suffer from this form of oppression and hence need to be liberated. Some animals do take on the values of humans, but it is not obvious that they suffer from a poor self-image as a result.

Since Singer's publication of *Animal Liberation* in the 1970s, there has been a new understanding of the mental life of animals, but there is still no evidence that any animals are autonomous or possess the capacities needed for liberation. Frans B. M. de Waal captures the difference in scientific understanding and attitudes this way: "Amid stern warnings against anthropomorphism, the then-prevailing view [among scientists] was that animals were mere robots, devoid of feelings, thoughts or emotions. . . . This thinking changed in the 1980s with the advent of cognitive approaches to animal behavior. We now use terms like 'planning' and 'awareness' in relation to animals. They are believed to understand the effects of their own actions, to communicate emotions and make decisions. . . . All of this goes far beyond fear, pain and anger: The emotional life of . . . animals is much closer to ours than once held possible."[24]

Many animals, DeGrazia claims, are capable of desires, beliefs, intentional actions, self-awareness, sociability, even certain kinds of moral agency. As a result, he asserts that some animals have a robust right to life since they can meet any reasonable set of conditions taken from this list.[25] DeGrazia's demonstration of the rich mental life of animals lends credibility to his doubts concerning the existence of autonomy in any animal. Autonomy, he says, requires "critical self-reflection"—an ability to "have preferences about [our] preferences," to "evaluat[e] and . . . sometimes modify . . . the preferences that move [us] to act."[26] He rightly does not regard autonomy as a requirement for the right to life. However, the requirements for liberation (which DeGrazia does not discuss) are probably similar enough to the requirements for autonomy to conclude that if animals cannot meet the conditions for autonomy, they probably cannot meet the conditions for liberation either.

Thus far I have argued that liberation presupposes an ability to construct one's own sense of self and one's own purposes. Although it is a necessary condition of liberation that individual beings liberate themselves, liberation should not be construed as simply a psychological task. It requires as well changes in the social structure. In order to highlight this dimension of liberation, I want to contrast liberation and the right to liberty. These have often been confused, but their clear difference emerges in examples of unliberated liberty such as the so-called sexual revolution.

In *Marriage and Morals*, Bertrand Russell discusses what he takes to be women's liberation, but what is in fact liberty.[27] He predicts that with the sexual revolution will come a relaxing of the double standard, and women will be as free as men to have as many sexual partners as they like. But now that we have lived through the sexual revolution—a benefit that Russell did not have—we know that women and men can be given the same liberties in this regard, and yet because of unequal power structures in our society, the same act can mean something different and have very different practical results, depending on whether it is done by a woman or a man. The classical liberal right to liberty challenges neither social structures nor psychological states. Liberation requires us to resist and restructure a whole system of social and psychological pressures, whereas the right to liberty is given to us within that system.

Some respects in which animals are treated badly are similar to situations in which women who are in need of liberation are treated badly. However, two things must be noted. First, according to Singer, the basic problems of animals are that they are tortured and eaten. Liberation is not the solution to these problems. Second, Singer's reduction of liberation movements to civil rights movements keeps us from thinking deeply about what liberation is and how it differs from the absence of discrimination or having rights.

POSTSCRIPT

I have construed the word "interest" throughout to mean, as Singer does, "desire." So when I say that animals have an interest in not experiencing pain or suffering, I mean that animals have a desire not to experience pain or to suffer. Although this use is typical in both contemporary utilitarian and rights theories, much of the literature in environmental ethics operates with a different idea of having interests, understanding it in terms of having "a good of one's own," so that what is in one's interests is what promotes one's own good whether or not it causes enjoyment or fulfills one's desires. If a being is liberated (at least in part) when it is treated by others as having a good of its own (which is not defined simply from the point of view of what serves others), animals (and not only animals) could be liberated. On this view wildflowers have a good of their own and can be liberated.

Paul Taylor, for example, takes a view like this in his book *Respect for Nature*.[28] In a move similar to Peter Singer's claim that species membership as such is irrelevant to moral standing, Taylor rejects sentience as the criterion that must be met in order for a being (or entity) to count for something morally speaking. Singer believes that the species one happens to be, like the race or sex one happens to be, is an arbitrary characteristic that has no moral significance. What matters, in his view, is whether a being can suffer. But Taylor, like others such as Kenneth Goodpaster[29] or the deep ecologists,[30] thinks that seeing sentience as all-important is as arbitrary as claiming the same for membership in Homo sapiens. Taylor describes his view as *biocentric egalitarianism*. According to him, all living beings have equal inherent worth, in that each living being is a goal-directed system pursuing its own good. Respect for nature is respect for these pursuits. However, his biocentric ethic is individualistic in contrast to a biocentric holism that places a moral value on the biosystem itself. In Taylor's view, according to reviewer T. L. S. Sprigge, "Total eco-systems only matter because individuals find their good within them; there is no over-all value of the whole, since the whole (it is claimed) is pursuing no good of its own."[31]

Taylor, as Sprigge points out, is prepared to push his individualistic biocentrism pretty far. For example, it is just as important for nonconscious individuals such as plants to achieve their goal as it is for a conscious individual.[32] Plants do not have to be conscious in order to be valued for their own sake or in order to be as valuable as human beings. Taylor says, "The killing of a wildflower, then, when taken in and of itself, is just as wrong, other-things-being-equal, as the killing of a human."[33]

One reason why environmental ethics might have taken this turn is that modern traditions in Western philosophical ethics such as theories of rights and utilities cannot account for the value of environmental objects such as plants and trees, rivers and streams. Peter Singer claims that plants have no conscious experiences, and thus there is nothing seriously wrong in pulling weeds from a garden.[34] If environmental objects are not sentient or conscious, it is hard to see how they would qualify for any basic rights even according to the view I have been developing. Rights, as I see it, presuppose certain psychological capacities such as sentience, autonomy, self-awareness, that explain why a being has, for example, a right not to be tortured, a right to liberty, a right to life. It would be absurd to claim that rocks have a right not to be tortured if they are incapable of suffering.

It is worth noting that it was the challenge to what is sometimes called the anthropocentric paradigm—the idea that only human beings have moral standing—that changed the character of the rights debate into one about capacities and the moral relevance of capacities. My disagreement with Taylor has to do in part with whether the capacity to live is relevant to moral standing, or more specifically to the possession of any rights, or to liberation. Living things such as kudzu and the AIDS virus lack self-awareness but have the capacity to live. Their capacity to live does not signify in my view a morally significant interest in their continued life.

Finally, and this point I will elaborate on in the last chapter, when one's good—as a human at least—becomes disconnected from or too far removed from one's own desires, an individual's authority about her or his own good is in danger of becoming irrelevant. It is not only the goal of wildflowers, as natural law theory attests, that may be determined by those like Taylor with Aristotelian tendencies.

We do, of course, want to say (before we pollute ourselves out of existence) that wildflowers and trees, rivers and streams (even if they are not alive), are valuable. However, we could, as Anthony Weston suggests, replace philosophical disputes about the earth's inherent or intrinsic value with an understanding that the earth is valuable because it is our home.[35]

9

Feminist Separatism

Feminist separatism is not exactly a popular topic these days. Witness Katha Pollitt's comment on embattled Boston College professor Mary Daly's most recent attempt to keep men out of her classroom. For many years, Daly has refused to admit male students into her classes and to respond to questions from males in her wider lectures, although she has offered to tutor separately the occasional male student who has wanted to take her class. This recent event, however, was apparently preconceived and recognized by Pollitt as such.[1] It does not seem to be a case of a young man genuinely seeking knowledge of feminist ethics. Nonetheless, Pollitt, columnist for the *Nation,* says that Daly should have "gracefully accept[ed] that pesky male instead of falling on the rusty sword of seventies style separatism and embarrassing the whole feminist movement."[2] Pollitt goes on to say of Daly's position that it "confirms every media stereotype of feminists as separatists, victimologizers and hypocrites."[3]

By hypocrisy Pollitt means that feminists cannot both use Title IX to gain sexual equality and then repudiate it as she believes Mary Daly has done. However, even Title IX, as Mary Daly's lawyer says, "recognizes that in some circumstances it is not discriminatory to treat men and women differently—to remedy past discrimination, to create more opportunities for women, to serve a valid educational goal."[4] So there is room for argument here that Pollitt does not acknowledge.

Separatism is no longer popular in feminist academic circles either. Various theoretical positions—deconstructionism, the critique of identities, the differences critique, cultural pluralism—have been nudging separatism off the feminist screen for quite some time now. Many of these views give rise to Marianne Janack's characterization of the "Third Wave of feminist theorizing and activism" as "a dissolution of the category of 'woman' as a category for political organizing."[5] In this new climate, separatism is seen as a relic of feminism's early strident days, necessary perhaps to gain attention but now passé.

As I noted in the chapter on postmodernism, there cannot be a women's movement if there are no women, that is, if "woman" is not a recognizable category. The differences critique—that women do not have the same experiences, the same interests, or experience a shared oppression—can form the basis of an antiseparatist position. Uma Narayan argues that the differences critique does have this implication. She urges feminists to "broaden the scope of their concerns, to not restrict their analyses, moral concern, membership and political agendas to issues pertaining to women."[6] Janack says further that "Third Wave feminist theorizing and activism have forced to the surface the illusory universalism implicit in the category 'woman,' just as the Second Wave worked the same magic on the category 'human.' "[7] But is it the same magic? Deconstructing the concept of "human" showed that women do exist, whereas the dissolution of the category "woman" has not created a new understanding of the parts that make up a larger whole but rather blurred them back into some older categories of race, class, and ethnicity.

A minimal but important form of feminist separatism is interest-group separatism. According to this version, women ought to organize as an interest group like any other interest group. The point of having an organization composed only of women is to enable women to develop an understanding of their political interests and a base for protecting and furthering those interests through legislation and political reform. In form, this theory is an extension of standard American pluralism. The only radical aspect of this theory is its assumption that women do have political interests as women rather than only as wives and daughters of union members or factory workers, as Jews or Catholics, and so on.

In the American suffrage movement it was clear that women had interests as women and that they could not depend on men to further these interests. Today, according to the 1993 United Nations Human Development Report, "there is no country in the world in which women's quality of life is equal to that of men, according to a complex measure that includes longevity, health status, educational opportunities, employment, and political rights."[8] Moreover, the global evidence suggests that heterosexual families (which are assumed by some economists to be cooperative units) are in fact "split apart, with some individuals doing well at the expense of the deprivation and misery of others"; that is, "males are quite often neglectful of the interests of females, whether wives or children, and make decisions inimical to those interests."[9]

Interest-group feminist separatism makes sense as long as women have at least some basic interests in common because they are female and as long as the barriers placed in their way are due to misogyny.[10] There is global evidence that women have fewer advantages, opportunities, and resources because they are female, and that men have more advantages, opportunities, and resources because they are male.[11] Furthermore, there is evidence that women simply cannot count on men to make things right.

Some feminist literature suggests that an old discussion of assimilation versus separatism has been replaced by assimilation versus pluralism.[12] But pluralism retains many of the same basic ideas as separatism, in that it attempts to preserve separate and distinct cultural traditions. The obvious difference is that cultural pluralism strives to keep the lines of communication open between groups and is more open to coalition politics. But it should be noted that many feminist separatists have always been open to coalition politics. Few separatists have advocated being (or been able to) separate from men altogether.

Separatism got a negative reception in the seventies as well. Adrienne Rich once said, "The deliberate withdrawal of women from men has almost always been seen as a potentially dangerous or hostile act, a conspiracy, a subversion, a needless and grotesque thing, while the exclusion of women from men's groups is rationalized by arguments familiar to us all, whether the group is a priesthood, a dining club, a fishing expedition, an academic committee, or a Mafioso rendezvous."[13] As one defender of Mary Daly said, "If Mary was a man who'd transformed his field as Daly has transformed hers, she'd have a comfortable sinecure someplace, and she'd be allowed to admit whomever she wants into her class."[14]

In the 1970s, only two articles dealing with the subject of feminist separatism appeared in philosophy journals, Virginia Held's "Marx, Sex, and the Transformation of Society" and Mihailo Marković's "Women's Liberation and Human Emancipation," and both construed the separatist position in purely negative ways with no appreciation of its positive elements.[15] Marković, for example, charged that it is " a specific form of sexism, a female chauvinism that consists in expressing resentment, hostility and even hatred for the opposite sex."[16] He showed no awareness of separatism as an affirmation of sisterhood, only as a rejection of men. Held's discussion of separatism focused on the fact that feminist separatists might not value love relationships between men and women rather than on the fact that separatism requires a commitment to women. Marković is even more extreme in his portrayal of separatism as primarily an expression of man-hating.

What was not recognized in early criticisms of separatism is that separatism is not sexism. The union meeting that excludes management is a more appropriate analogy to mainstream politics than is the board of directors of General Motors excluding women and minorities. The General Motors board has a responsibility to be nondiscriminatory, because admission to that group is admission to power; their exclusion of minorities and women from the group is blameworthy because they have important benefits to distribute. On the other hand, there is no particular moral objection to a group of Bowery winos being discriminatory; they have no power to distribute either fairly or unfairly. There is a moral difference between organizing to keep the presently powerless from power and organizing the powerless as such. Thus, Marković's accusation that feminist separatism is simply another form of sexism ignores the moral relevance of power and is comparable to claiming that labor unionism is simply a form of classism.

Feminist separatists do not exclude men because they hate them anymore than unions exclude management because they hate management. Certainly, individual union members hate either individual managers or management as such, but it would be absurd to claim that the principle of unionism consists in expressing hatred and resentment toward management. In her contemporary critique of separatism, Uma Narayan suggests that feminists should widen the scope of their concerns, arguing that "it is odd to care about or struggle for the interests of the wretched of the earth only as long as the wretched are women."[17] Although a "lack of caring" as a criticism is a more delicate charge than is man-hating, it is still a type of accusation that takes aim at a false target. A union, for instance, simply assumes that it works for the good of its own members, that working for the betterment of everybody is a fine goal but not the reason for the union's existence.

There is a distinction between power *over* others and keeping men from using the power of women against themselves. The union-management analogy is again helpful. Workers unionize in order to keep management from using workers' power against themselves. Unless they join together, workers often do not realize that they even have any power. But the workers do not have power *over* management. One thing 1970s feminist separatism did was to keep men from using women's power against themselves; it did not give women power *over* men.

This is an important distinction, if only because feminist separatists have been accused of playing men's games on men's terms, that is, using a power play. A referee, in commenting on a version of something I once read on separatism at the American Philosophical Association meetings, said, "Walking out on men in order to pressure them into changing . . . would not be getting away from the use of power, [it is] just another form of using it." One assumption here is that the use of power is bad and that any use of power is as bad as any other. Another assumption is that whatever feminists do they do in order to change men rather than to change women. Let me give one example of women acting in response to the needs and interests of women that simultaneously illustrates the two kinds of power I have distinguished.

In towns and cities that have shelters for battered women, it is possible for a woman who is beaten by her husband to go somewhere and begin to take charge of her own life. Women gave that power to other women by providing a place for them to go. Those familiar with the principles of nonviolence will understand this phenomenon as the refusal to be a victim. The power that husbands have over their wives is parasitic on the existence of victims. When feminists create structures such that wives can refuse to be victims, the power of the husbands is undercut. The power of the wives to walk out is the kind of power that Marilyn Frye talked about in her work on separatism, that is, being in a position to control access, to reject parasitism,[18] or, as I have phrased it, keeping your power from being used against you. More recently, Susan Moller Okin has offered as part of a solution to the inequality of gender-structured marriages the (economic and other sorts of) ability on the part of women to walk out of those marriages.[19]

In a conference discussion of discourse ethics, Naomi Scheman and Linda Nicholson suggested that feminists might sometimes have reasons for not engaging in discourse. The idea of using dialogue to solve ethical issues and social problems is popular among some feminist theorists these days. Emphasis is placed on talking issues through, using democratic procedures, empathizing and listening to others, trying to reach a consensus. Some of these ideas stem from "discourse ethics," which is rooted in the work of Jürgen Habermas in the 1970s.[20] In suggesting that there might be times when a feminist would say "no" to engaging in dialogue, Scheman referred to the "separatism inherent in any feminism."[21] The discussion then turned to the claim that there is a place for silence in the theory of discourse ethics. But Scheman was not talking about silence as a reason for not engaging in discourse; she was interjecting into the discussion a reference to the 1970s literature on separatism that is lost to much contemporary feminist theorizing. Marilyn Frye's explanation of the connection between access and power forms the background for Scheman's comment:

> The exclusion of men from [a] meeting not only deprives them of certain benefits (which they might survive without); it is a controlling of access, hence an assumption of power. . . . First: When those who control access have made you totally accessible, your first act of taking control must be denying access, or must have denial of access as one of its aspects. This is not because you are charged up with (unfeminine or politically incorrect) negativity; it is because of the logic of the situation. When we start from a position of total accessibility there *must* be an aspect of no-saying (which is the beginning of control) in *every effective* act and strategy, the effective ones being precisely those which *shift power,* i.e., ones which involve manipulation and control of access. Second: Whether or not one says "no," or withholds or closes out or rejects, on this occasion or that, the capacity and ability to say "no" (with effect) is logically necessary to control.[22]

As crucial as no-saying is, separatism has its positive features and ideals as well. The major ideals of separatism are those of solidarity, pride, and the celebration of common goals and an independent culture. The necessity of an independent culture rests in part on the assumption that the recognized culture of a society is that of the dominant group. The traditional dominant culture is particularly blatant in defining women's interests in terms of relationships with men. Thus, a woman is not offered any concept of woman as a being with her own needs, her own interests, her own concerns, rather than with a set of interests, needs, and concerns that she might have in virtue of her being related to a man. Indeed, the images of women provided by the dominant culture are so negative and derogatory as to cause some lesbians to claim that they are not women. But as Anna Stubblefield points out, most people think that lesbians are women, which is why "lesbians experience censure for not being feminine enough."[23]

The emotional and political rejection of a sense of inferiority is the major element of the notion of pride as it is used in liberation movements. If racism encourages blacks to be ashamed of being black, sexism encourages women to feel inferior as women, and heterosexism makes gay people hate their capacity to love, then the creation of pride and affirmation of oneself *as* a member of a previously despised group is crucial. In her discussion of lesbian pride, Claudia Card explains: "Owning with pride a lesbian identity steals thunder from whoever would manipulate one's fears of exposure. Neither chauvinistic nor sexually exhibitionist, the point of coming out is usually to avoid 'passing' or duplicity, to prevent extortion, to make political connections, to get others to see oneself in nonintimate contexts as lesbians see each other in such contexts, or to communicate that one is *not* ashamed and refuses to be shamed." She adds that "freedom from shame . . . need [not] involve any sense of elevation over others nor delusions regarding our virtues. . . . it does not even imply that one is a proud person."[24]

A call for organizations of dominant groups would presuppose an entirely different set of values. To the extent that any group is dominant, the recognized culture is its culture, and any attempt at consciously fostering pride is likely to be a development of arrogance rather than an overcoming of socially entrenched inferiority. Pollitt misses this point when she counts as an analogous case to Daly's exclusion of men from her classes a professor who barred "nonwhites from his whiteness studies seminar."[25]

Interestingly, Anna Stubblefield in a recent work argues that cultural pluralism does not work in the case of women because it inevitably leads either to separatism or to assimilation. Women, says Stubblefield, cannot maintain a cultural identity as women in any meaningful way without separatism in a fundamental sense. That is, the positive benefits of cultural identities for those who belong to that culture do not work in the case of women without separation. "If being a woman means experiencing constant pressures from norms that demand sexual and nurturing subservience to men," she argues, "and if trying consciously to resist those norms consumes as much energy and acknowledges the existence of those norms as much as conforming to them does, then affirming a women's culture in a way that would actually help remedy the problem would require separation."[26] However, Stubblefield is not recommending separatism, for the kind of separatism she says would be required here, that no women are sexually available to men, is so fundamental as to make a society unstable. This argument ends up in the same place that Virginia Held's arguments of twenty-five years ago did, namely, heterosexuality as we know it wins out over feminist separatism if the two are perceived to conflict.

It may be that only lesbians can separate from men in a fundamental enough way to model a positive image of what it means to be a female human being. If so, there is nothing scary or hopeless about this situation. On the contrary, having such a model should be helpful. Held painted a terrible picture of personal relations between women and men in 1975. She spoke of women having lessons in "not flying apart" and their "schizophrenic existence." A main thesis was that mutuality exists in sexual relations between men and women and that such relations should be used as models in extending mutuality to nonsexual relations between men and women: "A relation of mutual concern and respect as an immediate and purely sexual relation is not at present altogether rare. But when the same characteristics of genuine mutual concern are sought in other aspects of the relation between sexual partners, the more the other aspects are included, the more rare the relation becomes."

Held recommended expanding the "mutual concern and respect between man and woman . . . beyond a fleeting moment in a limited part of their lives to wider and more distantly related aspects of the relations between human beings."[27] The characterization of respect as a feeling that can be momentary and completely unconnected to the rest of a person's life is a somewhat peculiar notion of respect. Although the concept of respect that Held wanted us to aim at is perfectly coherent (respect is not using one another, each valuing the other for the other's sake, and so on), the same cannot be said of its starting point, which consists in a man who does not respect women having momentary flashes of respect for a woman as a person during sexual activities with her. Of course the argument that lesbians can be a better *model* of sexual equality does not rest on the assumption that all women will be lesbians.

Suppose all women were lesbians, or at least were not sexually available to men.[28] How would this scenario make society unstable? Stubblefield envisions that men and women would negotiate reproduction contracts and raise children separately. This arrangement, she claims, would lead to a genderless society. Her scenario assumes, however, that men will accept the fundamental separatism; she fails to take into account a number of alternative futures including the possibility of a violent response, that is, the possibility of rape or attempts to set up harems or to establish some kind of "Handmaid's Tale" society. According to Stubblefield, in raising their male children by themselves, men would either come to appreciate "women's perspectives and needs" or become "'women' (feminized)" themselves. Women would transmit their distinctive culture to their female children. Stubblefield concludes: "Thus, affirming a women's culture in the strong sense simply would not lead to a stable society with continuing differences between genders. It would evolve instead into a society that had transcended gender."[29]

In my view, the problem is not that separatism leads to assimilation (if indeed it does) or to any kind of instability. If pursuing a distinctive women's culture eventually led to a genderless society, why would this result not be good? The vision of a genderless society, Stubblefield says, is not a useful model for present-day policy because it does not address the gender-specific norms that are problematic today.[30] This statement may be true, but by the time we got to a genderless society, the vision or the model would fit the circumstances. Why does it matter if affirming a distinctive women's culture cannot be sustained indefinitely, if affirming such an identity *now* can help with problems *now*?

In fact, the recent struggle toward a genderless society is being carried out now, albeit tumultuously, in specifically lesbian events such as the Michigan Women's Music Festival. The participation of transgendered persons set off a firestorm of discussion among lesbians, with some insisting that "people are to be responsible for claiming their own gender . . . all people who *identify* as womyn need to be allowed in," and that "womyn-born-womyn have nothing to fear from MtoF [male to female] transexuals." Others argue that "it is not the women-born-men who pay the price" for admitting transgendered persons into the festival; rather "it is the androgynous womyn who *look* like men who pay," since these women cannot be free when "womyn are feeling unsafe and under attack—trying to figure out who really is a man."[31] Androgynous women who have to deal with being mistaken for men on a daily basis could use some separate space one week during the year where this does not happen to them. However, the further point is that gender as a concept is becoming ever more fluid despite Stubblefield's worries that it may destabilize society.

The problem now is that men do the defining of both who men are and who women are. Marilyn Frye's reaction to this situation is: "Make the arrogant 'A' [men who have consigned women to 'not-A'] *share* the universe."[32] In her recent article containing this comment, she argues for the possibility of and the desirability of a positive category of woman. Such a category, although still in the process of becoming, has been in the making for over two decades. Frye points to the associations and projects of women during this time, such as conferences, book fairs, music festivals, the National Women's Studies Association, and so on, as important to this process of solidarity and the construction of a positive identity. What women have been doing and continue to do is construct "a sociality, a symbolic order, a web of meanings of and among women" that does not depend in any way on "patriarchally constructed femininity."[33]

In Frye's view, feminist theory should account for these actual processes, not deny their existence as the excesses of postmodernism have done. (Recall Marianne Janack's characterization of the third wave of feminist theorizing as "a dissolution of the category of 'woman' as a category for political organizing.") In showing how to construct a positive category of woman that accommodates differences and is not essentialist, Frye's article is about the *logical* construction of categories; it is not about separatism. The word "separatism" is never mentioned, but her view *is* a kind of separatism. Who is going to construct this positive category of woman? Only those women who are and have been engaged in these associations and projects. Only those women who are defining and liberating themselves from patriarchal conceptions of themselves.

Separatism plays a fundamental and important role in making the sharing of definitional power come about. Implied in Frye's examples is the view that not all women have to be lesbians in order to extricate themselves from the norms of femininity, as Stubblefield puts it. But, of course, it does not hurt that many of them are. Nonetheless, all that is required is women devoting effort and emotional energy to relationships with other women and to organizations and groups of women—this in contrast to the traditional view, which claims that a woman's overriding emotional commitment is, and ought to be, to a man; that men are, and ought to be, the most important people in a woman's life; and that relationships between women are unimportant and trivial.

Separatism of various forms played a much larger role in the second wave of feminism than it has in the third. Women working together for women as women has done an enormous amount of good. Maybe it is time to get some of the rust off that sword.

10

Gay Marriage

"The effort to legalize gay marriage will almost certainly emerge as a major issue in the next decade," said law professor Nan D. Hunter in the October 1991 issue of *Nation*.[1] She was right. Why is this so? In part, what drives this issue is the practice of most U.S. employers and many institutions (such as the IRS) of giving significant benefits including health, life, disability, and dental insurance, tax relief, bereavement and dependent care leave, tuition, use of recreational facilities, and purchase discounts on everything from memberships at the local Y to airline tickets only to those in conventional heterosexual families. Although employee benefits are sometimes referred to as "fringe" benefits, they in fact make up a hefty portion of compensation. As such, married people are paid more than their nonmarried counterparts. Whether or not favoring the institution of marriage is justified, there remains the problem that those in heterosexual relationships at least have the option (indeed, the right) to marry, whereas lesbians and gay men in relationships do not (at least in the United States).[2]

Although I find monetary and benefit arguments convincing, what follows is a discussion of other types of considerations—legal, historical, ethical, and psychological—that are relevant to the issue of gay marriage. Of these, I find the so-called psychological ones most persuasive. Moreover, since some benefits can be gained by domestic partnership plans, the question of the comparative merits of marriage and domestic partnership needs to be addressed.

LEGAL ARGUMENTS

The 1993 Hawaii Supreme Court decision in *Baehr v. Lewin*[3] (now *Baehr v. Anderson*) was described at the time by the Lambda Legal Defense and Education Fund as "astonishing." The first same-sex marriage case to reach a state supreme court in twenty years, the Hawaii Supreme Court held in *Baehr* that "denial of marriage to same-sex couples is sex discrimination."[4] Overturning a lower court decision, the court sent the issue back for a trial at which the state was instructed to show compelling reasons for its discriminatory policy. According to Lambda, the Hawaii court refused to be satisfied with the "tortured and conclusory sophistry" of past court hearings on gay marriage and rejected the "tautological and circular nature" of the state's argument that same-sex couples cannot marry because marriage is inherently for opposite-sex couples.[5]

Indeed, the argument from definition cited so recently in the Hawaii case has been around for a long time. In 1971, the Minnesota Supreme Court defined marriage as "a union of man and woman,"[6] and in 1974, two men were denied a marriage license "because of the nature of marriage itself."[7] As Richard Mohr puts it so nicely, "The courts [have held] that gay access to marriage must be a form of grand theft." The charge, says Mohr, is "theft of essence. . . . straights wouldn't really be married if gays were. . . . the meaning of marriage would be revised beyond recognition if gays could marry."[8] Similar claims about the concept of "family" are commonplace in right-wing rhetoric today; it is said that so-called true families will be undermined if the concept of family is extended to include lesbian and gay couples.

Not everyone thinks that gay marriage is a threat to straight marriage. Andrew Sullivan, for example, argues that "gay marriage . . . [u]nlike domestic partnership . . . merely asks that gays be allowed in. . . . Gay marriage could only delegitimize straight marriage if it were a real alternative to it." In other words, gay marriage does not challenge the value of "a deeper and harder-to-extract-yourself-from commitment to another human being [which] would foster social cohesion, emotional security, . . . economic prudence," and a nurturing environment for children.[9]

Other possibilities for legal argument include privacy rights[10] and Kenneth Karst's interesting claim that the constitutional freedom of intimate association "extends to homosexual associations."[11] More recently, others have followed Karst's lead, arguing for same-sex marriage on grounds that the right to marriage is an "important institutional expression" of the "right to intimate life"[12] and that the "right to marriage" is a "reasonable corollary" to "the human right . . . to intimate life."[13] These ideas I simply mention, concluding my remarks on legal reasoning by noting arguments from sex discrimination in the Hawaii case and from the common benefits clause in the Vermont case. Crucial to all legal arguments vis-à-vis same-sex marriage is a 1967 Supreme Court case, *Loving v. Virginia,* which established the right to marry as a fundamental legal right. *Loving* overturned laws against interracial marriage in the United States. Presumably one can make an equal protection argument to the effect that even as the government cannot restrict choice of a marital partner by insisting on a particular race, so the government cannot restrict such a choice on the basis of sex. Of course, such an argument would only work in states where the category of sex is constitutionally protected from discrimination.

The holding in *Baker v. State,*[14] a 1999 gay marriage case decided by the Vermont Supreme Court, was based on the common benefits clause in the state constitution. The 1777 clause provides that "government is, or ought to be, instituted for the common benefit, protection, and security of the people, nation or community; and not for the particular emolument or advantage of any single man, family or set of men, who are a part only of that community."[15] The opening pages of the decision constitute an eloquent and wide-reaching essay on the clause, including its history, its implications for a principle of inclusion, and its distinct character vis-à-vis the equal protection clause of the Fourteenth Amendment of the U.S. Constitution. The common benefits clause "prohibits not the denial of rights to the oppressed, but rather the conferral of advantages or emoluments upon the privileged."[16] It is said to reflect the framers' resentment of "governmental favoritism" or "advantages" or "political preferences of any kind . . . toward not only groups or 'set[s] of men,' but also toward any particular 'family' or 'single man.'"[17] The court held "that the State is constitutionally required to extend to same-sex couples the common benefits and protections that flow from marriage under Vermont law."[18]

In sum, what is new on the legal scene is that advocates of gay marriage are making serious arguments that are at long last being taken seriously. The fact that good arguments are finally being recognized as such raises the level of discussion far above the ridicule and dismissal of the 1970s, but it does not guarantee that good arguments will prevail. The Hawaii Supreme Court could have affirmed the 1996 lower court ruling (which they themselves commissioned) that no compelling reason exists for denying the right to marry to lesbian and gay couples, or they could have reaffirmed their own 1993 decision that denial of the right to marry to same-sex couples is sex discrimination. Instead, after saying nothing for three years, they finally ruled *Baehr v. Anderson* moot in 1999 because of a 1998 state constitutional amendment against gay marriages that the court said removed "access to marriage licenses from the reach of the state constitution's equal protection clause."[19]

Although there is a huge difference between the Vermont case and the Hawaii case, not the least of which is that the Vermont decision is a victory (of sorts) for gay marriage and the Hawaii ruling is a loss, the cases are similar in that the Vermont justices also left the ultimate remedy up to the state legislature. Claiming that a marriage license is not the only route to the "benefits and protections that flow from marriage," the court left open the possibility of domestic partnership legislation as the remedy, ignoring the fact that the *status* of marriage is itself a benefit[20] and that a "separate but equal" solution is no more likely to stand in this case than it did in racially based education. Indeed, the legislature did choose this option, coining the secular yet respectful term "civil union." Nonetheless, a civil union is not equal to a marriage in that no federal benefits flow from civil unions, even to Vermonters, and the benefits and protections that are bestowed as a result of such unions are not transferable to other states.

Justice Denise R. Johnson, who concurred with the majority's holding but dissented from their "novel and truncated remedy," argued that, in declining to give gay and lesbian couples "any relief other than an exhortation to the Legislature to deal with the problem," the court abdicated its "constitutional duty to redress violations of constitutional rights."[21] Quoting a 1998 Canadian decision, she said: " 'Groups that have historically been the target of discrimination cannot be expected to wait patiently for the protection of their human dignity and equal rights while governments move toward reform one step at a time.' Once a court has determined that a discriminatory classification has deprived plaintiffs of a constitutionally ripe entitlement, the court must decide if the classification 'is demonstrably justifiable in a free and democratic society, not whether there might be a more propitious time to remedy it.' "[22]

If—or when—some state does legalize same-sex marriage, lesbian and gay couples will find themselves in the same position interracial couples did in the 1960s: their marriages will be legal in some states but not in others. Litigation will then take place under the full faith and credit clause in the U.S. Constitution to determine if states that do not issue marriage licenses to same-sex couples must respect the marriages performed in states that do. Vermont's compromise of civil unions does not clarify but only further complicates the issue.

QUEER VERSUS STRAIGHT: HISTORICAL ARGUMENTS

As the title of a recent article conveys, however, "Some Gays Aren't Wedded to the Idea of Same-Sex Marriage."[23] Writer Anna Quindlen expanded on this issue when she said: "Gay marriage is a radical notion for straight people and a conservative notion for gay ones. After years of being sledgehammered by society, some gay men and lesbians are deeply suspicious of participating in an institution that seems to have 'straight world' written all over it."[24] Queer things—queer theory, Queer Nation, the protest chant, "we're here, we're queer, we're fabulous, get used to us"—assume that respect for distinctiveness, an opportunity to pursue a life that is "not straight," is what is wanted.[25] Although some traditionalists have called same-sex marriage a slap in the face of tradition, and some queer theorists have repudiated the institution of marriage as not queer, both may have reason to pause.

If Yale historian John Boswell is right, Christian marriage rites between same-sex partners date back to the fourth century, earlier than the widespread performance of heterosexual ceremonies in the eleventh century.[26] Boswell claimed to have found gay marriage rites in liturgical manuals and early legal documents that constitute clear evidence that "gay unions were comparable to heterosexual marriage." "Both men and women were married using these rites, though evidence for lesbian unions is not as geographically widespread nor as ancient," Boswell said. He theorized that "gay marriage rites . . . appear to have started as a religious ceremony and were based principally on love . . . including an erotic dimension." He contrasted this history with heterosexual marriage, which he said started as a civil ceremony with property exchange and later, when appropriated by the church, emphasized progeny and worldly success.[27] So it appears that queer theorists could claim or reclaim an institution that is part of their history. Indeed, the good history—the part about love and eroticism—is queer.

EQUALITY, JUSTICE, LIBERATION

Whether being able to marry is a desirable political goal is a question pretty much outside of law and history. At the least, it is a question that requires ethical analysis of matters such as equality, justice, oppression, and dignity. Attorney Paula Ettelbrick, who doubts that marriage is the path to liberation for anyone, argues against lesbian and gay marriages on the grounds that they will not alter the elitist character of marriage, that they will at best "minimally transform" the oppressive character of marriage by "diluting its patriarchal dynamic," and that they will not transform society or bring about a just world. On the subject of a just world, Ettelbrick says: "Gay marriage will not help us address the systematic abuses inherent in a society that does not provide decent health care to all of its citizens . . . nor will it address the pain of the unmarried lesbian who is prohibited from entering the intensive care unit . . . solely because she is not a spouse or a family member. Likewise, marriage will not help the gay victim of domestic violence who, because he chose not to marry, finds no protection under the law to keep his violent lover away."[28]

Of course, allowing lesbians and gay men to marry will not address the issue of decent health care. Why, we might (indeed, *should*) ask, must a person be employed by a company or an institution of a certain size or be married to someone who is in order to get health insurance? Presumably, in a just world, folks could get health care because they are valuable in and of themselves. Ettelbrick is absolutely correct in her view about the notions of "equality" or "rights" or "equal rights" when she says, "A pure 'rights analysis' often fails to incorporate a broader understanding of the underlying inequities that operate to deny justice to a fuller range of people and groups." Despite her claim that rights and justice should be combined, she goes on to argue that gay marriage will gain rights for a few, will make some lesbians and gays "insiders," but will not correct the imbalance of power between the married and the nonmarried. Thus, "justice would not be gained."[29]

One answer to Ettelbrick, that she herself has put her finger on, is the way equality arguments usually work: on a limited scale. They do not do big jobs such as bringing about a just society. As Mary Midgley puts it so clearly, "Equality . . . is a rather abstract ideal. . . . Who is to be made equal to whom, and in what respect? Historically the answers given have mostly concerned rather narrow groups. . . . The formula needed is something like, 'let those who are already equal in respect x be, as is fitting, equal also in respect y.' . . . Outsiders . . . who are currently not equal in respect x, cannot benefit from this kind of argument. . . . The notion of equality is a tool for rectifying injustices within a given group, not for widening that group or deciding how it ought to treat those outside it."[30]

Ettelbrick does understand the limited and painfully slow way that equality arguments normally work when she suggests that "more marginal members of the lesbian and gay community (women, people of color, working class and poor) are less likely [than those more acceptable to the mainstream] to see marriage as having relevance to our struggles for survival." The fact that achieving the right to marry will not benefit everyone or benefit everyone equally or solve all the world's problems is not an argument against it. What good, asks Ettelbrick, "is the affirmation of our relationships (that is, marital relationships) if we are rejected as women, blacks, or working class?"[31] But the obvious answer to the question, "What good is a job in philosophy if I am discredited as a woman?" is "A lot of good."

Moreover, the exclusion of lesbian relationships from legal recognition directly affects survival issues that cut across class and race. As attorney Ruthann Robson notes, "A member of a lesbian couple who becomes incapacitated can be controlled by a person determined in accordance with relationships recognized under the rule of law, such as the father who does not believe she is a lesbian, the brother who abused her, or the husband she has not seen for twenty years but never divorced."[32] The long and well-publicized estrangement between partners Karen Thompson and Sharon Kowalski (after a car accident that left Kowalski partially paralyzed, her father assumed her guardianship and denied Thompson even any visitation rights) is a textbook example of Robson's point.

Ettelbrick dismisses the importance of equality not only because it is of more use to those "closer to the norm or to power" but also because "the concept of equality . . . only supports sameness." She continues: "The moment we argue . . . that we should be treated as equals because we are really just like married couples and hold the same values to be true, we . . . begin the dangerous process of silencing our different voices."[33] As we have seen, the assumption that equality is similarity is simplistic and not always justified. However, even if equality did entail similarity, sameness is not always bad. Of course, sometimes sameness is bad, and that is part of Ettelbrick's worry. She says that lesbians and gay men "end up mimicking all that is bad about the institution of marriage in our effort to appear to be the same as straight couples."[34] Cheshire Calhoun responds to this concern in an interesting way. She says:

> It is . . . important not to exaggerate the level of conformity involved in having familial status. . . . [F]amilies often fail to conform to gender, sexual, and family composition norms. This has not prevented heterosexuals from claiming that, their deviancy notwithstanding, they still have real marriages and real families, and are themselves naturally suited for marriage, family, and parenting. Thus, lesbians and gays who resist their construction as family outlaws are not bidding for access to one, highly conventional family form (such as the nuclear, two-parent, self-sufficient, procreative family). They are instead bidding for access to the same privilege that heterosexuals now enjoy, namely the privilege of claiming that *in spite of their multiple deviations* from norms governing the family, their families are nevertheless *real* ones and they them-

selves are naturally suited for marriage, family, parenting *however* these may be defined and redefined.[35]

Others who disagree with Ettelbrick think that the participation of lesbians and gay men in the institution of marriage will alter the institution for the better. For example, Thomas Stoddard said that "marriage may be unattractive and even oppressive as it is currently structured and practiced, but enlarging [it] to embrace same-sex couples would necessarily transform it into something new."[36] Susan Moller Okin, in her book *Justice, Gender and the Family,* certainly makes a strong case against what she calls *gender-structured* marriage, thereby tempting others to suggest that an alternative, especially an alternative that is not gender-structured, has got to be better.

Marriage and the family as currently practiced in our society, Okin says, "constitute the pivot of a . . . system of gender that renders women vulnerable to dependency, exploitation, and abuse."[37] The conventional family, she says, is "the linchpin of gender,"[38] and gendered relationships, private and public, are thoroughly unjust. Martha Nussbaum, in her review of Okin's book, says that Okin "plainly has a strong preference for the nuclear family in something like its modern Western form. . . . But she never tells us what benefits she believes the modern Western family provides, or why, in view of the many alternatives that have been conceived, she still prefers the pattern that has proven, as she herself demonstrates, so resistant to reform in the name of justice."[39]

If same-sex couples could marry, says Nan Hunter, "the profoundly gendered structure at the heart of marriage would be radically disrupted. Who would be the 'husband' in a marriage of two men, or the 'wife' in a marriage of two women? And either way—if there can be no such thing as a female husband or a male wife, as the right-wing argues with contempt; or indeed in some sense there can be, as lesbian and gay couples reconfigure these roles on their own terms—the absolute conflation of gender with role is shattered. What would be the impact on heterosexual marriage?"[40]

Unfortunately, Hunter does not answer this question. As we have seen, Thomas Stoddard was hopeful, Paula Ettelbrick is doubtful, and Martha Nussbaum suggests that trying something new might be justified because heterosexual marriage and the nuclear family are unjust institutions. I would not rest a case for the legalization of lesbian and gay marriage on the possibility that lesbians and gay men might improve the institution of marriage, for transformative values may not come about. Nonetheless, I am for trying something new. We ought to pull the pin and see what happens. However, at the least, arguments against lesbian and gay marriages, based on the oppressive character of marriage itself, should be rejected if the oppressive character referred to is caused by the currently accepted gender requirements of marriage.[41]

This type of argument, exemplified in the following remarks by Ruthann Robson and S. E. Valentine, has been widespread in lesbian writings: "Underlying the lesbian critique of marriage is the gendered perspective of marriage developed by feminists. . . . Marriage has remained interwoven with both the development and the perpetuation of patriarchy and women's status within the patriarchy."[42] Even if the oppressive nature of marriage historically did count as a reason for devaluing marriage per se, and therefore gay marriage, it still could be argued that lesbians and gay men should have the right to marry.[43] It is perfectly coherent to assert that lesbians and gay men should have the option to marry without claiming a necessary value for marriage, even as one can coherently claim that lesbians and gay men should have the option to serve in the military without valuing the military.[44]

Paula Ettelbrick has one last formulation of her antiequality argument. She says the idea of marriage is inconsistent with the goal of gay liberation, which is to recognize the legitimacy of many different kinds of relationships.[45] Interestingly, she favors domestic partnership plans that, she argues, better accomplish this goal. Such plans, on the part of municipalities and employers, almost universally define domestic partners as including lesbian and gay couples as well as unmarried heterosexual partners and extend to them some of the rights accorded to married couples. The qualifications for benefits approximate the qualifications for marriage, although in many instances they are more stringent. For example, domestic partnership requires couples to give evidence of commitment, whereas marriage does not.[46] On Ettelbrick's view, marriage is a "two-tier system of the 'haves' and the 'have-nots,'" and same-sex marriage would simply perpetuate "the elevation of married relationships and of 'couples' in general . . . further eclipsing other relationships of choice." Domestic partnership plans, on the other hand, "validate nonmarital relationships,"[47] thereby contributing to the goal mentioned above of recognizing many different kinds of relationships.

It does seem that the idea of domestic partnership is more inclusive of diverse relationships than is marriage, although creating such a category does not abolish the privileging of some relationships. For instance, sisters who are really siblings and not closeted lesbians posing as sisters could get minimal benefits if they set up a household and are financially interdependent.

KINSHIP ARGUMENTS

Despite the attractive potential of domestic partnerships, I think a separate and compelling argument can be made for lesbian and gay marriages. Although lesbians and gay men have made some progress in the area of individual rights in the United States, until very recently there has been an almost total nonrecognition of gay families. A chapter title of a recent book illustrates the exile of gays from kinship: "Is Straight to Gay as Family Is to No Family?"[48] And Justice Byron White, speaking for the Supreme Court's majority view that homosexual sex between consenting adults in their own bedroom is not protected by the right to privacy, said, in the *Bowers v. Hardwick* decision in 1986, "No connection between family, marriage, or procreation on the one hand and homosexual activity on the other has been demonstrated."[49] The right to privacy in *Bowers* protects only marital privacy.

Gay people were not seen by Justice White as being in relationships, nor were lesbians and gay men visible to him as couples, partners, families, kin. Had the Court interpreted the right to privacy as a right to sexual autonomy, gay people might have been seen, for all the Court had to be able to see then were individuals who desired autonomy and who had some kind of a sexual life. But when the Court said the right to privacy is the right to *marital* privacy, they saw no connection between marriage and gay people. A legal system or an ethical system based on principle will not be of any use to lesbians and gay men if they are not seen as the sorts of folks to whom these principles can apply.

Worse yet, think about an ethic based on sentiment. Take, for example, Mary Midgley's view: those nearest to us have special claims, claims that diminish in proportion to distance, either physical or social. Fortunately, Midgley says that those most distant need not always come at the end of the queue. Unfortunately, priority rankings among various kinds of claims are determined by the cultural maps worked out by individual societies, and nearness and kinship are real and important factors in our psychological makeup. The psychology presented here seems right to me. I care more about Morgan, my Maine Coon cat, than I do about the child I do not know who lives six blocks down the street. These feelings I have really matter, however much those folks who believe in universalizing ethical principles say that physical and social distance should not matter. However, appealing to sentiment as a way of justifying behavior as *ethical* can be as dangerous as it is comforting. It is, of course, comforting to hear that those folks we already care about are just the ones that we ought to care about (or ought to care most about). Such a psychology explains, at least in part, why ethical views based on sentiment have not been applied positively to lesbians and gay men who are perceived as strangers and not as kin in our society.

One would expect lesbians and gay men to get a better deal from ethics based on principle, but arguments based on principle often do not work for gay people—as evidenced by the 1986 *Bowers* case. A more recent example is the debate over Colorado's Amendment 2, which illustrated how all civil rights of lesbians and gay men can be jeopardized because lesbians and gay men are not perceived as kin or as having important relationships. In July 1993, the Colorado Supreme Court ruled that the voter initiative to outlaw gay rights laws must prove a compelling state interest in order to meet constitutional standards. The state's attorney general argued that "the State's desire to promote 'family values' provide[s] such a compelling interest."[50] Amendment 2 was declared unconstitutional by a district court judge on December 13, 1993, on the grounds that it violated equal protection by usurping "the fundamental right of an identifiable group to participate in the political process";[51] and, as we have seen, the U.S. Supreme Court continued in this lead. Nevertheless, the fact that anyone would offer "family values" as a good reason for the denial of equal rights is a measure of just how far lesbians and gay men are from being viewed as kin in our society. As one California court put it, in rejecting a similar initiative in Riverside, California, "All that is lacking is a sack of stones for throwing."[52]

In short, moral arguments based on existing sentiment will not work for gay people; arguments based on principle should work but often do not, in part because sentiment plays a role in even principled ethics and law. Until current sentiments in our society are changed, lesbians and gay men will not be able to expect that ethical (and legal) principles will be applied fairly to them. Thus, it is important for the sake of creating new sentiments to press for gay marriage so that lesbians and gay men can become visible as couples, partners, families, and kin. Pressing for registered partnerships—or what some have called gay near-marriage—may not do the job. Those folks who in 1986 could not even imagine lesbians and gay men in relationships need to know that many lesbians and gay men—to quote the Supreme Court—view their relationships as "noble" and "intimate to the degree of being sacred."[53]

CONCLUSION

In sum, I have raised the following issues: Married people are paid more than their nonmarried counterparts, while the possibility of choice regarding whether or not to marry has not been extended to lesbians and gay men. Marriage has been rejected as an undesirable political goal on the grounds that it is not queer, presumably meaning to a degree that marriage is not part of lesbian and gay history. But John Boswell's new discoveries of historical evidence indicate that marriage is, in a very important sense, queer. I have argued that the pursuit of equality should not be abandoned simply because it is often compatible with injustice. Nor should equality be discarded because it supposedly means "sameness," and sameness is bad. I have suggested that our assessment of the comparative merits of marriage and domestic partnership is to some extent a reflection of the respective values we place on equality and diversity. Although I have expressed my doubts about the transformative power of same-sex marriage, it seems to me that objections to gay marriage based on the gender-structure of heterosexual marriage are misplaced.

Finally, I have argued that Americans have been allowed for too long to view lesbians and gay men only as individuals, that is, not in relationships, and as strangers, that is, not as kin. I think that gay marriage needs to be on the political agenda for the sake of gaining a certain level of social awareness and acceptance of serious lesbian and gay relationships. I do not worry, as do some queer theorists, that pursuing a goal such as marriage will result in assimilation into invisibility or, as Ettelbrick puts it, let us "fade into the woodwork."[54] I think it is a far greater worry that the current invisibility as family is threatening to destroy any kind of a decent life at all for lesbians and gay men in the United States.

11

Natural Law Today

I wrote the earliest version of the opening chapter in this book, "Natural Law Language and Women," in 1971. It seemed to me at that time that natural law theory, while its lingering influence still had some power to shape contemporary philosophy and discourse, was deservedly on the way out. It was, after all, a theory formed in the earliest days of philosophy. In 1971 I thought that if people understood the underpinnings of "natural" as a value judgment, they would abandon such arguments, if not in popular literature, then at least as a thread in serious philosophy.

But it seems that natural law ethics has a good deal of staying power. It has not only remained into the nineties but has emerged in some new forms, asserting a new legitimacy by its allegiances with other and more contemporary philosophies. On the one hand are Christian thinkers such as Cristina L. H. Traina, who seek to salvage Thomistic thinking by linking it with feminist philosophy. I will examine her work in some detail, arguing that her attempts to merge the two result in a serious distortion of both. On the other hand is an attempt to discover a "new" natural law philosophy, based on observation of the natural world and relying on the intense credibility that science and empiricism have in this century. I discuss Edward O. Wilson's recent work *Consilience* and Bruce Bagemihl's *Biological Exuberance* as examples of this variation on the natural law idea. Indeed, Gabriel Rotello's ecology-based work, discussed in Chapter 5, illustrates another example of this new natural law trend. Both the science-based natural law theorists and the religion-based ones are still searching for those illusive natural laws that would bring clarity to the troubling questions of ethics.

REVISITING THOMISTIC NATURAL LAW

In 1999, Cristina L. H. Traina published *Feminist Ethics and Natural Law: The End of the Anathemas,*[1] claiming a reevaluation and a reconciliation of the Roman

Catholic natural law tradition and Anglo-American feminist ethics. She proposes to develop from these two supposedly antagonistic schools of thought a new feminist natural law. There can be, in my opinion, no such thing as a feminist natural law, at least not unless we change the meaning of natural law beyond recognition. Traina claims both that natural law needs feminism and that feminism need natural law. I will show that the dent that feminism can put in Thomistic natural law, if it exists at all, is small indeed. For the most part, however, I will proceed by looking in turn at the various benefits that Traina claims feminist ethics will gain from natural law and argue that feminism is better off without it.

First, however, it needs to be made clear that by feminist ethics Traina means *Christian* feminist ethics and by natural law she means *Christian* natural law. This distinction is not revealed in the title and is mentioned only sporadically within the book, but it is a clarification that is especially important to her claim that natural law and feminist ethics can be reconciled. The two schools of thought are not nearly so antagonistic if both are Christian.

Traina credits feminist deconstruction with revealing "the distinctively Christian character of natural law thought." Her view is that, far from destroying natural law by deconstructing its claims to "quintessential neutrality," deconstruction "relieves the pressure to make universal, neutral claims and permits natural law to identify itself as a religious ethic." She claims that "the ideal of expressing natural law as a universal, neutral ethic is a modern ideal"[2] now upset by postmodern analysis. But natural law ethics since the days of Plato has always presented itself as being based on secular reason, and it continues to do so today in the face of postmodern and other criticisms. For example, John Haas says: "The formulation and promulgation of laws is an activity natural to rational creatures whereby actions are ordered. The natural law is the human person's rational participation in the eternal law which itself orders all of creation. It is nothing other than the human person ordering his own actions reasonably."[3]

Of course, natural law never has been devoid of some value structure nor has it ever simply endorsed or reinforced the philosophical dictate to follow reason. Rather, the one constant view seems to be that the *specific* reasons or purposes for things are inculcated in the essential nature of those things and that those reasons or purposes have a moral dimension. For instance, when Aquinas said that "preserve yourself" is a natural law, he meant that suicide is both unnatural and is also morally wrong. If natural law theorists are telling us only to follow reason, they are saying something so general and vague that it has little directive content. After all, there may be good reasons for living and good reasons for not living.

Traditionally, natural law theorists have claimed more than a basis in reason alone. They have said that certain specific *moral* conclusions can be based on nature as well. Using "nature" as a model, they have asserted that suicide and euthanasia with consent are unnatural; that homosexuality, birth control, masturbation, in vitro fertilization, abortion, and interracial and gay marriages are unnatural; and that women engaging in the professions is unnatural. Furthermore,

Aquinas thought that natural law was looking not just for specific reasons but for the *right* reasons for actions. Ethicists, however, do not need the impetus of a Christian God to seek right reasons; and if we do discover right reasons for actions, as rational beings we should not need the backing of a God or nature to act according to those reasons.

When one hears that natural law tells us only to follow reason, the implication is that natural law morality is harmless and free of prejudice. How could anyone object to following reason? Then it somehow results that following natural law reasoning out to its ethical conclusions comes, in some Christian philosophers, to the very same set of beliefs as an unquestioning obedience to the will of God as promulgated by a particular denomination. Traina's natural law philosophy falls into this pattern. She says at one point, for example, that "unaided human reason is unreliable enough that God revealed many of the more basic, universal secondary precepts of natural law in the Old Law—chiefly in the Ten Commandments—and confirmed them in the New Law revealed in Christ."[4]

The alleged benefits of natural law to feminist ethics, according to Traina, are monumental; it offers an all-encompassing telos, that is, end or purpose; a foundation; and principles and norms to a scattered and diverse body of thought.

AN ALL-ENCOMPASSING TELOS

"Natural law's first contribution [to feminist ethics] is the insistence that a comprehensive, existentially compelling ethic demands an all-encompassing *telos,*" says Traina. "A constructive feminist ethic must have a *telos,* an end, that envelops and meaningfully connects the many particular dimensions of women's good." However, the only example she gives of such an end is "union with God." Such a union, she says, holds "great promise for a Christian feminist ethics." But she does not suggest, and there probably is not, an all-encompassing telos that would benefit a secular feminist ethics. Secular feminism can, indeed should, stop short of providing such an end in order to "leave room for a variety of ways of organizing goods and ends."[5] Thus feminism does not need an all-encompassing end. To the degree that Christian feminism does need such a telos, it becomes more Christian and less feminist.

For Traina, Martha Nussbaum's "capabilities approach" to ethics, which relies on Aristotelian essentialism but not Thomistic natural law, does not suffice for feminism because it does not provide us with any substantive telos for women.[6] Nussbaum's view focuses on "capabilities [for functioning], and not actual functions." Quality of life, Nussbaum argues, should be assessed on the basis of what people are able to do: "Government is not directed to push citizens into acting in certain valued ways; instead, it is directed to make sure that all human beings have the necessary resources and conditions for acting in those ways. It leaves the choice up to them."[7] It is precisely by not telling women what purposes they ought to achieve that Nussbaum is able to assert that the capabilities view is compatible with autonomy and choice. As she puts it, "By making opportunities available, government enhances, and does not remove, choice."[8]

A natural law view, on the other hand, is incompatible with autonomy in a fundamental way for reasons stated in Chapter 3. The functions or purposes of humans are determined by a fixed nature that is independent of the individual's will; the only choice is in choosing to fulfill or deny one's natural purpose. Traina's argument that the enveloping purpose of feminism is union with God does follow centuries of Thomistic thought, but it stands in stark contrast to the larger body of feminist philosophy.

FOUNDATIONAL CLAIMS

The second contribution of Thomistic natural law ethics, according to Traina, is providing a much needed foundation for feminist ethics. That foundation is provided in a view on an individual's good, or well-being, or flourishing. A taxonomy of the various kinds of views on well-being or flourishing will highlight the choices available to us and make clear why contemporary philosophers other than myself find natural law views on flourishing to be problematic.

David DeGrazia, in a discussion of interspecies well-being, critically outlines some possibilities with respect to theories on well-being.[9] There are, for example, desire-based theories and objective theories. Desire-based theories, as their name implies, hold that our well-being is intimately connected to the satisfaction of our desires. Of course, some desires are criticizable and need "tidying up," as DeGrazia would put it. If we push too far in this direction, however, we may end up with an objective theory of well-being. In "tidying up" desires we may begin to talk about what desires people *should* have, which in turn motivates talk about standards for desires that are "objective," that is, not related to the subject who is having the desires.

Objective theories, as DeGrazia uses the term, define an individual's good "by reference to conditions or factors that are independent of, and may diverge from, the individual's own desires, values, or authority." Natural law theories are objective theories. Although DeGrazia does not discuss natural law theories as such, he locates Aristotle's theory (which is the origin of the type of theory that Traina wants to perpetuate) as an example of perfectionist theories that "are not serious contenders today." Such theories "include a conception of the good life for humans, a particular ideal; one's well-being is then assessed in terms of how close one's life gets to that ideal. Aristotle, for example, argued that there was a human function or telos—namely rational activity (which he divided into two components)—and that humans flourished to the extent that they actualized their function." DeGrazia concludes: "But it is very doubtful that there is a human telos and, consequently, a single good life for humans—much less, that it is rational activity."[10]

But this conclusion is not the end of the matter. There can be *flexible* objective theories that, according to DeGrazia, are contenders. Such theories maintain that "some things in themselves make life go better." Some candidates here are "enjoyments, autonomy, accomplishment, and deep personal relationships." These are objective concepts whose specific contents are defined by the individual. A very important point here is DeGrazia's view that "any plausible items on the objective theory's list will be something we *tend* to find satisfying,"[11] which is a criterion that natural law does not meet. A woman's being pregnant when she does not want to be hardly seems to be a situation that she would find satisfying. Yet putting women in this situation is in part due to the idea that the only natural function or good of sex is procreation. Also playing a role here is the official Catholic view of marriage and marital sex: Only marital sex is legitimate (marital here is assumed to be heterosexual), and every act of marital sex is to be uncontracepted. Unless marriage partners are at least willing to have a baby every time they have sex (this is called self-gift), their sexual activity is considered selfish and indulgent, even sinful. A satisfactory sexual relationship is not a concept whose outlines are filled in by the individual, but a set of detailed behaviors and attitudes.

Following this line of thinking, homosexual sex is considered to be unnatural, indulgent, and incapable of self-gift because it is nonprocreative. Not only are homosexuals supposed to be celibate on this view, but they also are barred from marriage and, hence, according to Andrew Sullivan, barred from flourishing as well. "Matrimonial love," according to Sullivan, is held by the Catholic Church to be "intrinsic, for most people, to the state of human flourishing." As Sullivan puts it, "If homosexuality is overcome by a renunciation of homosexual emotion and sexual union, . . . the human being is liberated into sacrifice and pain . . . to a less than fully realized life. . . . [the] renunciation of such love is not guided toward some ulterior or greater good as celibacy of the religious orders is designed to intensify their devotion to God. Rather, the loveless homosexual destiny is precisely toward nothing, a negation of human fulfillment."[12] Obviously, this type of situation does not meet DeGrazia's criterion of satisfying experiences.

More generally, the official Catholic view on sexual ethics does not qualify as a flexible objective theory of an individual's good because it is not flexible. What makes an objective theory flexible, according to DeGrazia, is that it includes goods that are or tend to be "good in any life." Also, goods such as autonomy and enjoyments are "sensitive to individual differences."[13] Viewing sex as having the single good of potential biological parenthood is neither a good in any life nor sensitive to individual differences.[14] Some philosophers, such as L. W. Sumner, have gone so far as to suggest that perfectionist theories "do not even address what is good for the individual."[15]

So why does Traina think that Thomas Aquinas's natural law views with their perfectionist emphases can ground feminism? Often Traina sticks with generalities of good that no one could object to, that is, such Thomistic values as rationality, integrity, integral flourishing, and the like. On occasion she does offer a specific line of argument, at one point noting that for Aquinas, moral reason is practical reason, prudence is part of practical reason, and prudence entails taking experience into account. If we are allowed to take experience into account in our reasoning, then conclusions may vary with individual circumstances. Thus, we may get some feminist conclusions. Traina admits, however, that "although Thomas clearly allows in theory for variation and change in practical moral conclusions, he just as clearly does not expect that the amplitude of their oscillations will be very large."[16]

Lisa Sowle Cahill, who like Traina is interested in deriving feminist conclusions from Thomist philosophy, gives an example that shows just how constricted these oscillations are. Cahill, like Traina, points out that for Thomas Aquinas ("Catholicism's model for natural law philosophy"), the principles of speculative reason or general principles are necessary and "contain the truth without fail," whereas practical reason deals with contingent matters surrounding action, and therefore "truth or practical rectitude is not the same for all."

Cahill's example has to do with new reproductive technologies that she says are contingent matters. "The applicable principle," she says, "is undisputed: unity of love, sex, and procreation."[17] She concedes that in the official view "the inseparable unity of these ends is to be maintained in each and every sexual act. Further, this unity is thought to entail certain specific prohibitions: against artificial birth control, conception without sexual acts, sexual acts outside marriage, and reproduction outside marriage."[18] Cahill argues that if Catholic officials would put more emphasis on personal relationships than on sexual acts and also acquaint themselves with the experiences of infertile couples, they might not categorically rule out such procedures as homologous in vitro fertilization, a process in which the gametes are provided by the spouses and there are no third parties.

She concludes: "Biological manipulation of one (or both) of two persons already within a morally good relationship (marriage), in order to further a proper end of that relationship (procreation), is morally acceptable."[19] But even this tiny departure is contested by those who see homologous in vitro fertilization as "manufacturing" children and "subject[ing] the child to the domination of technology" in a way that is incompatible with the child's "innate worth and dignity."[20]

What Cahill does do, and Traina does not, is to give an example of the relationship between speculative and practical reason that shows just how little flexibility there is in this particular objective theory. There is certainly no hope of flourishing for homosexuals as long as these connections between love, sex, and procreation are necessary ones. Even in Cahill's example, the necessary connections are maintained in the necessary general principle. It is this principle that needs to go.

Ultimately, Traina's endorsement of empirical methods extends to the establishment of ideals, moral principles, and moral wisdom—far beyond anything Aquinas had in mind. She states: "There is no single ideal of flourishing, no final and authoritative set of moral principles, no unique path to moral wisdom. The task is rather to discern, in each place and age, which ways of life, guidelines, and ways of moral discernment seem best to respect and promote the integral good of particular people." Credible morally normative definitions of human nature are "open, tentative, and inductively defined." Moreover, inductive methods must be inclusive.

If we are to figure out what it means for women to flourish, we are going to have to find out something about women's lives, their needs, and their situation at least in part by asking them. In Traina's words, "natural law ethics has been developed, organized, and articulated by small, fairly homogenous groups of scholars, and feminism provides important alternative procedural models." Elsewhere she says that the "barriers to clear vision are methodological and procedural." Those with unclear vision are Aquinas and the natural law revisionists, who lack a "truly comprehensive method" that includes not only listening to but giving moral and epistemological preference to "those who are generally excluded from both integral flourishing and the process of authoritative moral deliberation."[21]

With this defense of experiential knowledge, Traina has shown that feminists who are in, and want to remain in, the Thomist tradition need to push to the limits the view that Aquinas can accommodate empirical and inclusive methods in order for some modest feminist conclusions to emerge from that tradition. However, feminist ethics does not need natural law as a foundation in order to adopt empirical and inductive methods.

PRESERVING PRINCIPLES

Knowing that feminist maneuverability is severely limited within established principles of natural law makes a mystery of Traina's third alleged advantage of feminist ethics uniting with natural law, namely that "natural law provides a tradition of principles and norms [and] a method of criticizing and altering them." When we look at the principles and norms that the natural law tradition provides, a feminist will have to spend all her time "criticizing and altering." Why would any feminist take this on? Why would Traina take this on? Principles from the tradition that she cites are examples of abstraction that are totally at odds with her inductive and inclusive methods and the flexibility she claims is inherent in practical reason. For example, a feminist criticism described by Traina as "persistent and trenchant" and at odds with both traditional and contemporary or revisionist natural law is that "natural law objections to abortion value abstract or potential human life over the lives of particular, pregnant women, and, often, their families."

Or, to give another example, in the Vatican Instruction *Donum Vitae* (Gift of Life), the value placed on genetic connection between parents and children is so abstracted from other considerations that Traina says of it: "It gives the impression that the conjugal relationship itself is the being whose good is to be pursued, an entity whose good seems to supercede even that of the persons who compose it."[22]

The tradition of principles and norms that natural law provides consists of abstractions created by authors who often go out of their way to disconnect from the realities of people's lives. It is not plausible that principles such as these would be useful to Traina, or any feminist thinker, given her method of formulating principles.

NATURAL LAW TURNED ON ITS HEAD

Traina's conception of natural law stands in marked contrast to traditional natural law and official Catholic interpretation of natural law today. While insisting that women have a telos or an ideal, Traina is vague about what it is. Here is an interesting clue: "No telos that categorically excludes or ignores any dimension of women's good can be acceptable." But in traditional natural law theory, the reasoning is just the other way around. The telos of women is defined first and then the good of women (or what it means for them to flourish) is defined in terms of their fulfilling their telos. Traina has made the idea of flourishing basic, but it is not basic in natural law theory; that theory depends on first defining the natural purposes of women and/or men and/or human beings. Nor is there any way in traditional natural law ethics to rule out certain purposes or principles if they conflict with feminist views. But, says Traina, any human telos or principle that depends on political or economic sexist oppression can be disqualified as unjust.[23]

In one sense, Traina's "natural law" view is just not a traditional natural law view because she makes flourishing basic rather than a notion dependent on natural purposes. In another sense, she has redefined what is natural to particular people as being their good or their flourishing. Suppose we tried to discern, in this place and age, what best respects and promotes the good of women by asking them. We would not necessarily come up with a feminist view. We might find women who argue passionately that marriage is an oppressive patriarchal institution, just as we might find women who agree with the 1999 Southern Baptist proclamation that women ought to be subordinate to their husbands. But the likelihood of coming up with a feminist view is much greater with inductive and inclusive methods than with deductive and exclusive methods.

On the other hand, suppose we take lesbians and gays to be the particular people in Traina's framework. Here we see a vast difference between social, cultural, and institutional views that would promote the flourishing of gays as natural to them and those traditional natural law views that see homosexuality as intrinsically evil or as an objective disorder. The latter views must always work against gay flourishing as long as the basic purpose of sexuality is perceived as reproduction and human flourishing is perceived as accomplishing that purpose.

The idea of flourishing, good as it sounds, is too vague to stand alone. Traina, for example, suggests that both scholars such as Mary Daly and Martha Nussbaum who oppose female genital mutilation and scholars who defend it "would say they are defending women's genuine flourishing within particular social contexts."[24] If the idea of flourishing is really that vague, it points up the need for a rights view that at least can be made specific enough to protect certain individual interests.

RIGHTS AND NATURAL LAW

In Traina's opinion, one last advantage of natural law to philosophy in general is that it "walks the line" between universals and relativism.[25] Traina does not want to cede feminism entirely to the deconstructionists, even though she believes that feminist deconstructionists have had important insights, because deconstructionism leads to moral relativism. She says she wants to be able to assert, for example, that genital mutilation of girls and women is wrong even in a culture that condones it. But a rights view can also walk the line here. Rights are universal principles that can consistently coexist with cultural diversity. It is not clear that a Thomist natural law view can protect these women at all. What traditional natural law principle would cover this case as long as the possibility of pregnancy is preserved? And Traina's natural law, so heavily dependent on empirical methods, may run into trouble if women in these cultures condone these practices.

There is a further problem with recommending to a natural law theorist that rights replace natural law. Rights may not be rejected by natural law theorists, but if rights are accepted, they likely will not be allowed to stand on their own feet. Typically, rights are said to be grounded in natural law. For example, Traina says that "in an historicist and pluralist era, which has all but discredited such terms, even to allude to universals or nature or givenness is touchy business. I have stressed one pressing practical reason for doing so: without them one cannot make rights arguments stick."[26] Although no argument is provided, the clear implication here is that rights need a foundation in natural law, and such foundational claims are not without consequence.

Grounding rights in natural law can change the character of rights, that is, not only will some classical rights be left out, but novel rights will be created. For example, the 1987 Vatican Instruction "Gift of Life" claims that "a child has the right to be conceived, carried in the womb, brought into the world and brought up within marriage: it is through the secure and recognized relationship to his own parents that the child can discover his own identity and achieve his own proper human development."[27] Such a right that devalues family members who are chosen but have no genetic connection to their parent or parents is only possible with certain traditional natural law assumptions in place.

Martha Nussbaum counters relativism in the matter of female genital mutilation by combining the idea of flourishing with rights and the idea of participatory dialogue with an account of deformed preferences. Moreover, her idea of capabilities for functioning as opposed to insisting that certain functions be performed brings her to a different conclusion than would the tradition of natural law. She says that "female genital mutilation means the irreversible loss of the capability for a type of sexual functioning that many young women value highly, usually at an age when they are far too young to know what value it has or does not have in their own life." Girls who undergo this mutilation do not have the choice of sexual pleasure later on. Moreover, Nussbaum claims, the practice is linked with male domination: "Sex relations constructed by the practice are relations in which intercourse becomes a vehicle for one-sided male pleasure rather than for mutuality of pleasure." In addition she notes many other relevant facts, such as the use of physical force, the suffering involved, and the possibility of serious, lifelong health problems.[28]

Note the differences here from a natural law approach. First of all, consequences matter, particularly the consequences to the woman herself. Second, the function is different, with an emphasis on preserving the woman's future choice of functions rather than on the single function of childbearing. While I am not saying that one can never reach any feminist conclusions by working within the natural law tradition, I do argue that natural law theory is not an asset to feminist ethics; it is a weight dragging one down. Notice that Nussbaum could not reach the conclusions she does if she confined herself to an Aristotelian framework. She takes the idea of flourishing as basic, substitutes choice for the performing of certain functions, adds a list of liberal liberties, and includes participatory dialogue.

There is no argument in Aristotle for women's autonomy to develop their own life plans, no women's participation in political dialogue, no women's need to resist male domination. As a *secular* thinker, however, Nussbaum is free to disconnect from Aristotle at any point and not bring his natural law (or any other) baggage along. Another example here of successful disconnect is Lisa Tessman's contention that oppression interferes with flourishing and that women can develop virtues for resistance against oppression.[29] Traina insists, on the other hand, that Thomistic natural law philosophy can be retrieved for feminism while still tied to the principles and norms of that tradition as well as its commitment to an overarching telos and foundational status.

REVISITING ARGUMENTS FROM ANIMAL BEHAVIOR

Biologist Bruce Bagemihl's 1999 book, *Biological Exuberance: Animal Homosexuality and Natural Diversity,*[30] was greeted by a popular magazine as finally refuting the timeworn argument against homosexuality that it is unnatural.[31] It is true that one form of the argument from naturalness has seemingly been put to rest by scientific research. Sexual behavior studies in animals, as Simon LeVay puts it, "challenge one particular sense of the dogma that homosexual behavior is 'against nature': the notion that it is unique to those creatures who, by tasting the fruit of the tree of knowledge, have alone become morally culpable."[32] The evidence simply refutes the old argument that "animals don't do it, therefore it is unnatural." However, LeVay, warns, this does not prevent people from saying "animals *do* do it, therefore it's bestial."[33] Nonetheless, as Alfred Kinsey observed several decades ago, "The sexual acts which are demonstrably part of the phylogenetic heritage of any species cannot be classified as acts contrary to nature, biologically unnatural, abnormal or perverse."[34]

What Bagemihl does is claim that biological exuberance with all of its gender variations and sexual possibilities is natural. Homosexuality, transgender, and nonreproductive heterosexuality are all part of biological diversity, which is intrinsically valuable.[35] Indeed, the whole idea of biological exuberance suggests a complexity of sexuality in the animal world that reflects a natural extravagance, an excess, an abundance in life itself. Crediting Georges Bataille, Bagemihl asserts that excess and exuberance are more basic to biological systems than scarcity or functionality, that is, "usefulness."[36] He suggests that "reproduction is not the ultimate 'purpose' or inevitable outcome of biology. It is simply one consequence of a much larger pattern of energy 'expenditure,' in which the overriding force is the need to use up excess. In the process, many organisms end up passing on their genes, but just as many lead lives in which reproduction figures scarcely at all. Earth's profusion simply will not be 'contained' within procreation: it wells up and spills over and beyond this."[37]

I noted in Chapter 1 that the *facts* of animal behavior do not prescribe how human beings *ought* to act, and there are plenty of graphic examples to back up this point. For instance, a female praying mantis may start chewing off the male's head while they are still in the process of mating. Here the "naturalistic fallacy" is relevant: normative conclusions are not logically entailed in descriptions of matters of fact. However, even though there is no logical entailment between "what is" and "what ought to be," there is generally an impact on people's lives and attitudes that comes from knowing what seem to be the facts.

Consider the following passage from Ovid's *Metamorphoses:*

> Cows do not burn with love for cows, nor mares for mares;
> The ram is hot for the ewe, the doe follows the stag.
> So also do birds mate, and among all animals
> No female is seized with desire for the female.[38]

From Ovid to the story of Noah's ark, the impact on gay people of these well-known construals of fact can be one of loneliness in the universe, of feeling like an aberration in nature. John Boswell reports an unknown late Roman thinker who tried to give a different interpretation to the accepted facts: "Is it any wonder that, since animals have been condemned by nature not to receive from the bounty of Providence any of the gifts afforded by intellect, they have with all else been deprived of gay desires? Lions do not have such a love, because they are not philosophers either. Bears have no such love, because they are ignorant of the beauty that comes from friendship. But for humans wisdom coupled with knowledge has after frequent experiments chosen what is best, and has formed the opinion that gay love is the most stable of loves."[39] Interestingly, the Roman's comments are consistent with studies today that show a correlation between gay experience and high levels of education. But even those interpretations are not very accurate, since many animals do form wonderful friendships with each other and with humans.

If continual exposure to the falsehoods and influential myths of the past can have a negative impact, perhaps one can only read so many hundreds of pages of accounts of animal homosexuality with their kisses and nuzzles and lifelong pair-bonds without its having some countering positive impact. A few examples of new findings follow. Bagemihl's definitions are helpful. He defines *heterosexuality* as "courtship, affectionate, sexual, pair-bonding, and/or parenting behaviors between animals of the opposite sex, while *homosexuality* is defined as these same activities when they occur between animals of the same sex."[40]

- "Male ostriches perform a unique 'pirouette dance' only when courting other males, while female Rhesus Macaques engage in courtship games such as 'hide-and-seek' that are unique to lesbian interactions."[41]
- "Some dolphins appear to engage in a sort of sonic 'foreplay': male Atlantic Spotted Dolphins have been observed stimulating their partner's genitals with pulsed sound waves, using a type of vocalization known as a genital buzz. . . . male Botos occasionally insert the penis into a male partner's blowhole (on the top of his head!)."[42]
- "In 1988 a sheep farmer came to the United States Department of Agriculture's Sheep Experimental Station in Dubois, Idaho, with a problem: every year, about 10 percent of the rams that had been raised to be studs failed to perform; when paired with estrous ewes, they showed no sign of sexual arousal and refused to mount. . . . many of the rams that had expressed no sexual interest in ewes did readily mount and copulate (anally) with other rams."[43]
- "Entire lizard species . . . consist only of females who reproduce by virgin birth and also have sex with each other."[44]
- "Among Lions and Elephants . . . the bond between male companions is closer and longer-lasting than any heterosexual bonds (which, in these and many other species, are virtually nonexistent beyond mating)."[45]

Of course, the impact of such information can be blunted. For example, some have said that although homosexual behavior is widespread in animals, exclusive homosexual orientation is not. Bagemihl contests this claim with examples, adding that documentation of either exclusive heterosexuality or exclusive homosexuality in animals is hard to achieve because both claims presuppose lifelong observations.[46] Moreover, many scientists through the years have read their own beliefs about perversion into their observations. One of most blatant, Bagemihl notes, is a 1987 published article on homosexuality in butterflies entitled, "A Note on the Apparent Lowering of Moral Standards in the Lepidoptera."[47] Then there are the scientists who celebrate biological diversity but never mention that gender variation and homosexuality are part of this diversity.

In fact, it seems that using "what animals do" as the normative version of "natural" is convenient when it serves to bolster antifeminist prejudices or maintain the status quo vis-à-vis women, and it is conveniently ignored when it suggests that homosexuality is just one sexual variation among many that the world affords. For example, basing his views in part on comparative primate data, Lionel Tiger argued in his 1969 book *Men in Groups*[48] that a male biological propensity to bond with other males may account for male domination in the political-religious-business scene. This "genetically programmed behavioral propensity" became engrained over the centuries by continual participation in hunting, which required cooperation, aggression, and organizational ability, all characteristics of a bond.[49] His views were reported by the press in even more extreme ways than Tiger himself proposed.

For example, Melvin Maddocks of the *Christian Science Monitor* pointed to what he called Tiger's "ultimate shocker," namely that "ancient occupational differences between males and females have produced 'brain-process differences' which no amount of militant feminism can change."[50] Tiger argued only that males have a "deep predisposition" to success that would require "more than just routine education and emancipation" to overcome in the name of equity.[51] The longevity of biology-based claims like his is evidenced by Barbara Ehrenreich's comment in a recent forum between herself and Tiger in which she blames him for precluding a fruitful discussion of gender and evolution and finally ends up saying to him, "I personally resent the fact that I can't even open up the subject of human evolution with my feminist friends without wasting half an hour refuting you."[52]

Praising Tiger's studies, leading American scientist Edward O. Wilson argues for a similar sociobiologist thesis, albeit the sexist implications are muted in comparison. In his new book *Consilience: The Unity of Knowledge,* Wilson asserts that "there is a biologically based human nature that is relevant to ethics and religion."[53] *Consilience* is the interlocking of explanatory theories, that is, fact-based theories across disciplines. Wilson believes that it is possible to extend consilience beyond the success he says it has had in the natural sciences to include the humanities, social sciences, arts, and religions. To believe in the possibility of consilience is to believe in the unity of knowledge and to accept an Enlightenment view that things have a fundamental order. But it is much more than that. It is the view that Philosophy—and more importantly for our purposes, Ethics—should be turned into science. According to Wilson, "Philosophy, the contemplation of the unknown, is a shrinking dominion. We [philosophers and scientists] have the common goal of turning as much philosophy as possible into science."[54]

Wilson sees his view as reductionist and believes that it will be perceived as such by professional philosophers, who, he says, see his subject matter as their domain. They will "indict" his view, he says, as "*conflation, simplism, ontological reduction, scientism,* and other sins made official by the hissing suffix. To which I plead guilty, guilty, guilty." In sum, in Wilson's own words, "The central idea of the consilience world view is that all tangible phenomena, from the birth of the stars to the workings of social institutions, are based on material processes that are ultimately reducible, however long and tortuous the sequences, to the laws of physics."[55]

THE SORRY STATE OF ETHICS TODAY

Ethics, Wilson says, is not "informed by anything that would be recognizable as authentic theory in the natural sciences. Both ethics and political science lack a foundation of verifiable knowledge of human nature sufficient to produce cause-and-effect predictions and sound judgments based on them." Ethical systems or ways of thinking, he claims, are either transcendental or empirical. Ethics today, insofar as it is centered in theology and philosophy, is transcendental. We must choose, Wilson says, whether to leave ethics there or to shift it "toward a science-based material analysis."[56]

"In transcendental thinking," Wilson maintains, "the chain of causation runs downward from the given ought . . . to individual choice. The argument from transcendentalism takes the following general form: *There is a supreme principle, either divine or intrinsic in the order of nature, and we will be wise to learn about it and find the means to conform to it.*" [57] In striking contrast, Wilson's "natural laws" are bottom up, discovered empirically, reversing the chain of causation by claiming that moral behavior has biological roots that predispose us to make certain choices.

Although traditional natural law theory fits Wilson's definition of transcendental, rights do not; they come from human sources alone. Yet rights are not established by methods that Wilson would call empirical. For example, when a feminist claims that women's autonomy, like men's autonomy, is valuable and ought to be protected by a right to liberty, she/he is not necessarily committed to the view that women's autonomy is consistent with some genetic predisposition. But some biological basis for women's autonomy would have to be established here in order to meet Wilson's standards for empirically based ethical rules. How we might ever do this or how many decades it might take are issues that Wilson does not address. Indeed, he does not even talk about women's autonomy.

All we know from him is that there is a biologically based human nature that is relevant to ethics as well as his further assertion (without argument or elaboration) that "on average many of the [biologically based] propensities differ according to . . . gender."[58] At least this much seemingly follows from Wilson's view. We could not just extend the value of autonomy for women from its value for men assuming we could establish the latter, that is, could prove that the male desire for autonomy is biologically based. What Wilson would require of feminist ethics is made clear by what he does demand of other ethical theories such as John Rawls's theory of justice. Wilson says: "Rawls ventured no thought on where the human brain comes from or how it works. He offered no evidence that justice-as-fairness is consistent with human nature, hence practicable as a blanket premise."[59]

A POINT IN FAVOR OF RAWLS

Rawls's thought experiment involving the veil of ignorance is not empirical in Wilson's sense. Rawls is not talking about choices that we are biologically predisposed to make; he is talking about choices that we would make under certain hypothetical conditions. Doing so makes Rawls guilty of relying on abstractions, as has been pointed out by pragmatists and many feminists, but it does not make him a transcendentalist if by that is meant someone whose ethics depends upon a divine command or the so-called natural order of things. There is no point in denying that Rawls's view is dependent upon abstractions. Doing his thought experiment requires that we abstract ourselves from the very particularities that make up our actual lives. So the issue here is when, if ever, abstract procedures such as the one Rawls suggests are of value to us.

Such procedures are rejected by pragmatists who want us to grapple with our real-life problems, not abstractions. We should work through our problems together trying to find a harmony of values or, failing that, a compromise.[60] Some feminists think what is needed is not a disinterested self but an empathetic self. Some adherents of discourse ethics and some feminists think that we ought to be trying to achieve an actual consensus, not a hypothetical consensus, on matters such as justice and equality. Discourse ethics says forget thought experiments; we need empirical discourse. What Rawls has to offer is a hypothetical consensus: what would people agree to if they did not know the ways in which they are significantly self-interested?

Rawls's view, while not based on God, nature, fact, reality, empirical discourse, or brain research, has the potential to end injustice quickly. Take pay equity as an example. Suppose that we were trying to decide if a policy of paying women less for doing the same work as men is just or fair. We do in fact follow this policy in our society today, but the question is whether or not this is a good policy; should we aspire to this way of doing things or should we dispense with it? The Rawlsian thinks that we would not agree to this policy under the veil of ignorance, and the fact that we would not agree proves the policy is unjust or unfair so let us end it now. Note that all three objections to Rawls—the pragmatist, the discourse ethicist, the scientist—have the effect of being conservative in the sense of keeping things as they are and putting off change. The pragmatist says, "Wait until we work it out"; the discourse ethicist and some feminists say, "Wait until we have an actual consensus"; and the scientist says, "Wait until someone proves this to be consistent with human nature."

REDUCTIONISM

Making ethics into science will not account for normative conclusions. In the end, choosing the good is different from knowing the facts, which is not to say that facts discovered by science are never useful in helping us determine what is good. Ecological facts translate rather easily into values, assuming we want to survive or care about future generations or both. With other scientific facts, the normative implications are not so obvious. For example, it is unclear how one gets from genetics to ethics. Wilson argues against genetic determinism, saying that genes do not "prescribe behavior in a simple one-on-one manner." Instead, there are *epigenetic rules* that direct behavior, although, for the most part, Wilson says that we do not know what these rules are. Moreover, in some instances these rules are not specific enough to give any guidance at all. Further, Wilson "concedes that moral codes are devised to conform to some drives of human nature and to suppress others."[61] If moral codes are devised for both encouraging and suppressing human nature, science or empirical methods cannot tell us which purpose is desirable.

EPIGENETIC RULES

"Epigenetic rules," Wilson says, "predispose individuals to view the world in a particular innate way and automatically to make certain choices as opposed to others."[62] If there is a biological basis of ethics, the ensuing natural laws would have to be specific enough to guide behavior. Some epigenetic rules, according to Wilson, are rigid or narrow in scope, resembling the hard instincts in animals. Rules of this type would give us the kind of specificity we are looking for. Wilson says there is at least one such rule relevant to ethics: avoid incest. However, epigenetic rules may also be broad in scope, characterized by him as "more generalized rational algorithms that function across a wide range of behavior categories."[63]

Discovering what rules there are and which rules are which is part of the work that needs to be done. Without doing this work, there will be little in the way of specific rules that are relevant to ethics. Indeed, the point of Wilson's book is to convince those in the humanities, social sciences, and arts to abandon their current separateness from the natural sciences and to do the kind of research that will be concilient with the conclusions of the natural sciences.

In art, for example, scientists have demonstrated that the brain responds optimally to a certain level of order that is achieved in various drawings, pictographs, and some abstract art including certain pieces by Piet Mondrian. Having shown that Mondrian produces art that we like, genetically speaking, Wilson looks elsewhere for epigentic rules relevant to aesthetics. He chooses "the beauty of a young woman's face." It seems that scientists who identify features thought to be attractive in female faces can exaggerate them in composites and show that "an average face is attractive, but not optimally attractive."[64] In other words, an optimally attractive face is one that few, if any, women have.

Males desiring females who do not exist is claimed by Wilson to be common in animal species. Called the *supernormal stimulus*, it is defined as the "preference . . . for signals that exaggerate the norms even if they rarely if ever occur in nature." As an example, Wilson cites the male silver-dappled butterfly that recognizes and chases female butterflies of his own species by their color and movement but does not prefer them. These male butterflies will leave females and fly toward plastic replicas that have "the biggest, brightest, and most rapidly moving wings." Wilson concludes from these experiments that "males of the silver-washed fritillary appear to have evolved to prefer the strongest expression of certain stimuli they encounter, with no upper limit."[65]

Two other examples include male anole lizards that like "photographs of other members of the same species, even though the images are the size of a small automobile," and herring gulls that prefer large painted wooden eggs to their own.[66] We do not know from Wilson's examples the sex of those in the photographs or the sex of the herring gulls. We might like to know, because this knowledge would be relevant to understanding whether the supernormal stimulus is characteristic of only males or of only heterosexual males. Of course, we might also like to know why scientists would be spending their time on such experiments in the first place!

What Wilson gets out of all this discussion is the following: "The entire beauty industry can be interpreted as the manufacture of supernormal stimuli. Eyelid shadow and mascara enlarge the eyes, lipstick fills out and brightens the lips, rouge brings a permanent blush to the cheeks, pancake makeup smoothes and reshapes the face toward the innate ideal, fingernail paint adds blood circulation to the hands, and teasing and tinting render the hair full-bodied and youthful."[67] He does not in any way criticize the beauty industry or what Sandra Bartky calls the "fashion-beauty complex" after the "military-industrial complex." Wilson takes the beauty industry to be a perfectly normal reaction to a biologically based notion of female attractiveness.

Feminists, on the other hand, do not see the beauty industry as simply an aesthetic matter. Bartky, for example, compares the subjective effects of the fashion-beauty complex to the church: "The church cultivates in its adherents very profound anxieties about the body, most particularly about bodily appetites and sexual desires. It then presents itself as the only instrument able, through expiation, to take away the very guilt and shame it has itself produced. The fashion-beauty complex refines and deepens feminine anxieties which would accompany the status of sex-object in any case; like the church, it offers itself, its procedures and institutions as uniquely able to diminish these anxieties."[68] Stubblefield uses clothing as an example of the web of femininity that women are caught in regardless of whether they resist or conform: "Unfeminine clothing may be chosen because it is more comfortable or practical. But there are costs . . . because others perceive [such a choice] as a resistance to femininity, even if that was not the intent. Women experience censure (frequently severe—being fired, beaten, raped) for appearing to resist femininity . . . as much from other women as from men. Furthermore, women who resist or appear to resist norms of femininity are held up as examples of why it is so important to conform to these norms: 'You don't want to look like that—she'll never get a date.' Their acts of nonconformity are used by others to reinforce feminine norms."[69]

Wilson's system of thought allows for critical reflection here, because social and ethical regulation rightly repress some natural desires and encourage expression of others. So why does Wilson not suggest that we downplay these unrealizable desires on the part of males? He worries that we will make ourselves into computers when we are in a position to alter our genetic structure and advises us not to stray too far from our biological heritage when the time comes that we actually have that choice. He worries that we will destroy the environment even now but does not seem to worry that we are or will become sexist.

CONCLUSION

When human beings are able to alter their genes, perhaps that will finally be the end of natural law claims. In the meantime, feminists can continue to challenge the concept of "nature" as normative or to claim nature as Bagemihl does, for different and more progressive values. The latter is Traina's intent, but I have argued that, among other things, the Thomist tradition in natural law is too inflexible at too specific a level to accomplish this task. Thirty years ago, claiming nature for feminist[70] or lesbian and gay purposes was unthinkable. When Lionel Tiger wrote *Men in Groups,* women were not heading up construction companies or serving as secretary of state.[71] As the unthinkable happens, it becomes more "natural," more acceptable. Note Cheshire Calhoun's talk about lesbians and gays as "naturally suited" for family life in Chapter 10. Years ago I argued that calling more and more things natural was not helpful and only contributed to a vague if not vacuous support for more and more values.[72] But perhaps now it is not a bad strategy, if not a good foundation for ethics.

Nature, whether defined as an immutable religious principle or a conclusion from empirical data, may always be held up to reason as either a challenge or a verification. Although I have argued that natural law as derived from Aristotelian or Thomist views has no place in contemporary ethics and that natural law theory evolving from science has yet to be more than a compilation of information, still I realize that the very persistence of bolstering one's values by claiming they are natural argues for its attraction. However, the tradition of rights in ethical theory has given autonomy and independence to those who have been oppressed by natural law claims; that alone makes rights a better alternative for ethics than natural law.

Notes

INTRODUCTION

1. Aristotle, *Physics,* 205a10, 230b25, trans. R. P. Hardie and R. K. Gaye, in *The Basic Works of Aristotle,* ed. Richard McKeon (New York: Random House, 1941).

2. Richard D. Mohr, *Gays/Justice: A Study of Ethics, Society, and Law* (New York: Columbia University Press, 1988), 34.

3. The journal *Social Philosophy and Policy,* for example, will devote a whole issue to "Natural Law and Modern Moral Philosophy" 18 (2001).

CHAPTER 1. NATURAL LAW LANGUAGE AND WOMEN

1. *Bradwell v. The State,* 83 U.S. 130, 141 (1872).

2. *Encyclical Letter of Pope Pius XI on Christian Marriage* (Boston: St. Paul Editions, n.d.), 32; emphasis added.

3. Etienne Gilson, *The Christian Philosophy of Saint Thomas Aquinas,* trans. L. K. Shook (New York: Random House, 1956), 298.

4. George Will, "How Can Women Be Happier? Marry Young and Have Youngsters Pronto," *Raleigh (NC) News and Observer,* 5 February 1999.

5. Ibid.

6. Oriana Fallaci, "An Interview with Mary Hemingway," *Look,* 6 September 1966, 66.

7. Bruce Bagemihl, *Biological Exuberance: Animal Homosexuality and Natural Diversity* (New York: St. Martin's Press, 1999), 23–26.

8. Ibid.

9. Aristotle, *The Politics,* 1254b5, trans. T. A. Sinclair (Baltimore: Penguin Books, 1962).

10. Aristotle, *The Politics,* 1260a13, trans. T. A. Sinclair.

11. Aristotle, *Politics,* 1260a13, trans. Benjamin Jowett, in *The Basic Works of Aristotle,* ed. Richard McKeon (New York: Random House, 1941).

12. Plato, *Republic,* 455d, trans. Allan Bloom (New York: Basic Books, 1968). A full discussion of Plato's argument appears in the next chapter.

13. Aristotle, *The Politics,* 1254b14, trans. T. A. Sinclair.

14. Aristotle, *Politics,* 1260a21–24, trans. Benjamin Jowett.

15. Aristotle, *The Politics,* 1260a30, trans. T. A. Sinclair.

16. Alisdair MacIntyre gives a similar account of some of Aristotle's virtues in his book, *A Short History of Ethics* (New York: Macmillan, 1966), 78–79. More recently, MacIntyre has viewed the Aristotelian legacy in a more flattering light.

17. Lon Fuller, *The Morality of Law* (New Haven: Yale University Press, 1964).

18. Amartya Sen, "Gender Inequality and Theories of Justice," *Women, Culture, and Development,* ed. Martha Nussbaum and Jonathan Glover (Oxford: Clarendon Press, 1995), 270.

19. Ibid., 262.

20. Morton Hunt, "Up Against the Wall, Male Chauvinist Pig," *Playboy,* May 1970, 209.

21. Michael Moore, "Why Doesn't GM Sell Crack?" chap. 34 of *Downsize This!* (New York: Crown Publishers, 1996), 282–287.

22. Hunt, "Up Against the Wall," 207.

23. Fallaci, "Interview with Mary Hemingway," 66.

24. Aristotle, *The Politics,* 1253b38.

25. Hunt, "Up Against the Wall," 209.

26. Barbara Ehrenreich, "Who Needs Men? Addressing the Prospect of a Matrilinear Millennium, A Forum with Barbara Ehrenreich and Lionel Tiger," *Harper's,* June 1999, 41.

27. Hunt, "Up Against the Wall," 209.

28. Sigmund Freud, "The Unconscious," in *New Introductory Lectures on Psycho-Analysis,* trans. and ed. James Strachey (1933), reprinted in E. Kuykendall, ed., *Philosophy in an Age of Crisis* (New York: Harper and Row, 1970), 122.

CHAPTER 2. EROS AND EPISTEMOLOGY

1. Some of the ideas in this chapter were developed in correspondence with Ellen Shapiro in the late 1970s. In particular, the line of argument pursued on pages 23–25 was first suggested to me by her in "The Epistemological Significance of Homosexuality in Plato (*Symposium* and *Phaedrus*)" (Trinity College, 1977).

2. Natalie Harris Bluestone, *Women and the Ideal Society: Plato's Republic and Modern Myths of Gender* (Amherst: University of Massachusetts Press, 1987).

3. Summaries and examples of Bluestone's types are taken from her text, 23–73, and my "Equality: *Republic* V," *Monist* 57, no.1 (1973).

4. Ernest Barker, *The Political Thought of Plato and Aristotle* (1906; reprint, New York: Russell and Russell, 1959); reprinted as "Communism in Plato's *Republic,*" in *Plato's Republic, Interpretation and Criticism,* ed. Alexander Sesonske (Belmont, CA: Wadsworth Publishing, 1968), 88.

5. Richard Nettleship, *Lectures on the Republic of Plato* (London: Macmillan, 1967), 173.

6. Plato, *The Republic,* 455d, trans. Allan Bloom (New York: Basic Books, 1968).

7. Stephen Halliwell, author of a recent (and the first separate) commentary in English on Book V of *The Republic,* objects to "talk of women's (equal) opportunities" (*Plato: Republic 5* [Warminster, England: Aris and Phillips, 1993], 33). The word "equal" is not the problem. Halliwell says it is "true" and "important" that Plato's "proposal for female Guardians does represent a case for the equal treatment of women with men" (14). He also finds the term "role-equality" ("employing women alongside men in all activities") an acceptable representation (15). But, he says, "it is quite misplaced to speak of 'opportunities' or 'freedom of action' for women in this context" (14). He explains that "the term 'opportunity' has become inescapably linked with liberal ideals and policies" (33). Halliwell rightly objects to portraying Plato as a "proponent of the rights or freedoms of women"(14). Since Plato does not think anyone has rights or individual freedoms, this statement seems especially misleading, although Gregory Vlastos, a well-respected Plato scholar, characterizes female philosophers in Book V as having equality of rights; see "Was Plato a Feminist?" *Times Literary Supplement,* 17–23 March 1989. Even Halliwell admits that there may be some superficial plausibility in saying that women of the ruling class have the same rights as their male counterparts (14), but he will not allow even superficial plausibility for the term "opportunity." This refusal seems puzzling given that the objection to "opportunity" is its association with the concept of liberty. Of course, people today do associate opportunity with liberty, but it is also associated with an opening and having a chance at something important. In Plato's *Republic,* women would get an equal chance along with men to be considered for the role of guardian on the basis of their talents or merits. The fact that Plato was motivated by the desire for a well-run state instead of the fulfillment of the satisfactions of individuals shows his rejection of freedom of role choice, but it does not rule out the notion of an opportunity. Plato's real interest is in the meritocracy, but an opportunity given in order to not waste talent is still an opportunity.

8. Plato, *The Republic,* trans. Allan Bloom, with notes and interpretive essay by Allan Bloom (New York: Basic Books, 1968), 383.

9. Jean Bethke Elshtain, *Public Man, Private Woman: Women in Social and Political Thought* (Princeton: Princeton University Press, 1981), 27.

10. Bluestone, *Women and the Ideal Society,* 140, 141.

11. Michael Ruse, *Homosexuality* (Oxford: Basil Blackwell, 1988), 181.

12. Bluestone, 141, 144, 146.

13. *Symposium,* 211C, trans. Alexander Nehamas and Paul Woodruff (Indianapolis: Hackett Publishing, 1989).

14. Susan Moller Okin, *Women in Western Political Thought* (Princeton: Princeton University Press, 1979), 25.

15. Ibid.

16. Bluestone, *Women and the Ideal Society,* 142.

17. Okin, *Women in Western Political Thought,* 25.

18. This is Shapiro's argument referred to in my introductory note. I am also indebted to her for pointing out the similarities between Plato and Simone de Beauvoir and the suggestiveness of Bertrand Russell's terminology for determining what Plato is getting at.

19. Bertrand Russell, *The Problems of Philosophy* (New York: Oxford University Press, 1959), 46, 47.

20. Gregory Vlastos, "The Individual As an Object of Love in Plato," *Platonic Studies* (Princeton: Princeton University Press, 1973), 24.

21. K. J. Dover, *Greek Homosexuality* (Cambridge: Harvard University Press, 1978), 164.

22. *The Symposium,* 211A, trans. Walter Hamilton (London: Penguin Books, 1951).

23. Simone de Beauvoir, *The Second Sex* (New York: Bantam Books, 1961), 391.

24. *Phaedrus,* 255E, 256A, trans. R. Hackforth (New York: Bobbs-Merrill, 1952).

25. *Phaedrus,* 255D, trans. R. Hackforth.

26. Evelyn Fox Keller, *Reflections on Gender and Science* (New Haven: Yale University Press, 1985), 27.

27. Keller, *Reflections,* 24, quoting Dover, *Greek Homosexuality,* 162.

28. Keller, *Reflections,* 30, 31.

29. Bluestone, *Women and the Ideal Society,* 145.

30. Elizabeth V. Spelman, *Inessential Woman: Problems of Exclusion in Feminist Thought* (Boston: Beacon Press, 1988), 30.

31. Virginia Valian, "Success and Failure: Expectations and Attributions" (Hunter College, 1989).

32. L. S. Fidell, "Empirical Verification of Sex Discrimination in Hiring Practices in Psychology," in *Woman: Dependent or Independent Variable?* ed. R. K. Unger and F. L. Denmark (New York: Psychological Dimensions, 1975), 774–782.

33. Luce Irigaray, *Speculum of the Other Woman,* trans. Gillian C. Gill (Ithaca, NY: Cornell University Press, 1985), 246–247, 311, 352.

34. Ibid., 317, 339.

35. Laura S. Brown, "New Voices and Visions: Toward a Lesbian/Gay Paradigm for Psychology," presidential address, American Psychological Association, Atlanta, August 1988.

CHAPTER 3. NATURAL LAW AND MORAL RIGHTS

1. Alan Donagan, *The Theory of Morality* (Chicago: University of Chicago Press, 1977).

2. Ibid., 66, 75.

3. Immanuel Kant, *The Foundations of the Metaphysics of Morals,* trans. Lewis White Beck (New York: Bobbs-Merrill, 1959), 41.

4. Donagan, *Theory of Morality,* 80.

5. Kant, *Foundations,* 40.

6. Immanuel Kant, *The Critique of Judgement,* trans. James Creed Meredith (Oxford: Clarendon Press, 1980).

7. Views on the end of the vegetable and animal kingdoms and "man" as the ultimate end are found in "The Critique of Teleological Judgement," in Kant, *Critique of Judgement,* 88, 92. Views on the nature of woman are found in Kant's "Observations on the Feeling of the Beautiful and the Sublime," trans. John T. Goldthwait, in *History of Ideas on Woman: A Source Book,* ed. Rosemary Agonito (New York: Putnam's Sons, 1977), 133. See also idem, "The Philosophy of Law: An Exposition of the Fundamental Principles of Jurisprudence as the Science of the Right," trans. W. Hastie (T. and T. Clark, 1887), in *Woman in Western Thought,* ed. Martha Lee Osborne (New York: Random House, 1979), 161–163.

8. Immanuel Kant, *Lectures on Ethics,* trans. Louis Infield (Indianapolis: Hackett Publishing, 1979), 240.

9. Plato, *The Republic,* 455d, trans. Allan Bloom (New York: Basic Books, 1968).

10. Mary Anne Warren puts the point this way in "The Abortion Issue," *Health Care Ethics,* ed. Donald VanDeVeer and Tom Regan (Philadelphia: Temple University Press, 1986).

11. Donagan, *Theory of Morality,* 83, 167.

12. Ibid., 169.

13. Etienne Gilson, *The Christian Philosophy of St. Thomas Aquinas,* trans. L. K. Shook (New York: Random House, 1956), 298.

14. Donagan, *Theory of Morality,* 28.

15. Ibid., 170.

16. Alan Donagan, "Natural Law and Moral Rights: Comments on a Paper by Christine Pierce," delivered at a meeting of the American Philosphical Association, Western Division, Columbus, Ohio, April 1982.

CHAPTER 4. HOLES AND SLIME: SEXISM IN SARTRE'S PSYCHOANALYSIS

1. Jean-Paul Sartre, *Being and Nothingness,* trans. Hazel Barnes (New York: Washington Square Press, 1966), 636. Barnes points out that the pronouns referring to the For-itself (in French, "il") can be read indifferently as "he" or "it" (677).

2. Ibid., 766.

3. Simone de Beauvoir suggests that even such qualities as vitality and sensitivity are not "ready-made" parts of our nature, but are ways of casting ourselves into the world, a matter of generosity. See *The Ethics of Ambiguity,* trans. Bernard Frechtman (New York: Citadel Press, 1967), 41–42.

4. William Barrett, *Irrational Man* (Garden City, NY: Doubleday Anchor Books, 1962), 258.

5. Ibid., 254, 258.

6. Ibid., 254–258.

7. Ibid., 261.

8. Ibid., 260.

9. Jean-Paul Sartre, *Nausea,* trans. Lloyd Alexander (New York: New Directions Publishing, 1964), 76.

10. Ibid., 128.

11. Jean-Paul Sartre, *The Age of Reason,* trans. Eric Sutton (New York: Bantam Books, 1959), 14.

12. Although there is a semantic difference between female and feminine as terms referring, respectively, to physical and cultural concepts, sexual anatomy, and sexual role, there is no evidence, linguistic or otherwise, that Sartre employs or implies such a distinction. He consistently uses the word *feminin,* which translates interchangeably as female or feminine. Thus, females may or may not possess feminine characteristics, and insofar as one discourages "feminine" behavior in females (or males), one may be antifeminine without being antifemale or sexist. To escape a charge of sexism, one needs to make such a differentiation, and Sartre does not do so.

13. Sartre, *Being and Nothingness,* 746–747.

14. Ibid., 747.

15. Ibid., 752.

16. Ibid.
17. Ibid.
18. Ibid., 751.
19. Jean-Paul Sartre, *No Exit,* trans. Stuart Gilbert (New York: Vintage Books, 1969), 42.
20. Ibid., 45.
21. Sartre, *Nausea,* 59.
22. Ibid.
23. Maurice Cranston, *Sartre* (London: Oliver and Boyd, 1962), 78.
24. Barrett, *Irrational Man,* 253.
25. Jean-Paul Sartre, *Troubled Sleep,* trans. Gerard Hopkins (New York: Vintage Books, 1973), 73.
26. Jean-Paul Sartre, *The Reprieve,* trans. Eric Sutton (New York: Vintage Books, 1973), 27, 109, 410.
27. Sartre, *Troubled Sleep,* 213, 215.
28. Sartre, *The Age of Reason,* 29.
29. Ibid., 38.
30. Ibid., 73–74.
31. Sartre, *The Reprieve,* 43.
32. Sartre, *Troubled Sleep,* 104.
33. Iris Murdoch, *Sartre* (London: Collins Press, 1953), 98.

CHAPTER 5. AIDS AND *BOWERS V. HARDWICK*

1. *Bowers v. Hardwick,* 478 U.S. 186 (1986).
2. Note, "The Constitutional Rights of AIDS Carriers," *Harvard Law Review* 99 (1986): 1274.
3. Richard Goldstein, "A Plague on All Our Houses," *Village Voice,* Literary Supplement, September 1986, 17.
4. Barbara Herbert, quoted in "Lesbian/Gay Health Conference," *Off Our Backs,* May 1986, 3.
5. L. H. Calabrese and K. V. Gopalakrishna, "Transmission of HTLV-III Infection from Man to Woman to Man," *New England Journal of Medicine* 314, no.15 (1986): 987.
6. John Langone, "AIDS," *Discover,* December 1985, 40–41.
7. Some prefer the term "alternative insemination" for the obvious and good reason that "artificial" is in opposition to "natural."
8. Lawrence K. Altman, "AIDS May Be Spread Outside of Bloodstream," *New York Times,* 14 December 1986.
9. David Black, *The Plague Years: A Chronicle of AIDS, The Epidemic of Our Times* (New York: Simon and Schuster, 1986), 99.
10. Ibid., 97.
11. Goldstein, "A Plague on All Our Houses," 17.
12. Ibid.
13. Gabriel Rotello, *Sexual Ecology: AIDS and the Destiny of Gay Men* (New York: Plume, 1998), 75.
14. Ibid.

15. Ibid., 15.
16. Ibid., 75.
17. Ibid., 46.
18. Ibid., 47.
19. Ibid., 89.
20. Ibid., 219.
21. Ibid., 212.
22. Ibid., 213.
23. "World Scientists' Warning to Humanity," reprinted in *The Environmental Ethics and Policy Book,* 2d ed., ed. Donald VanDeVeer and Christine Pierce, (Belmont, CA: Wadsworth Publishing, 1998), xxiii.
24. Ibid., xxv.
25. *Raleigh (NC) News and Observer,* 1 July 1999.
26. John M. Klink, speech to the organization Women Affirming Life, 24 September 1994, reprinted in *The Holy See and the International Conference on Population and Development, Cairo, Egypt, 5–13 September 1994* (New York: Permanent Observer Mission of the Holy See to the United Nations, n.d.), 197. Klink mentions in the same address that he is pleased with some revisions of wording that made specific reference to "husband and wife," thus "effectively sidelining the desire on the part of certain parties to make the language as ambiguous as possible so as to allow for same-sex marriages" (198).
27. *Raleigh (NC) News and Observer,* 13 August 1999.
28. Rotello, *Sexual Ecology,* 260.
29. "World Scientists' Warning to Humanity," xxiv.
30. Edward O. Wilson, *Consilience: The Unity of Knowledge* (New York: Alfred A. Knopf, 1998), 278.
31. The facts surrounding Hardwick's arrest are found in an interview with him in the *Advocate,* 2 September 1986, 38–41,110; see also Donahue transcript no. 07116 (Cincinnati: Multimedia Entertainment, 1986).
32. Charged with heterosexual rape and forcible sodomy of his seventeen-year-old-niece, Anthony Powell was found not guilty. However, in his defense, he admitted to consensual oral sex with her. Given Georgia's sodomy law, he was convicted on this charge, but the conviction was overturned when Georgia voided that law. Although it took a heterosexual case to put an end to Georgia's sodomy law, the court struck down the statute in its entirety, "declaring that private, consensual sex between adults, gay or non-gay, cannot be criminalized" ("'Sodomy Law' Reform," *Lambda Update,* Winter 1999, 19). See also Kevin Sack, "Georgia's High Court Voids Sodomy Law," *New York Times,* 24 November 1998.
33. *Romer v. Evans,* 517 U.S. 620 (1996).
34. The wording here relies heavily on the *New York Times* account; see Linda Greenhouse, "Gay Rights Laws Can't Be Banned, High Court Rules," 21 May 1996.
35. 517 U.S. 620, 632 (1996).
36. 517 U. S. 620, 635 (1996).
37. David A. J. Richards, *Women, Gays, and the Constitution: The Grounds for Feminism and Gay Rights in Culture and Law* (Chicago: University of Chicago Press, 1998), 444.
38. Ibid., 414.
39. Joel Feinberg, *Offense to Others* (New York: Oxford University Press, 1985), xiii.
40. Ronald Dworkin, "Lord Devlin and the Enforcement of Morals," in *Morality and the Law,* ed. Richard Wasserstrom (Belmont, CA: Wadsworth Publishing, 1971), 63.

41. 478 U.S. 186, 193, 194 (1986). By "today" the Court means 1986. In 1999, "bans on private consensual oral and anal sex still exist in 18 states" ("Lambda Helps End Sex Ban in Georgia," *Lambda Update,* Winter 1999, 7).

42. 478 U.S. 186, 196 (1986).

43. *Loving v. Virginia,* 388 U.S. 1, 3 (1967).

44. 388 U.S. 1 (1967).

45. 388 U.S. 1, 3 (1967).

46. 478 U.S. 186, 196 (1986).

47. "Sex Busters," *Time,* 21 July 1986, 22. See also "Poll Shows Americans Disapprove of Ruling," *Advocate,* 5 August 1986, 11.

48. In his dissenting opinion, Justice John Stevens comments, "Interestingly, miscegenation was once treated as a crime similar to sodomy" (478 U.S. 186, 216 [1986]).

49. Petitioner's brief, 20.

50. See Chapter 2.

51. Petitioner's brief, 37–38.

52. See also the discussion of Plato's views on homosexuality in the *Laws* in Martha Nussbaum, "Platonic Love and Colorado Law," in *Sex and Social Justice* (New York: Oxford University Press, 1999).

53. David A. J. Richards, *Sex, Drugs, Death, and the Law: An Essay on Human Rights and Overcriminalization* (Totowa, NJ: Rowman and Littlefield, 1982), 31.

54. Ibid., 52.

55. Ibid., 55.

56. Immanuel Kant, *Lectures on Ethics,* trans. Louis Infield (Indianapolis: Hackett Publishing), 170.

57. 478 U.S. 186, 206 (1986).

58. The following sketch of the constitutional status of privacy serves only the limited functions of explaining why Justice Blackmun and others thought the Court in earlier cases was developing a right to sexual autonomy and of providing some background for the ensuing critical discussion of Dworkin.

59. 381 U.S. 479 (1965).

60. 405 U.S. 438 (1972).

61. 410 U.S. 113 (1973).

62. 394 U.S. 557 (1969).

63. 394 U.S. 557, 565 (1969).

64. 478 U.S. 186, 191 (1986).

65. Nan D. Hunter, "Banned in the U.S.A.: What the Sodomy Ruling Will Mean," *Village Voice,* 22 July 1986, 15–16.

66. 478 U.S. 186, 199 (1986).

67. "Sex Busters," 21; "Women Ask Judge to Block Ala. Law on Sex Toys," *Raleigh (NC) News and Observer,* 18 February 1999.

68. Dworkin, "Lord Devlin and the Enforcement of Morals," 64.

69. Joel Feinberg, "'Harmless Immoralities' and Other Offensive Nuisances," *Rights, Justice and the Bonds of Liberty* (Princeton: Princeton University Press, 1980), 83.

70. Michael Ruse, *Homosexuality: A Philosophical Inquiry* (New York: Basil Blackwell, 1988), 188–192. See also the discussion of Bruce Bagemihl's book on animal homosexuality in Chapter 11.

71. Brief of Amici Curiae, American Psychological Association and American Public Health Association in Support of Respondents, 22, 27.

72. Ibid., 24–27. The following footnote in the brief explains the associations' claim that the transmissability of the AIDS virus from women to men is an area where falsification of information may have occurred: "A study of military personnel done at Walter Reed Army Medical Center shows a much higher incidence of female-to-male transmission of HTLV-III/LAV virus than most other United States reports. The question of the incidence of female-to-male transmission is an important area of current inquiry. It is possible that the other reports show an artificially low incidence of such transmission. But another explanation for the disparity is that the military personnel in the Walter Reed study were reluctant to admit to homosexual activity or intravenous drug use, either of which could lead to discharge."

73. Dale Van Atta, "Faint Light, Dark Point: Roy Cohn, AIDS, and the Question of Privacy," *Harper's*, November 1986, 56–57.

74. "Married Prisoners Will Get Condoms," *Auburn (NY) Citizen*, 23 December 1986.

75. Archbishop Renato R. Martino, interview given to Vatican Radio, 16 September 1994, reprinted in *The Holy See and the International Conference on Population and Development*, 197.

76. *Boston Gay Community News*, "Condom Ads Make TV," 1–7 February 1987.

77. Ellen Goodman, "Equal Opportunity Offender," *Raleigh (NC) News and Observer*, 17 August 1999. As Levitt puts it, "I think children have better outcomes when mothers want them and have the resources and inclination to have them."

78. Hardwick has since died of AIDS. Bowers (the decision and the man) has caused a great deal of trouble for lesbians and gay men. For example, on the grounds that she was in violation of the state's (then) sodomy law, Attorney General Michael Bowers terminated an offer of employment to attorney Robin Shahar when he learned that she was preparing for a Jewish marriage ceremony with another woman, this despite his own subsequent admission to commiting adultery, which was at the time—and still is—illegal in Georgia.

79. See Joseph W. Hovermill, "A Conflict of Law and Morals: The Choice of Law Implications of Hawaii's Recognition of Same-Sex Marriages," *Maryland Law Review* 53 (1994): 450–493. The arguments from definition, however, have lost some of their thunder in the courts. See the discussion of *Baehr v. Lewin* in Chapter 10.

80. John Finnis, "Law, Morality, and 'Sexual Orientation,'" in *Symposium on Sexual Orientation, Notre Dame Journal of Law, Ethics and Public Policy* 9, no. 1 (1995): 30.

81. Richard F. Duncan, "Homosexual Marriage and the Myth of Tolerance: Is Cardinal O'Connor a 'Homophobe?'" *Notre Dame Journal of Law, Ethics and Public Policy* 10, no. 2 (1996): 595.

82. Richards, *Women, Gays, and the Constitution*, 444.

83. See Paul J. Weithman, "A Propos of Professor Perry: A Plea for Philosophy in Sexual Ethics," *Notre Dame Journal of Law, Ethics and Public Policy* 9, no. 1 (1995), and idem, "Natural Law, Morality, and Sexual Complementarity," in *Sex, Preference, and Family: Essays on Law and Nature*, ed. David M. Estlund and Martha C. Nussbaum (New York: Oxford University Press, 1997).

84. Weithman, "A Propos of Professor Perry," 79.

85. Ibid.

86. Nothing changes here when Finnis adds the good of friendship, because the good of friendship is inseparable from the good of procreation.

87. Richards, *Women, Gays, and the Constitution*, 444–445.

88. *Baker v. State*, 744 A.2d 864 (Vt. 1999).

89. Ibid., 882.

90. Ibid.

91. Ibid.

92. Ibid., 881.

93. *Baker* cannot go on to the Supreme Court because it was decided on the basis of a common benefits clause in the Vermont Constitution that has no counterpart in the U.S. Constitution. For more details, see Chapter 10.

94. Richards, *Women, Gays, and the Constitution,* 456.

95. See Cheshire Calhoun, "Family's Outlaws: Rethinking the Connections between Feminism, Lesbianism, and the Family," in *Feminism and Families,* ed. Hilde Lindemann Nelson (New York: Routledge, 1997).

96. Ruth E. Harlow, "How Far Can *Romer* Reach?" Lambda Legal Defense and Education Fund, 1 February 1997, *http://www.lambdalegal.org.*

CHAPTER 6. RIGHTS AND RESPONSIBILITIES

1. Susan Bordo, "Feminism, Postmodernism, and Gender-Scepticism," in *Feminism/Postmodernism,* ed. Linda J. Nicholson (New York: Routledge, 1990), 137.

2. Carol Gilligan, *In a Different Voice: Psychological Theory and Women's Development* (Cambridge: Harvard University Press, 1982).

3. I tell this story and the experience as I remember it from the Women and Moral Theory Conference at the State University of New York at Stony Brook, 22–24 March 1985. Diana Tietjens Meyers refers to the fable as one about the moles and the porcupine. This discrepancy suggests that my memory of a monogamous relationship is incorrect, but fortunately the difference has no bearing on the points about rights and care. See "The Socialized Individual and Individual Autonomy," in *Women and Moral Theory,* ed. Eva Feder Kittay and Diana Tietjens Meyers (Totowa, NJ: Rowman and Littlefield, 1987), 148.

4. Samantha Brennan made this point about rights but in a different context. She says that character may explain those people who make an annoyance of themselves by claiming too many rights as well as those who claim too few. See "Feminist Rights Theories: Assessing the Reconstruction of Rights as Relational," paper presented at the Feminist Ethics Revisited Conference, Tampa, Florida, 1–3 October 1999.

5. Sara Ann Ketchum, "Liberalism and Marriage Law," in *Feminism and Philosophy,* ed. Mary Vetterling-Braggin, Jane English, and Frederick Elliston (Totowa, NJ: Littlefield, Adams, 1977), 274.

6. *Ritter v. Ritter,* 31 Pa. 396, 398 (1858); quoted in Ketchum, "Liberalism and Marriage Law," 274.

7. Ketchum, "Liberalism and Marriage Law," 274.

8. John Ladd, "Legalism and Medical Ethics," *Journal of Medicine and Philosophy* 4 (1979): 75.

9. John Ladd, "Legalism and Medical Ethics," in *Contemporary Issues in Biomedical Ethics,* ed. J. W. Davis, C. B. Hoffmaster, and S. Shorten (New York: Humana Press, 1978), 34, holds that there is a right to informed consent, but the existence of such a right is not what is at issue here, only the appropriateness of asserting it.

10. Dana Hawkins, "Risky Recycling," *U.S. News and World Report,* 20 September 1999.

11. Ibid., 62, 63.

12. Ibid., 63, 67.

13. See Diana Tietjens Meyers, ed., *Feminists Rethink the Self* (Boulder, CO: Westview Press, 1997), and Uma Narayan, *Dislocating Cultures: Identities, Traditions, and Third-World Feminism* (New York: Routledge, 1997). See also a review of these two books by Marianne Janack, "Struggling for Common Ground: Identity Politics and the Challenge to Feminist Politics," *Social Theory and Practice* 25, no. 2 (1999): 325–335.

14. Brennan, "Feminist Rights Theories."

15. Eva Feder Kittay, in discussion, Feminist Ethics Revisited Conference. See also her book *Love's Labor: Essays on Women, Equality, and Dependency* (New York: Routledge, 1998).

16. Ladd, "Legalism" (1979), 76.

17. Aristotle, *Nicomachean Ethics,* 1156b 7–8, trans. W. D. Ross, in *The Basic Works of Aristotle,* ed. Richard McKeon (New York: Random House, 1941).

18. Aristotle, *Nicomachean Ethics,* 1158b 13–15, trans. W. D. Ross.

19. Aristotle, *Nicomachean Ethics,* 1161a 19–20, trans. W. D. Ross.

20. Ladd, "Legalism" (1979), 79. Aristotle maintained that when there are great discrepancies of wisdom (or virtue or wealth, and so on) between people, those people do not even expect to be friends; see *Nicomachean Ethics,* 1158b 33–1159a 2.

21. "Attempts to vindicate rights as the basic category for moral decision-making, e.g., medical decision-making, are bound to fail because they abstract the concept of rights from the context in which it is designed to function, namely, the context of politics, law, institutions, and public life in general. To take rights as providing general guidelines for conduct outside of these contexts leads, as I have suggested, to irresponsible behavior" (Ladd, "Legalism and Medical Ethics" [1978], 33, 34).

22. Ibid., 11; emphasis added.

23. Ladd, "Legalism" (1979), 78.

24. Ibid.

25. Ibid., 76.

CHAPTER 7. POSTMODERNISM AND OTHER SKEPTICISMS

1. A brief description of postmodern philosophy follows: "Within the last decade, there have emerged . . . radical arguments against claims of objectivity in the academy which have been tied to broad analyses of the limitations of modern Western scholarship. The proponents of such analyses, linked under the label of 'postmodernists,' have argued that the academy's ideal of 'a God's eye view' must be situated within the context of modernity, a period whose organizing principles they claim are on the decline. The postmodernist critique of modernity is wideranging; it focuses on such diverse elements as the modern sense of the self and subjectivity, the idea of history as linear and evolutionary, and the modernist separation of art and mass culture. I will focus, for the moment, on the postmodernist critique of the idea of a transcendent reason.

"Postmodernists have gone beyond earlier historicist claims about the inevitable 'situatedness' of human thought within culture to focus on the very criteria by which claims to knowledge are legitimized. The traditional historicist claim that all inquiry is inevitably influenced by the values of the inquirer provides a very weak counter to the norm of objectivity. The response can be made that while values and culture might affect the choice of questions the scholar brings to her or his inquiry, they cannot affect the truth or falsity of the answers the scholar gives to such questions. This is because the criteria which determine the truth or falsity of such answers are themselves independent of the specific perspective of the inquirer. But the more radical move in the postmodern turn was to claim that the very criteria demarcating the true and the false, as well as such related distinctions as science and myth or fact and superstition, were internal to the traditions of modernity and could not be legitimized outside of these traditions. . . . Therefore, the postmodern critique has come to focus on philosophy and the very idea of a possible theory of knowledge, justice, or beauty" (Linda J. Nicholson, introduction, *Feminism/Postmodernism* [New York: Routledge, 1990], 3–4).

2. Jane Flax, "Postmodernism and Gender Relations in Feminist Theory," *Signs: Journal of Women in Culture and Society* 12, no. 4 (1987): 633.

3. Ibid., 625.

4. Ibid.

5. Robert Paul Wolff, "Social Philosophy: The Agenda for the Nineties," *Journal of Social Philosophy* 20, nos. 1, 2 (1989): 5, makes a similar point about limitations on advances in knowledge, but his remarks are not directed at postmodernists.

6. Jane Flax, "Beyond Equality: Gender, Justice, and Difference," lecture at Duke University, 12 February 1990.

7. Although there are many feminist criticisms of John Rawls in many different areas of his work, it is still possible that some feminists may see some value in his thought experiment. See Chapter 11 for further discussion of this possibility.

8. Susan Bordo, "Feminism, Postmodernism, and Gender-Scepticism," in *Feminism/Postmodernism,* ed. Linda J. Nicholson (New York: Routledge, 1990), 139.

9. Joan C. Tronto, "Beyond Gender Difference to a Theory of Care," *Signs: Journal of Women in Culture and Society* 12, no. 4 (1987): 649.

10. See Bordo, "Feminism, Postmodernism, and Gender-Scepticism," 135.

11. Aristotle, *Metaphysics,* 1010a 12–13 and 1010a 1–15, trans. W. D. Ross, in *The Basic Works of Aristotle,* ed. Richard McKeon (New York: Random House, 1941).

12. Teresa de Lauretis, *Technologies of Gender: Essays on Theory, Film, and Fiction* (Bloomington: Indiana University Press, 1987), 9–10. See also Denise Riley's discussion of the problem in "Am I That Name?" *Feminism and the Category of "Woman" in History* (Minneapolis: University of Minnesota Press, 1988), chaps. 1 and 5.

13. Carol Gilligan, keynote speaker, Women and Moral Theory Conference, State University of New York at Stony Brook, 22–24 March 1985.

14. Bordo, "Feminism, Postmodernism, and Gender-Scepticism," 139.

15. Flax, "Beyond Equality," 1–3.

16. Ibid., 3–4.

17. Richard Wasserstrom, "The University and the Case for Preferential Treatment," *American Philosophical Quarterly* 13, no. 2 (1976): 165–170.

18. Andrea Nye, *Feminist Theory and the Philosophies of Man* (New York: Routledge, 1989), 194–195.

19. Sarah Lucia Hoagland, *Lesbian Ethics: Toward New Value* (Palo Alto, CA: Institute of Lesbian Studies, 1988), 257.

20. Alisa Solomon, "Sins of Omission: Is the Church Undermining Public Health?" *Village Voice,* 20 February 1990, 28.

21. The stated principle, I think, is not what is in fact motivating Catholic policy-makers. My point here is about what principle would justify the reasoning if it were true rather than about what principle is motivating them.

22. Hoagland, *Lesbian Ethics,* 10.

23. Ibid., 11.

24. "State Amendment Allows Hawaiian Court to Close Its Doors on Gay Marriages," *Raleigh (NC) News and Observer,* 11 December 1999. For more details concerning the Hawaii Supreme Court case, see Chapter 10.

25. Matthew Daniels, "Rule of Law," *Wall Street Journal,* 14 June 1999.

26. Joel Feinberg, *Offense to Others* (New York: Oxford University Press, 1985), 25–26.

27. Ibid., 43.

28. Ibid., 27–29.

29. *Paradise Lost* (IV, 296–299) in *John Milton's Complete Poems and Major Prose,* ed. Merritt Y. Hughes (New York: Odyssey, 1957), 285.

30. Charlene Haddock Seigfried holds this view; see "Where Are All the Pragmatist Feminists?" *Hypatia* 6, no. 2 (1991): 1–20, and idem, "The Missing Perspective: Feminist Pragmatism," *Transactions of the Charles S. Peirce Society* 27, no. 4 (1991): 405–416.

31. I take issue here with Audre Lorde's often quoted advice to feminists that "the master's tools will never dismantle the master's house." Of course, Lorde did not anticipate in her remarks a deconstructionism that would undercut assertion altogether; see *Sister/Outsider: Essays and Speeches* (Trumansburg, NY: Crossing Press, 1984), 112.

CHAPTER 8. CAN ANIMALS BE LIBERATED?

1. Peter Singer, *Animal Liberation* (New York: New York Review of Books, 1975).

2. Ibid., x.

3. Michael Tooley, "In Defense of Abortion and Infanticide," in *The Problem of Abortion,* 3d ed., ed. Susan Dwyer and Joel Feinberg (Belmont, CA: Wadsworth Publishing, 1997).

4. Tooley does not commit himself on this point. He says some animals may have a right to life.

5. Hence, Tooley's conclusion that abortion and even infanticide can be justified. In contrast, Phillip E. Devine, who has argued against Tooley, says that "the prospect of continued life is possessed as much by a foetus or an infant as by an adult" ("Abortion, Contraception, Infanticide," *Philosophy* 58, no. 226 [1983]: 517.) Note that the "prospect" of continued life does not depend on any desire or capacity. However, wildflowers also have a prospect of continued life. See my discussion of Paul Taylor and wildflowers in the postscript to this chapter. Also, what if a person's prospects at the end of life are not good, but she or he still desires to live? Devine's book, *Natural Law Ethics,* is to be published by Greenwood Press in 2000.

6. David DeGrazia, *Taking Animals Seriously: Mental Life and Moral Status* (New York: Cambridge University Press, 1996).

7. Ibid., 269. As is noted further on, a right to liberty is not needed here, according to DeGrazia, because the principle of equal consideration or even serious consideration is adequate to prohibit this sort of confinement.

8. Anthony Weston, *Toward Better Problems: New Perspectives on Abortion, Animal Rights, the Environment, and Justice* (Philadelphia: Temple University Press, 1992), 81.

9. Frans B. M. de Waal, "The Limits of Animal Rights," *Raleigh (NC) News and Observer,* 22 August 1999.

10. Ibid.

11. Singer, *Animal Liberation,* 24.

12. Ibid., 2.

13. Ibid., 2–3.

14. Gary L. Francione, *Rain Without Thunder: The Ideology of the Animal Rights Movement* (Philadelphia: Temple University Press, 1996), 57.

15. Interestingly, Gary Varner argues that scientific researchers who do animal experimentation "agree to a surprising extent" with Singer's ethical principles. "Where they disagree with Singer is at the level of policy; they see the same ethical theory implying different things in practice. . . . So the disagreement between Singer and the research establishment is largely empirical, about how likely various kinds of research are to lead to important human benefits" ("The Prospects for Consensus and Convergence in the Animal Rights Debate," the Hastings Center, reprinted in Donald VanDeVeer and Christine Pierce, *The Environmental Ethics and Policy Book,* 2d ed. [Belmont, CA: Wadsworth Publishing, 1998], 125, 126).

16. Francione, *Rain Without Thunder,* 137.

17. DeGrazia, *Taking Animals Seriously,* 47.

18. Ibid., 45.

19. Ibid., 280.

20. Ibid., 281. Of my list, only no. 2 and no. 5 "clearly depend on equal consideration" (281).

21. Ibid., 37.

22. Mihailo Marković, "Women's Liberation and Human Emancipation," *Philosophical Forum* 5 (1973–1974): 165.

23. Example from Claudia Card.

24. De Waal, "The Limits of Animal Rights." See also "Can Animals Think?" *Time,* 6 September 1999. Interestingly, the above title is given on the cover and at the beginning of the article. However, in the table of contents, the same article is entitled "What Are Animals Thinking?" indicating that we have moved beyond the "can animals think" question.

25. DeGrazia, *Taking Animals Seriously,* 265.

26. Ibid., 207, 208, 278.

27. Bertrand Russell, *Marriage and Morals* (New York: Liveright, 1957).

28. Paul Taylor, *Respect for Nature* (Princeton: Princeton University Press, 1986).

29. Kenneth E. Goodpaster, "On Being Morally Considerable," *Journal of Philosophy* 75, no. 6 (1978): 308–325.

30. Included in this category are Arne Naess, Bill Devall, and George Sessions.

31. T. L. S. Sprigge, "Some Recent Positions in Environmental Ethics Examined," *Inquiry* 34, no. 1 (1991): 117.

32. This remark is a paraphrase of a point made by Sprigge; ibid., 116.

33. Paul Taylor, "In Defense of Biocentrism," *Environmental Ethics* 5 (1983): 242; quoted in Sprigge, "Recent Positions in Environmental Ethics," 116.

34. Peter Singer, *Practical Ethics* (Cambridge: Cambridge University Press, 1979), 92.

35. See Weston, *Toward Better Problems*, 110–117.

CHAPTER 9. FEMINIST SEPARATISM

1. "22-year-old Duane Naquin—perhaps because he was a Young Republican backed by the right-wing Center for Individual Rights (CIR)—insisted on being a full member of the class and threatened to sue. . . . In a world in which right-wingers are trolling for lawsuits, potential targets have to mind their Ps and Qs" (Katha Pollitt, "No Males Need Apply?" *Nation*, 23–30 August 1999, 10).

2. Ibid. Gloria Steinem and Eleanor Smeal supported Mary Daly, so not all feminists were embarrassed.

3. Ibid.

4. Gretchen Van Ness, attorney for Mary Daly, "Exchange," *Nation*, 11 October 1999, 2.

5. Mary Janack, "Struggling for Common Ground: Identity Politics and the Challenge to Feminist Politics," *Social Theory and Practice* 25, no. 2 (1999): 325.

6. Uma Narayan, "The Scope of Our Concerns: Reflections on 'Woman' as the Subject of Feminist Politics," plenary address delivered at the Feminist Ethics Revisited Conference, Tampa, Florida, 1–3 October 1999.

7. Janack, "Struggling for Common Ground," 335.

8. *Women, Culture, and Development*, ed. Martha C. Nussbaum and Jonathan Glover (Oxford: Clarendon Press, 1995), 2.

9. Ibid., 6, 7. These observations are used by Amartya Sen and Martha Nussbaum to challenge models in economic theory that assume that heads of households (which are invariably male) are altruistic with respect to the families' interests.

10. See Marilyn Frye, *The Politics of Reality: Essays in Feminist Theory* (Trumansburg, NY: Crossing Press, 1983), 1–16, for her distinction between oppression as a set of barriers and suffering because bad things happen to folks.

11. Ibid., 16.

12. See Iris Young, *Justice and the Politics of Difference* (Princeton: Princeton University Press, 1990). See also Diana Tietjens Meyers, "Cultural Diversity: Rights, Goals, and Competing Values," in *Jewish Identity*, ed. David Theo Goldberg and Michael Krausz (Philadelphia: Temple University Press, 1993).

13. Adrienne Rich, *Of Woman Born* (New York: W. W. Norton, 1976; Bantam edition, 1977), 94.

14. Laura Flanders, quoting a Boston-area educator, "Feminist De-tenured," *Nation*, 26 July–2 August 1999, 5.

15. Both articles are published in *Philosophical Forum* 5 (1975).

16. Marković, "Women's Liberation and Human Emancipation," 165.

17. Narayan, "The Scope of Our Concerns," 12.

18. Frye, *The Politics of Reality*, 95–109.

19. Susan Moller Okin, *Justice, Gender, and the Family* (New York: Basic Books, 1989).

20. Jürgen Habermas, "Discourse Ethics: Notes on a Program of Philosophical Justification," from *Moral Consciousness and Communicative Action,* trans. Christian Lenhardt and Shierry Weber Nicholsen (Cambridge, MA: MIT Press, 1990). Alison Jaggar is writing a book on discourse ethics from a feminist point of view.

21. In discussion, Feminist Ethics Revisited Conference.

22. Frye, *The Politics of Reality,* 104.

23. Anna Stubblefield, "Beyond Pluralism and Assimilation in the Politics of Gender," in *On Feminist Ethics and Politics,* ed. Claudia Card (Lawrence: University Press of Kansas, 1999), 161.

24. Claudia Card, *Lesbian Choices* (New York: Columbia University Press, 1995), 155–156.

25. Pollitt, "No Males Need Apply," 10.

26. Stubblefield, "Beyond Pluralism and Assimilation," 165–166.

27. Virginia Held, "Marx Sex, and the Transformation of Society," *Philosophical Forum* 5 (1975): 174, 176–177, 182.

28. Stubblefield says that men living separately would "presumably look to each other for sexual satisfaction" ("Beyond Pluralism and Assimilation," 166). She does not say whether women living separately would look to other women for same.

29. Ibid., 166, 167.

30. Ibid., 168–170.

31. "Responses," *Lesbian Connection,* January/February 2000, 16, 17, 18.

32. Marilyn Frye, "The Necessity of Differences: Constructing a Positive Category of Women," *Signs: Journal of Women in Culture and Society,* 21, no. 4 (1996): 998.

33. Ibid., 998, 1002.

CHAPTER 10. GAY MARRIAGE

1. Nan D. Hunter, "Sexual Dissent and the Family," *Nation,* October 1991, 441. Nan Hunter was formerly an attorney with the American Civil Liberties Union, which has endorsed lesbian and gay marriage since 1986.

2. At the international level, registered partnerships are recognized in Denmark, Norway, Sweden, Greenland, Iceland, and the Netherlands. Such partnerships offer most of the benefits and protections of civil marriage and typically offer more benefits and protections than does domestic partnership in the United States. The Netherlands is considering legislation that would offer civil marriage to same-sex couples. See "International Recognition of Same-Sex Relationships," Lambda Legal Defense and Education Fund, 14 July 1999, *http://www.lambdalegal.org.*

3. *Baehr v. Lewin,* 852 P.2d 44 (Haw. 1993).

4. "*Baehr v. Anderson,*" Lambda Legal Defense and Education Fund, 9 December 1999, *http://www.lambdalegal.org.*

5. Evan Wolfson, "Hawaii Supreme Court Paves Way for Same-Sex Marriage," *Lambda Update*, Summer 1993, 23.

6. *Baker v. Nelson,* 291 Minn. 310 (1971); appeal dismissed, 409 U.S. 810 (1972).

7. *Singer v. Hara,* 11 Wash. App. 247 (1974).

8. Richard Mohr, *Gay Ideas, Outing, and Other Controversies* (Boston: Beacon Press, 1992), 90.

9. Andrew Sullivan, "Here Comes the Groom: A (Conservative) Case for Gay Marriage," *New Republic,* 28 August 1989, 22.

10. See, for example, Hannah Schwarzschild, "Same-Sex Marriage and Constitutional Privacy: Moral Threat and Legal Anomaly," *Berkeley Women's Law Journal* 4 (1988): 94–127.

11. Kenneth L. Karst, "Freedom of Intimate Association," *Yale Law Journal* 89 (1980): 682.

12. William N. Eskridge Jr., *The Case for Same-Sex Marriage: From Sexual Liberty to Civilized Commitment* (New York: Free Press, 1996), and Mark Strasser, *Legally Wed: Same-Sex Marriage and the Constitution* (Ithaca, NY: Cornell University Press, 1997); cited in David A. J. Richards, *Women, Gays, and the Constitution: The Grounds for Feminism and Gay Rights in Culture and Law* (Chicago: University of Chicago Press, 1998), 441.

13. Richards, *Women, Gays, and the Constitution,* 443.

14. *Baker v. State,* 744 A.2d 864 (Vt. 1999).

15. Ibid., 874.

16. Ibid.

17. Ibid., 875.

18. Ibid., 887.

19. "Preliminary Notes on the Hawaii Supreme Court's 12/9/99 Decision," Lambda Legal Defense and Education Fund, 10 December 1999, *http://www.lambdalegal.org.*

20. This point was made by attorney for the plaintiffs Beth Robinson in the opening arguments for the case.

21. *Baker v. State,* 744 A.2d 864, 898.

22. Ibid., 904. Quoting *Rosenberg v. Canada,* docket no. C22807, Ontario Court of Appeals, 23 April 1998, at 17–18 (quoting *Vriend v. Alberta,* [1988] S. C. J. No. 29 [Q. L.], at para. 122).

23. Peter Freiburg, "Some Gays Aren't Wedded to the Idea of Same-Sex Marriage," *Advocate,* 1 August 1989.

24. Anna Quindlen, "Evan's Two Moms," *New York Times,* 5 February 1992.

25. There is a variant of this protest chant that does not seek social acceptance of even things queer: "we're here, we're queer, we're fabulous, don't fuck with us."

26. Steve Bryant and Demian, eds., "The Ancient History of Same-Sex Marriage," in *An Indispensable Guide for Gay and Lesbian Couples: What Every Same-Sex Couple Should Know* (Seattle: Sweet Corn Productions, 1993), 43. This article consists of notes by Timm Peterson on a public lecture given by John Boswell; the lecture summarized ideas that are discussed more fully in Boswell's book, *Same-Sex Unions in Premodern Europe* (New York: Villard Books [Random], 1994).

27. Bryant and Demian, "The Ancient History of Same-Sex Marriage," 43.

28. Paula Ettelbrick, "Since When Is Marriage a Path to Liberation?" *Outlook*, Fall 1989, 17.

29. Ibid., 14.

30. Mary Midgley, *Animals and Why They Matter* (London: Penguin Books, 1983), 67.

31. Ettelbrick, "Since When Is Marriage," 16.

32. Despite her recognition that these practical difficulties arise from the fact that lesbian partners are legal strangers, Robson, *Lesbian (Out)Law: Survival Under the Rule of Law* (Ithaca, NY: Firebrand Books, 1992), 117, 126, 127, opposed both gay marriage and

domestic partnership, arguing instead that marriage should be abolished. Attorney Thomas Stoddard, "Why Gay People Should Seek the Right to Marry," *Outlook,* Fall 1989, 13, welcomed abolishing marriage for all couples as an alternative to extending the right to marry to lesbians and gay men but found replacement of marriage by a new legal entity unlikely.

33. Ettelbrick, "Since When Is Marriage," 14, 15, 16.

34. Ibid., 15.

35. Cheshire Calhoun, "Family's Outlaws: Rethinking the Connections between Feminism, Lesbianism, and the Family," in *Feminism and Families,* ed. Hilde Lindemann Nelson (New York: Routledge, 1997), 147.

36. Stoddard, "Why Gay People Should Seek," 13.

37. Susan Moller Okin, *Justice, Gender, and the Family* (New York: Basic Books, 1989), 135, 136.

38. Ibid., 170.

39. Martha Nussbaum, "Justice for Women!" *New York Review of Books,* 8 October 1992, 46.

40. Hunter, "Sexual Dissent and the Family," 411.

41. Cheshire Calhoun is writing a book on the thesis that heterosexist domination is a separate axis of oppression not reducible to gender domination.

42. Ruthann Robson and S. E. Valentine, "Lov(h)ers: Lesbians as Intimate Partners and Lesbian Legal Theory, *Temple Law Review* 63 (1990): 536. For further examples of arguments to the effect that gay marriage should be rejected because marriage is "het" or "patriarchal" or oppresive to women, see Freiburg, "Some Gays Aren't Wedded to the Idea," 18; Catherine Saalfield, "Lesbian Marriage . . . [K]not!" in *Sisters, Sexperts, Queers: Beyond the Lesbian Nation,* ed. Arlene Stein (New York: Penguin Books, 1993), 191; and Suzanne Sherman, ed., *Lesbian and Gay Marriage: Private Commitments, Public Ceremonies* (Philadelphia: Temple University Press, 1992), 113, 217. Robson now says that "since 1995, the general shift has been away from a feminist critique of same-sex marriage to an acceptance of marriage as a civil right" (in correspondence, August 1998).

43. Thomas Stoddard took this position.

44. See Claudia Card, *Lesbian Choices* (New York: Columbia University Press, 1995), chap. 9.

45. Ettelbrick, "Since When Is Marriage," 16.

46. Marrying for the sake of a green card is an exception here.

47. Ettelbrick, "Since When Is Marriage," 16, 17.

48. See Kath Weston, *Families We Choose: Lesbians, Gays, Kinship* (New York: Columbia University Press, 1991).

49. *Bowers v. Hardwick,* 478 U.S. 186, 191 (1986).

50. Dirk Johnson, "Colorado Ban on Gay Rights Laws Is Ruled Unconstitutional: Violation Found on Rights to Equal Protection," *New York Times,* 14 December 1993.

51. "Colorado Gay Rights Ban Ruled Unconstitutional," *Washington Post,* 15 December 1993.

52. Tamar Lewin, "Colorado Ban on Gay Rights Laws Is Ruled Unconstitutional: Gay Rights Groups See Ruling as Curb on Other States," *New York Times,* 14 December 1993.

53. Stoddard, "Why Gay People Should Seek," 12, quoting from the Supreme Court's 1965 decision to strike down an anticontraception statute.

54. Ettelbrick quoted in Freiburg, "Some Gays Aren't Wedded," 18.

CHAPTER 11. NATURAL LAW TODAY

1. Cristina L. H. Traina, *Feminist Ethics and Natural Law: The End of the Anathemas* (Washington, DC: Georgetown University Press, 1999).

2. Ibid., 320.

3. John Haas, "The Natural and the Human in Procreation," in *Gift of Life: Catholic Scholars Respond to Vatican Instruction*, ed. Edmund D. Pellegrino, John Collins Harvey, and John P. Langan (Washington, DC: Georgetown University Press, 1990), 103.

4. Traina, *Feminist Ethics and Natural Law*, 63.

5. Ibid., 158, 159, 315.

6. Ibid., 315.

7. Martha C. Nussbaum, "Human Functioning and Social Justice: In Defense of Aristotelian Essentialism," *Political Theory* 20, no. 2 (1992): 225.

8. Ibid. See also Martha C. Nussbaum, *Sex and Social Justice* (New York: Oxford University Press, 1999), 49.

9. David DeGrazia, *Taking Animals Seriously: Mental Life and Moral Status* (New York: Cambridge University Press, 1996).

10. Ibid., 216, 217.

11. Ibid., 217, 226.

12. Andrew Sullivan, "Alone Again, Naturally: The Catholic Church and the Homosexual," *New Republic*, 28 November 1994, 54.

13. DeGrazia, *Taking Animals Seriously*, 217.

14. The same can be said of the twin goods of procreation and friendship when the two are inseparable.

15. L. W. Sumner, footnote in DeGrazia, *Taking Animals Seriously*, 217.

16. Traina, *Feminist Ethics and Natural Law*, 69.

17. Lisa Sowle Cahill, "What Is the 'Nature' of the Unity of Sex, Love and Procreation? A Reply to Elio Sgreccia," *Gift of Life: Catholic Scholars Respond to Vatican Instruction*, 144, 145.

18. Ibid, 140.

19. Ibid., 143.

20. Hass, "The Natural and the Human," 112.

21. Traina, *Feminist Ethics and Natural Law*, 13, 160, 308, 311.

22. Ibid., 303, 317, 324.

23. Ibid., 321, 333.

24. Ibid., 5.

25. Ibid., 4–7.

26. Ibid., 13.

27. *Instruction on Respect for Human Life in Its Origin and on the Dignity of Procreation*, in *Gift of Life: Catholic Scholars Respond to the Vatical Instruction*, 21.

28. Nussbaum, *Sex and Social Justice*, 123–124.

29. Lisa Tessman, "Critical Virtue Ethics: Understanding Oppression as Morally Damaging," paper presented at the Feminist Ethics Revisited Conference, Tampa, Florida, 1–3 October 1999.

30. Bruce Bagemihl, *Biological Exuberance: Animal Homosexuality and Natural Diversity* (New York: St. Martin's Press, 1999).

31. Max Harrold, "Creature Comforts" *Advocate,* 16 February 1999, 61.

32. Simon LeVay, *Queer Science: The Use and Abuse of Research into Homosexuality* (Cambridge, MA: MIT Press, 1996), 209.

33. Ibid., 195.

34. James Weinrich, "Is Homosexuality Biologically Natural?" in *Homosexuality: Social, Psychological, and Biological Issues,* ed. William Paul et al. (Beverly Hills, CA: Sage Publications, 1982), 204.

35. Bagemihl, *Biological Exuberance,* 252.

36. Ibid., 253.

37. Ibid., 255.

38. John Boswell, *Christianity, Social Tolerance, and Homosexuality: Gay People in Western Europe from the Beginning of the Christian Era to the Fourteenth Century* (Chicago: University of Chicago Press, 1980), 152.

39. Ibid., 153.

40. Bagemihl, *Biological Exuberance,* 12.

41. Ibid., 15.

42. Ibid., 15, 19.

43. LeVay, *Queer Science,* 199.

44. Bagemihl, *Biological Exuberance,* 260.

45. Ibid., 23.

46. Ibid., 47.

47. Ibid., 89.

48. Lionel Tiger, *Men in Groups* (New York: Random House, 1969).

49. LeVay notes Amy Parish's claim that female bonobos bond; see *Queer Science,* 206–207.

50. Melvin Maddocks, *Christian Science Monitor,* 10 July 1969, 11.

51. Tiger, *Men in Groups,* 103, 112.

52. Barbara Ehrenreich, "Who Needs Men? Addressing the Prospect of a Matrilinear Millennium, A Forum with Barbara Ehrenreich and Lionel Tiger," *Harper's,* June 1999, 42.

53. Edward O. Wilson, *Consilience: The Unity of Knowledge* (New York: Alfred A. Knopf, 1998), 264.

54. Ibid., 12.

55. Ibid., 11, 266.

56. Ibid., 240, 255.

57. Ibid., 250.

58. Ibid., 205.

59. Ibid., 249.

60. See Anthony Weston, *Toward Better Problems: New Perspectives on Abortion, Animal Rights, the Environment, and Justice* (Philadelphia: Temple University Press, 1992).

61. Wilson, *Consilience,* 193, 251.

62. Ibid., 193.

63. Ibid., 172.

64. Ibid., 230.

65. Ibid., 231.

66. Ibid.

67. Ibid., 232.

68. Sandra Lee Bartky, *Femininity and Domination: Studies in the Phenomenology of Oppression* (New York: Routledge, 1990), 41.

69. Anna Stubblefield, "Beyond Pluralism and Assimilationism," in *On Feminist Ethics and Politics,* ed. Claudia Card (Lawrence: University Press of Kansas, 1999), 164.

70. No one took seriously Ashley Montagu's book, *The Natural Superiority of Women* (New York: Collier Books, 1952).

71. "I am proposing that 'human nature' is such that it is 'unnatural' for females to engage in defense, police, and by implication, high politics" (Tiger, *Men in Groups,* 112).

72. This was in the original Basic Books version: "Natural Law Language and Women," from *Woman in Sexist Society,* ed. Vivian Gornick and Barbara K. Moran (New York: Basic Books, 1971).

Selected Bibliography

The materials listed in this bibliography influenced my thinking on the issues discussed in this book, even though some are not specifically cited in the notes. However, some individual articles contained in special issues, symposia, and collections listed here are referenced in the notes.

Annas, Julia. "Plato's *Republic* and Feminism." *Philosophy* 51 (1976): 307–321.

Appiah, K. Anthony. "Homosexual Wedlock." *New York Review of Books* 42 (1996): 48–52, 54.

Baier, Annette. "Trust and Antitrust." *Ethics* 96 (1986): 231–260.

Baird, Robert M., and Stuart E. Rosenbaum, eds. *Same-Sex Marriage: The Moral and Legal Debate*. Amherst, NY: Prometheus Books, 1997.

Balian, Habib A. " 'Til Death Do Us Part: Granting Full Faith and Credit to Marital Status." *Southern California Law Review* 68 (1994–1995): 397–426.

Bar On, Bat-Ami, ed. *Engendering Origins: Critical Feminist Readings in Plato and Aristotle*. Albany: State University of New York Press, 1994.

Bolte, Angela. "Do Wedding Dresses Come in Lavender? The Prospects and Implications of Same-Sex Marriage." *Social Theory and Practice* 24 (1998): 111–131.

Bonsor, Jack A. "Homosexual Orientation and Anthropology: Reflections on the Category 'Objective Disorder.'" *Theological Studies* 59 (1998): 60–83.

Boonin-Vail, David. "A Defense of 'A Defense of Abortion': On the Responsibility Objection to Thomson's Argument." *Ethics* 107 (1997): 286–313.

Brownworth, Victoria A. "Tying the Knot or the Hangman's Noose: The Case Against Marriage." *Journal of Gay, Lesbian, and Bisexual Identity* 1 (1996): 91–98.

Card, Claudia. "Pluralist Lesbian Separatism." In *Lesbian Philosophies and Cultures*, edited by Jeffner Allen, 125–141. Albany: State University of New York Press, 1990.

———, ed. *Feminist Ethics*. Lawrence: University Press of Kansas, 1991.

———, ed. *On Feminist Ethics and Politics*. Lawrence: University Press of Kansas, 1999.

Clark, Lorenne M. G., and Lynda Lange, eds. *The Sexism of Social and Political Theory:*

Women and Reproduction from Plato to Nietzsche. Toronto: University of Toronto Press, 1979.

Donovan, Josephine. "Animal Rights and Feminist Theory." *Signs: Journal of Women in Culture and Society* 15 (1990): 350–375.

Duncan, Richard F. "Who Wants to Stop the Church: Homosexual Rights Legislation, Public Policy, and Religious Freedom." *Notre Dame Law Review* 69 (1994): 393–445.

Estlund, David M., and Martha C. Nussbaum, eds. *Sex, Preference, and Family: Essays on Law and Nature*. New York: Oxford University Press, 1997.

Feder, Ellen K., and Eva Feder Kittay, eds. *Special Issue: The Family and Feminist Theory. Hypatia* 11 (1996).

Finnis, John. *Natural Law and Natural Rights*. New York: Oxford University Press, 1980.

Finnis, John, and Martha Nussbaum. "Is Homosexual Conduct Wrong? A Philosophical Exchange." *New Republic* 15 November 1993, 12–13.

Francione, Gary L. *Animals, Property, and the Law*. Philadephia: Temple University Press, 1995.

Friedman, Andrew H. "Same-Sex Marriage and the Right to Privacy: Abandoning Scriptural, Canonical, and Natural Law Based Definitions of Marriage." *Howard Law Journal* 35 (1992): 173–225.

Frye, Marilyn. *Willful Virgin: Essays in Feminism*. Freedom, CA: Crossing Press, 1992.

Gaard, Greta. "Toward a Queer Ecofeminism." *Hypatia* 12 (1997): 114–137.

Garside, Christine. "Can a Woman Be Good in the Same Way As a Man?" *Dialogue* 19 (1971): 534–544.

Hardin, Russell, ed. *Symposium on Feminism and Political Theory. Ethics* 99 (1989).

Hohengarten, William M. "Same-Sex Marriage and the Right to Privacy." *Yale Law Journal* 103 (1994): 1495–1531.

Homer, Steven K. "Against Marriage." *Harvard Civil Rights–Civil Liberties Law Review* 29 (1994): 505–530.

Kamm, F. M. *Creation and Abortion: A Study in Moral and Legal Philosophy*. New York: Oxford University Press, 1992.

Kittay, Eva Feder, and Diana T. Meyers, eds. *Women and Moral Theory*. Totowa, NJ: Rowman and Littlefield, 1987.

Kymlicka, Will. "Rethinking the Family." *Philosophy and Public Affairs* 20 (1991): 77–97.

LeVay, Simon. *The Sexual Brain*. Cambridge, MA: MIT Press, 1993.

McAlister, Linda Lopez, ed. *Symposium on Sandra Lee Bartky's Femininity and Domination: Studies in the Phenomenology of Oppression. Hypatia* 8 (1993).

McNaron, Toni A. H., Gloria Anzaldúa, Lourdes Arguëlles, and Elizabeth Lapovsky Kennedy, eds. *Special Issue: Theorizing Lesbian Experience. Signs: Journal of Women in Culture and Society* 18 (1993).

Mendelsohn, Daniel. "The Stand: Expert Witnesses and Ancient Mysteries in a Colorado Courtroom." *Lingua Franca*, September/October 1996, 34–46.

Meyers, Diana Tietjens. *Inalienable Rights: A Defense*. New York: Columbia University Press, 1985.

———. *Subjection and Subjectivity: Psychoanalytic Feminism and Moral Philosophy*. New York: Routledge, 1994.

Mohr, Richard D. *A More Perfect Union: Why Straight America Must Stand Up for Gay Rights*. Boston: Beacon Press, 1994.

Nelson, Hilde Lindemann, ed. *Feminism and Families*. New York: Routledge, 1997.

Nussbaum, Martha C. "Aristotle on Human Nature and the Foundations of Ethics." In *World,*

Mind, and Ethics: Essays on the Ethical Philosophy of Bernard Williams, edited by J. E. J. Altham and Ross Harrison, 86–131. Cambridge: Cambridge University Press, 1995.
———. "Non-Relative Virtues: An Aristotelian Approach." In *Ethics: Classical Western Texts in Feminist and Multicultural Perspectives,* edited by James P. Sterba, 439–457. New York: Oxford University Press, 2000.
Okin, Susan Moller. "Philosopher Queens and Private Wives: Plato on Women and the Family." *Philosophy and Public Affairs* 6 (1977): 345–369.
———. *Women in Western Political Thought.* Princeton: Princeton University Press, 1979.
Paul, Ellen Frankel, ed. *Human Flourishing. Social Philosophy and Policy* 16 (1999).
Pettit, Philip. "The Cunning of Trust." *Ethics* 24 (1995): 202–225.
Pierce, Christine, and Donald VanDeVeer, eds. *AIDS: Ethics and Public Policy.* Belmont, CA: Wadsworth Publishing, 1988.
Plumwood, Val. *Feminism and the Mastery of Nature.* New York: Routledge, 1993.
Pomeroy, Sarah B. "Feminism in Book V of Plato's *Republic.*" *Apeiron* 8 (1974): 32–34.
Povelones, Arthur A., ed. *Symposium on Sexual Orientation. Notre Dame Journal of Law, Ethics and Public Policy* 9 (1995).
Reath, Andrews, Barbara Herman, and Christine M. Korsgaard, eds. *Reclaiming the History of Ethics: Essays for John Rawls.* Cambridge: Cambridge University Press, 1997.
Regan, Tom. "The Case for Animal Rights: A Decade's Passing." In *A Quarter Century of Value Inquiry: Presidential Addresses of the American Society for Value Inquiry,* edited by Richard T. Hull, 439–459. Atlanta: Rodopi, 1994.
Seigfried, Charlene Haddock. *Pragmatism and Feminism: Reweaving the Social Fabric.* Chicago: University of Chicago Press, 1996.
Shenkman, Ethan G., ed. *Symposium on Sexual Orientation and the Law. Virginia Law Review* 79 (1993).
Slicer, Deborah. "Your Daughter or Your Dog." *Hypatia* 6 (1991): 108–124.
Soble, Alan, ed. *Sex, Love, and Friendship: Studies of the Society for the Philosophy of Sex and Love, 1977–1992.* Atlanta: Rodopi, 1994.
Sterba, James. *Three Challenges to Ethics.* New York: Oxford University Press, 2000.
Sullivan, Andrew. *Virtually Normal: An Argument About Homosexuality.* New York: Alfred A. Knopf, 1995.
———, ed. *Same-Sex Marriage: Pro and Con: A Reader.* New York: Vintage Books, 1997.
Thom, Paul. "Stiff Cheese for Women." *Philosophical Forum* 8 (1976): 94–107.
Trosino, James. "American Wedding: Same-Sex Marriage and the Miscegenation Analogy." *Boston University Law Review* 73 (1993): 93–120.
Vaid, Urvashi. *Virtual Equality: The Mainstreaming of Gay and Lesbian Liberation.* New York: Anchor Books, 1995.
Walker, Margaret Urban. *Moral Understandings: A Feminist Study in Ethics.* New York: Routledge, 1998.
Weston, Anthony. "Before Environmental Ethics." *Environmental Ethics* 14 (1992): 321–338.
Wolfson, Evan. "Crossing the Threshold: Equal Marriage Rights for Lesbians and Gay Men and the Intra-Community Critique." *New York University Review of Law and Social Change* 21 (1994–1995): 567–615.
Wolgast, Elizabeth. *Equality and the Rights of Women.* Ithaca, NY: Cornell University Press, 1980.
Zita, Jacquelyn N., ed. *Special Issue: Third Wave Feminism. Hypatia* 12 (1997).

Index